S0-BSP-846

A Place in the Rain

A Place in the Rain

DESIGNING THE WEST COAST GARDEN

Advice from Over 40 Experts

Edited by MICHAEL LASCELLE

whitecap

Copyright © 2004 by Michael K. Lascelle
Whitecap Books

All rights reserved. No part of this publication may be reproduced, stored in a
retrieval system, or transmitted in any form or by any means, electronic, mechanical,
photocopying, recording or otherwise, without prior written permission of the
publisher. All recommendations are made without guarantee on the part of the
authors or Whitecap Books Ltd. The authors and publisher disclaim any liability
in connection with the use of this information. For additional information, please
contact Whitecap Books, 351 Lynn Avenue, North Vancouver, British Columbia,
Canada v7J 2C4.

Edited by Elaine Jones
Proofread by Marial Shea
Cover and interior design by Brian Morgan
Photographs and illustrations by Michael K. Lascelle
     except where noted
Front cover photograph by Adam Gibbs

Printed and bound in Canada

National Library of Canada Cataloguing in Publication

A place in the rain : designing the west coast garden /
editor, Michael Lascelle. -- 1st ed.

Includes bibliographical references and index.
ISBN 1-55285-519-8 (pbk.)

1. Gardening--British Columbia. 2. Gardening--Northwest, Pacific.
I. Lascelle, Michael Kenneth, 1961-

SB453.3.C2P53 2004   635'.09711'1   C2004-900366-6

The publisher acknowledges the financial support of the Government of
Canada through the Book Publishing Industry Development Program for our
publishing activities.

For gardens and gardeners past

Michael Lascelle's great-great-grandparents,
George and Elisabeth Turner, in their Folkestone
English garden, *circa* 1920s.

ACKNOWLEDGEMENTS

I HAVE BEEN A GARDENER, in one form or another, for well over 20 years now and although I get a little tired of the politics from time to time, I am no less excited about seeing a new plant or garden than I was two decades ago. So I guess that means that I must still be a gardener at heart, and that is all it really takes to keep me in this business called horticulture.

We all have times when we get discouraged with the daily grind. And it is often during these moments that I find my solace in "ordinary" gardeners, people like Marge Saunders and Jack Gunther, who enjoy the company of fellow gardeners and take great pleasure in the trees, shrubs and perennials they tend in their own landscapes. They are not only generous in spirit and free with their garden stories, they have helped to renew my faith in humanity and also in my chosen career.

On the writing end of things, I would like to thank the staff at Whitecap Books for picking up and following through on a project made complex by the sheer number of people involved. Thanks also should go to the staff at the *Maple Ridge/Pitt Meadows News*, in particular Roxanne Hooper (who has since moved on) and Simone Ponne, who do a great job of organizing the text and photography for my regular garden column.

As a nursery manager, I rely heavily on local wholesale nurseries, which not only provide me with great stock but also keep me well informed about the latest plant introductions. Specifically, I would like to thank Hans and Marianne van der Pouw Kraan of Erica Enterprises, Lyle Courtice of Golden Eagle Tree Farms, Casey VanVloten and Ray LaForest of Van Vloten Nurseries, Erwin Gygli of Heimat Farms and Christine Mullens of Piroche Plants.

I am also greatly indebted to the people who took time out of their very busy schedules in order to be a part of this book. Names like David Tarrant and Blasig Landscaping are synonymous with horticulture in British Columbia, but all of the contributors here run thriving businesses and many also teach, write and lecture on gardening regularly. Saying they are just "busy" is an understatement. The contributors are the heart and soul of this endeavour and all of them share my vision of a landscape design book that all gardeners, regardless of their background, can understand and make use of.

Last but not least are my wife and daughters, who become what my wife calls "book widows" every time I get engrossed in a project such as this one. Without their patience and support, I would not have had the time to organize and write this material.

CONTENTS

Saunders landscape late
1940s, Maple Ridge, B.C.
(Photo: Marge Saunders)

Introduction

BEFORE I EVEN BEGAN THIS PROJECT, I asked myself one simple question: do we really need another landscape design book?

The market is flooded with such volumes, many featuring beautiful photography of elaborate landscapes or visual guides to what some consider essential for a "tasteful" garden. Many of these books are English in origin and books with local content are often limited to the plant selection, garden tour or how-to genres.

I have come across few Canadian works on landscape design that weren't trying to achieve coffee table status with their oversize format and lush photography, and most don't come close to meeting the needs of average gardeners. Don't get me wrong, I enjoy a good coffee-table book as much as the next person, but if success means that it stays on the coffee table, to be stacked and dusted weekly, then I hope this will never be a successful book.

This is a working volume, one that gardeners of average means can use for information relevant to their landscapes. I won't pretend to be an expert in all the fields presented in this book, although 23 years as an estate gardener, landscape foreman, garden designer and nursery manager have given me a familiarity with most aspects of garden design and installation. This also applies to the many contributors: landscape contractors, garden designers, professional horticulturists or landscape architects — all are seasoned veterans in their fields and that is obvious from the wisdom found in each piece.

You will notice an absence of preconceived garden designs (which rarely suit existing sites anyway) and there is no listing of suggested plants, containers and landscape features necessary to recreate a specific plan. What you will find is an insightful volume on how to plan your landscape properly, how to assess your garden site, how to use your property to its best advantage and how to create a design that really suits you and the site. This is a design book that is meant to help both novice and seasoned gardeners — before they even begin to design or renovate their landscape.

It is also a unique window on garden design as it exists in British Columbia today and it showcases the talented horticulturists of the province. Yet it is relevant in any temperate garden…be it the Pacific Northwest,

Saunders landscape late
1930s, Maple Ridge, B.C.
(Photo: Marge Saunders)

England, continental Europe, New Zealand or even the eastern seaboard of the United States.

The emphasis is on planning, honestly assessing your needs, and budgeting. Beyond that, we delve into design aesthetics, installation techniques, long-term maintenance considerations and organic options.

This is meant to be a working volume, one which you carry out into the landscape or share with your gardening friends. It is my hope to eventually see a few well-worn copies in the hands of gardeners shopping for plants at their local nursery or purchasing materials at the landscape supply store. To me, this would be a true measure of success.

CLIMATE ZONES

ALTHOUGH THIS BOOK deals primarily with landscape design, many of the contributors mention specific trees, shrubs, perennials and vines they deem important. Some of these lists include the climate zone, which is basically an indicator of the lowest minimum temperature that the plant will endure under normal circumstances. There are other limitations to plant growth, including soil type, annual rainfall and wind exposure (among others), but the lowest minimum temperature is probably the most crucial. Hardiness zones in Canada are expressed in digits from 1–9; 1 is the coldest and 9 the warmest. Here are the temperature listings for Zones 1 through 9, which will help you determine which plants are suitable for your garden. (Note that temperatures are approximate and based on the USDA zone ratings.)

	FAHRENHEIT	CELCIUS
Zone 1	Below −50	Below −46
Zone 2	−50 to −40	−45 to −40
Zone 3	−40 to −30	−40 to −35
Zone 4	−30 to −20	−35 to −29
Zone 5	−20 to −10	−29 to −23
Zone 6	−10 to 0	−23 to −18
Zone 7	0 to 10	−18 to −12
Zone 8	10 to 20	−12 to −6
Zone 9	20 to 30	−6 to −1

CHAPTER 1

Landscaping 101

*A garden is not made in a year; indeed it is never made in the
sense of finality. It grows, and with the labour of love should
go on growing.*
    Frederick Eden, *A Garden in Venice* (1903)

The first thing a gardener learns is that nothing ever goes as
planned. Nature always seems to have a mind of her own and is
more than willing to send a late spring frost, a horde of ravenous
slugs or even a few fungus spores to thwart our plans. It is only
persistence and a lot of hard work that make the difference between a forgettable landscape and one that has the neighbours
peering over the fence in envy.

That said, it is still important to have a strong grounding
in the basics before you set out to design your dream garden.
Quite often, it is simply a matter of honestly assessing what we
want and what we need in our landscapes, against what we can
really afford or physically accommodate on the property. And
if there is one common theme in this section, it is that a simple
garden design can be as elegant and satisfying as one with rare
plants or elaborate hard landscape features.

The basics also go beyond the obvious — plants, hard landscaping and layout. More subtle details, such as soil quality,
drainage and the presence of beneficial insects, play an important role in the long-term health of your garden. Landscaping
your own yard can be one of life's most rewarding experiences;
do it properly and it will continue to bring you pleasure for
many years to come.

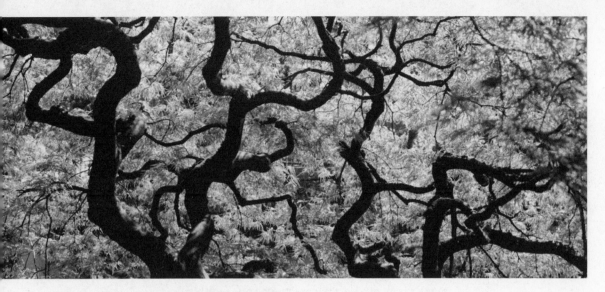

Making Your Garden Wish List
AYUKO INOUE, GARDENS BY DESIGN, VANCOUVER, B.C.

The ways we view and use our gardens have changed over the years. For many, the yard used to be just a space around the house — a place for the barbecue, an area for drying laundry or simply a view from the windows that provided a few seasonal colours. The garden of yesteryear was often treated as a static or passive space.

Today, gardens have become much more personal and intimate. Our gardens provide a place to retreat from our busy lives, to entertain or to enjoy gardening itself. This is particularly true for North American gardens, because they tend to be larger than those in many other places and the climate is more suitable for such outdoor living.

Curiously though, no matter how much garden space you have, it never seems to be enough. Whether you live in the suburbs with a sizeable garden or in the city with a small backyard or patio area, the biggest challenge you face when designing a landscape is often one of accommodation.

For many of us, gardens are closely tied to our dreams. This is especially true if you love gardening or plants, or feel spiritually involved with the natural world. You may wish to create many different features in your landscape. You can just imagine a warm summer evening, and see yourself sitting on a brick patio with the scent of jasmine filling the air....

However, before you plunge into creating your dream garden, take time to discuss your own and your family's expectations for this new landscape. You will need to assess whether these ideas can be realistically achieved in light of the physical conditions that exist in your garden and the budget available. After that, review your list and see how many wishes can, in fact, be accommodated. While it is certainly not easy to eliminate some of your treasured dreams, after the design process you will end up with a more realistic wish list and the process of building a garden can become more enjoyable and rewarding.

NEEDS

Most of us need a garage or a space to park the car and access to the house, from both the front street and the back lane. Not surprisingly, many of us already have these features. However, do they serve your purposes as they stand? More importantly, are they still in good condition or should you consider replacing them?

Remember to include storage areas for garbage cans, gardening tools and recreational equipment in your plans. Compost bins are becoming familiar sights, even in city landscapes. Will you need one in your garden? If you have one already, is it satisfactory, or do you need a larger structure?

Some practical features may turn out to be wishes rather than needs. For instance, you may like the idea of an outside drying area for laundry, but it may or may not be a necessity for your family.

Do you have children or pets? How old are your children? Will they need a play area or are they teenagers who may not use a garden often, except for occasional reading or a snooze in a hammock? Perhaps they want a swimming pool to share with family and friends. Will your pets need a special space? What are the requirements of other family members? Special interests may dictate setting aside a part of your garden for growing vegetables or raising herbs.

Many of us would like to have an outdoor area that could serve as an extension of our living room, dining room or even family room. Some of us feel the need to be closer to nature, and that can be as simple as doing light pruning or weeding, or just being out in the fresh air. Any patio, deck or sitting area can look very appealing when it is well furnished with suitable paving, trellises, comfortable chairs, tables and pots full of flowers. If such an exterior room is on your wish list, how will you use this area — daytime entertaining, evening parties or just a place for morning coffee on the weekends? Or perhaps you just need an attractive hideaway where you can relax with a magazine and a glass of wine after a hard day's work.

If you expect to do a lot of entertaining during the summer months, consider a built-in barbecue with wood, charcoal or gas storage. If you plan to start your barbecue parties early in the season, you may want to look into an outdoor heating system. Garden lighting will definitely help to create a more festive atmosphere and provide some degree of safety when entertaining in the garden in the evening.

While you're dreaming about your garden, consider the issue of privacy. A quiet retreat should be sheltered from other family members and the eyes of neighbours. This can be accomplished with a privacy screen — either by building a structure or fence to block the view, or planting suitable trees or shrubs.

AESTHETIC CONSIDERATIONS

Many of us have a preference for a particular style of landscape design — perhaps the English cottage garden, the Japanese minimalist type or the architectural Italian landscape. Generally, it is not advisable to have many different styles within one garden, although you might have a small, well-hidden section that has a completely different character of its own. This special area could be treated more as a "secret garden" than a contribution to the overall landscape effect.

The first thing to consider when choosing a garden style is whether it will complement the architecture of the house. The landscape can be brimming with wonderful features and rare plants, but if it does not complement the house, it will appear incongruous. A large, sprawling Tudor-style house with a Japanese garden, complete with stone lanterns and shaped pines, might attract attention because of its eccentricity, but it would hardly be considered a harmonious landscape.

Such contrasts may also be at odds with the surrounding neighbourhood. Examine the gardens of other houses around you. The landscape styles in each neighbourhood will vary, depending on the general lot sizes and their surroundings. Mixed shrub borders with flowing lines seem to abound in suburbs with large-sized lots and tall, mature trees. More compact, detailed gardens are usually found in cities and these may include a gate, formal hedge and intricate plantings that face the residence.

Do you want your garden to subtly blend into the neighbourhood, or do you want it to really stand out? You can create an exotic landscape that stands out in your neighbourhood, but in that case it had better be a good one, because everyone will be stopping to have a close look at it!

All your wishes will have to be carefully assessed against existing features that you already have in your garden. If the dominant tree in your front garden is a beautiful, mature Japanese maple, then it may be more of a challenge to create a formal garden with clipped boxwood parterres.

PRACTICAL CONSIDERATIONS

While drawing up your wish list, it is imperative that you consider the amount of garden area you actually have. Many good intentions have been thwarted because there was just not enough space! If such is your case, this is an area where you need to be disciplined and realistic. In a medium-sized city plot, it would be difficult to accommodate more than three areas of different character.

Simplicity is vital when designing a garden. A landscape with only a few features will look superior if each feature is well placed, well built and well maintained. The worst kind of garden is the one with too many features — none of which were properly built or are kept in good repair — and where the plants are generally not cared for. (Unless, of course, benign neglect is the look you are aiming for. Benign neglect, however, only works if the features are very well built to start with — otherwise, cheap and messy may be a more apt description.)

Remember that even after the landscape has been installed, the question remains: Who is going to look after the garden? Even if you have enough resources to budget adequately for a quality landscape, that garden will have to be maintained properly for it to continue to look attractive as the plants grow and hard structures take on that wonderful look of age and permanence. Do you have time to maintain the garden yourself? Even if you have the time at present, what about the future? Perhaps you have other interests that will occupy your time. If you decide to hire professionals to look after your landscape, can you find those who are knowledgeable about plants and their care at a cost you can afford or are willing to pay?

Even a matter as simple as watering requires careful consideration. Plants need consistent watering during the first two or three seasons, until they are established. If you are thinking of having a lot of plant material with differing water requirements, how would you feel about spending many of your summer hours watering them? Should you consider installing an irrigation system?

Often the choice is between expenditure of money or time. If you have an irrigation system, you will not have to spend the time watering, but you will have a significant initial outlay of money. On the other hand, a simple planting of drought-tolerant shrubs and perennials may be the way to go. These will need occasional watering, but the demands will be far less than a garden of hostas and rhododendrons.

Most of us have limited resources, so it is essential to consider your garden budget and apply your available resources to do fewer things better. This is another reason why making a wish list and realistically assessing it will help you to achieve your dreams in the garden.

A FINAL WORD

Listing and critiquing your wants and needs may not be the most popular stage of the design process, as it is an exercise that requires much thought, discipline and restraint. However, it is a necessary process that helps to clarify your own desires. Armed with your wish list, you will be able to allot space in the garden for those items important to you and your family, and achieve it within your budget.

Bulletproof Plants for the Gardening Impaired

MICHAEL LASCELLE, AMSTERDAM GARDEN CENTRE, PITT MEADOWS, B.C.

Not everyone is born with a green thumb and I know more than a few self-confessed "plant killers" who are desperate for something to grow in their garden. The reasons for a high plant failure rate can be quite varied, but the most common causes are adverse soil conditions, poor drainage, an unsuitable exposure (such as shade plants in full sun) or even competition from large, established trees such as *Thuja plicata* (western red cedar). The solution may be as simple as providing adequate moisture when the plant is young; even drought-tolerant shrubs need to become established before they can endure those dry soil conditions.

At the other end of the spectrum are those gardeners who love their plants to death by overwatering, adding too much fertilizer or piling the mulch so deep around the stem that the bark begins to rot. Occasionally, even a successful landscape can be plagued with small dead zones, where nothing seems to grow. These can sometimes be more difficult to diagnose, but some of the circumstances I have encountered in the past include persistent cats who prefer your dirt over their litter box, damage from road salt used to control ice on the front sidewalk, unwanted foot traffic or even the pool guy depositing the chlorine-laden skimmer sludge over the rhododendron beds.

Here is a short list of what I call bulletproof plants. It includes trees, shrubs, vines and perennials that tolerate a wide range of conditions, are relatively disease resistant and require little maintenance. These proven plants will not only enhance your landscape but they will also help to raise your self-esteem as a gardener.

Viburnum plicatum **'Summer Snowflake'** If ever there was a deciduous shrub that embodied a "plant and bloom" quality, 'Summer Snowflake' is it. Not only does it bear white lacecap flowers from late May through to frost in the Pacific Northwest, it is also quite tolerant of diverse soil conditions and will thrive in partial shade to full sun. While this is not a particularly compact viburnum, it does exhibit an attractive tiered growth habit. Averages 6 feet (2 m) tall. Zone 4.

Clematis montana **'Rubens'** If you are one of those gardeners who has trouble growing clematis, then this sturdy cultivar is for you. The deep pink flowers (May to June) are not as large as some clematis, but they are borne in such profusion that the foliage is often not visible. 'Rubens' is a vigorous plant, so you should eventually expect to accommodate up to 25 feet (8 m) of vine. Zone 6.

Hemerocallis **'Stella de Oro'** Daylilies in general are probably some of the easiest herbaceous perennials to grow, as they tolerate everything from modest drought to wet soil conditions, and they are generally disease free. The popular 'Stella de Oro' is a long bloom-

Hydrangea arborescens 'Annabelle' ('Annabelle' hydrangea)

ing (late May to November), dwarf cultivar that features slightly ruffled blooms of a golden yellow. Its compact size makes it ideal for containers or as an accent among the summer flowers. Averages 14 inches (35 cm) high. Zone 2.

Hydrangea arborescens **'Annabelle'** I have included this flowering shrub for those gardeners who may have a family member afflicted with "compulsive pruning disorder." 'Annabelle' blooms on current wood, so it can be hard pruned to stubs in spring and it will still bloom later that summer. This plant is rated Zone 3, so it is much hardier than the typical *Hortensia* or macrophylla-type hydrangeas. Expect a very full display of flattened mophead flower clusters (from midsummer on) that emerge pale green and mature to a beautiful pure white. Averages 6 feet (2 m) tall. Zone 3.

Liquidambar styraciflua **'Worplesdon'** Sweet gum is a favoured tree among homeowners who want a privacy screen, as it has a tendency to hold its glossy, maple-like leaves well into early December. 'Worplesdon,' in particular, features very attractive autumn tones of a deep wine red with some apricot highlights, and generally has smooth bark. This symmetrical tree tolerates moist soils and is usually unaffected by any pests or diseases. Averages 40 to 60 feet (13 to 20 m) tall. Zone 4.

Miscanthus sinensis **'Rotsilber'** To be honest, I have never met a *Miscanthus* that I didn't like. The best-coloured plumes are to be found on 'Rotsilber' (German for red-silver) — a mid-sized cultivar with attractive autumn tones of reddish-orange.

The other cultivar that is a must for its unusual foliage and form is *M.* 'Strictus' (porcupine grass). It combines a stiff, upright growth habit with whimsical variegation of horizontal gold bands. If space is limited, try 'Yaku Jima', a reliable dwarf form. It averages 3 to 5 feet (90 cm to 1.5 m) tall. Zones 5–6.

Rosa 'Bonica' or 'Royal Bonica' Have you ever wondered about those beautiful pale to mid-pink roses that seem to thrive in the narrow parking lot beds at your local shopping centre or gas station? The name is 'Bonica' (or the improved 'Royal Bonica') and this spring-to-frost bloomer was the first shrub rose to win an All-American Rose Selection award. While it will occasionally develop a little black spot when crowded, it is still considered one of the most disease resistant and easy-care roses on the market. Averages 3 to 5 feet (90 cm to 1.5 m) tall. Zone 4.

Putting Your Landscape Design on Paper
THOMAS MEYER, T.M. LANDSCAPE DESIGN & CONSULTING,
NEW WESTMINSTER, B.C.

A good landscape design will allow you to plan, schedule, avoid unexpected costs and start your garden renovation with peace of mind. This is what you can have when you start your project by getting it down on paper first!

WHAT DO YOU REALLY WANT?
The best place to start a comprehensive and effective landscape plan is with a clear analysis of three things: your needs, the site and your goals. While needs and goals may seem similar, they serve different functions. A review of your needs will help you establish goals, and having a sense of those goals will guide you through the process of evaluating your needs.

Needs
To establish your needs, start with the process of doing a family inventory. This can be as simple as sitting down with your family and writing down everything that each person needs or wants out of the garden. The inventory can be informal, or it can take the form of a detailed document. The family inventory provided here is one example of how this can be done — but it is important that the inventory be tailored to the reality of your situation in order to be relevant.

The inventory will assess which aspects of your family impact the landscape and detail elements of the garden that impact your family and lifestyle. For example, in trying to decide how big to make your patio, determine how everyone wants to use it. If the general consensus is that you do a lot of entertaining, you will want to ensure you get the maximum use of the outdoor space. The patio should be large enough and have some capacity to be used for extended hours. This might consist of using ornamental propane heaters to take the evening chill out of the air in early summer, adding night lighting or installing a screened-in porch. These details make the difference between just being outside and fully enjoying being outside.

Family Needs Inventory Checklist

The following inventory is intended as a guide only. There may be many other things you want to consider. Write down everything you can think of and create your own unique family needs inventory.

Family Members

Name	Age	Sex	Hobbies

Name	Age	Sex	Hobbies

Name	Age	Sex	Hobbies

Name	Age	Sex	Hobbies

Name	Age	Sex	Hobbies

Front or Main Entry Area

Driveways	Lanes	Number of cars in household

Extra parking needed	Guest parking	Location

Privacy from street needed	Entry walk	Entry courtyard

Safety lighting (where?)

Structures needed (gates, fences, etc.)

Backyard or Living Area

Paving or wooden deck needed	Type of surface preferred

Entertaining Large groups	Small groups	Formal or informal

Outdoor furniture Large table with chairs	Built-in seating

Benches	Bench height	Planters or walls

Covered area required   Screened-in space   Umbrella

Shade needs   Arbour or pergola   Outdoor heater

Landscape lighting   Location

Gas or propane barbecue   Cover needed

Outdoor kitchen   Water   Sink   Electrical

Sculpture   Type   Location

Lawn Area and Use

Games   Badminton   Croquet   Putting green

Tetherball   Shuffleboard   Basketball   Soccer

Mower needs   Push reel mower   Electric   Gas

String trimmer   Other garden equipment

Equipment storage area   Safe fuel storage

Swimming Pool and/or Hot Tub

Local regulations

Liability insurance   Legal responsibilities

Size needed   Swimming   Wading   Diving

Electrical Above-ground   In-ground

Method of enclosure   Changing areas   Pool house

Access to swimming pool   Night lighting

Safety concerns

Children's Play Areas

Tree house or fort   Monkey bars   Slide   Swings

Climbing equipment   Low impact surfacing

Shade requirements   Paved surface for riding

Trees and shrubs   Toy storage

Sandbox   Cover needed

Garden Areas

Maintenance levels   Family allergies

Cut flower garden   Herb garden   Perennial border

Mixed shrub border   Fruit trees   Vines

Seasonal interest Winter   Spring   Summer   Fall

Container plantings   Vegetable garden

Greenhouse   Location   Compost area

Window boxes   Cold frames   Garden storage

Other

Water features Pond   Fountain

Fish   Aquatic plants

Clothesline Permanent   Retractable   Regular use   Occasional

Pets Dogs   Cats   Other

Doghouse   Dog run   Other pet needs

Recreational vehicle storage	Size needed	Boat storage

Watering Sprinklers	Hose access

In-ground system	Controller location

Number of zones	Rain shutoff

Garbage cans	Recycling Box	Location	Access

Wildlife Bird feeders	Birdhouses	Bird baths

Squirrel protection	Cat protection

Plants to attract butterflies or beneficial insects

Evaluation

To make informed choices and remove as many unknowns as possible, a thorough evaluation of the site is needed. In other words, you need to really get to know your landscape.

A site analysis evaluates such things as sun direction, drainage, soil, climate, views of your neighbours (or their views of you), privacy, street noise and wind. The following is an example of a site analysis.

Site Inventory Checklist

Answer each of these questions with a yes or no.

Drainage

1. Does water drain away from the house and other structures?
2. Does water drain onto the property from surrounding areas?
3. Are there low spots where water sits?
4. Are there areas that are eroding due to water impact?
5. Does the water percolate through the soil evenly?
6. Are patio areas draining poorly due to settling?
7. Are all the drains working properly?

Structures

1. Are the structures on the property in good repair?
2. Are they placed where you want them?
3. Are they the right size for their use?
4. Do they blend with the landscape (or proposed landscape)?
5. Do any areas need to be hidden (compost bin, air conditioner, potting area)?

6. Do you need walls, retaining walls, fences or gates?

7. Can you incorporate seating into walls and retaining walls?

8. Are the patios or decks in the right location, vis-a-vis wind, sun etc.?

9. Is your patio or deck large enough?

10. Are there any structures (gazebos, for instance) you want to add?

Climate

1. Is there a need for wind breaks?

2. Is there a need for shade or sun breaks?

3. Are you aware of the maximum and minimum temperatures?

4. Do these temperatures affect your desired plant choices?

5. Are you aware of the average minimum and maximum rainfall levels?

6. Are there long periods of drought?

7. Is there an extended rainy season?

8. Is there dependable snowcover (in colder areas)?

9. Do your plants need supplemental watering?

* Note the sunny, wet, dry, boggy and windy areas in your garden.

Soil

1. Have you had a soil test done?

2. Do you know if your soil is acidic or alkaline?

3. Does your soil need additional organic matter?

4. Is your soil drainage adequate?

5. Is your soil (or growing medium) deep enough?

* If soil varies in different parts of your garden, complete for each area.

Plants

1. Do some trees or shrubs need to be removed?

2. Do some trees or shrubs need to be moved to a new location?

3. Is your lawn performing well and able to withstand winter conditions?

4. Are your plants grouped with plants with similar needs?

5. Is the yard overplanted, causing crowding and poor plant health?

6. Are the plants you have the ones you want?

7. Are your desired plant choices correct for your garden?

8. Do the design and plant choices minimize the need for pest control?

9. Is the yard friendly to birds and beneficial insects?

Existing Features

1. Are there any existing natural features you want to highlight?

2. Are there large rocks you can incorporate or use in the design?

3. Is there an opportunity to take advantage of a "borrowed landscape"?

4. Are there views you want to focus on?

Driveways and Walks

1. Are the walks and drives adequate for your needs?
2. Are you happy with the material of the walks and driveways?
3. Are the walks and driveways safe?
4. Do you need additional walkways to access buildings or areas on the property?
5. Do the walkways follow the natural flow of the yard?
6. Are there walkways that can be expanded to allow for seating or pots?
7. Are there attractive and interesting things to see along the walkways?
8. Are the sight lines clear from the driveway to the road?

Water Needs

1. Is your irrigation system equipped with a rain sensor or shut-off?
2. Is your irrigation system designed to deal with the different watering needs of various plants (lawn, trees, shrub border, etc.)?
3. Can you retrofit your existing irrigation to become a drip system?
4. Are the water features located on site safe?
5. Do you need to eliminate standing water to reduce mosquito breeding?
6. Are the hoses and hose bibs easy to access?

Other

1. Do you want landscape lighting?
2. Are there areas where you need safety lighting?
3. Do you need more privacy from the street?
4. Do you need privacy from your neighbours?
5. Do you need a buffer from noise?
6. Are you familiar with Integrated Pest Management?
7. Do you want to reduce chemical pesticide and fertilizer use on the property?
8. Are there any landscape areas that need to be made safer?
9. Are there good views from the inside looking out, as well as from the outside looking in?
10. Are you aware of local building and landscaping regulations or codes?
11. If hiring a landscaper, have you checked for certification or insurance coverage?
12. Are you going to change the grade of the property?
13. Will any grade changes affect the existing trees and shrubs?
14. Does the colour of your house or roofing material affect the plantings or choice of hard materials?

Many garden books have different versions of site analysis. To get the most use from your own analysis, it helps to have the site plan drawn up. You will be able to orient yourself more easily and cover site elements more thoroughly.

Before you undertake a site analysis, you may want to have your soil tested. Most urban areas have a few reputable soil laboratories that will, for a fee, give you a thorough analysis of your soil. A soil test is one of the first places where your needs and site analyses support each other. Let's say, for instance, that your soil is adequate for growing a lawn but you have determined that you want to grow vegetables. Let the soil lab know this and they can make recommendations for soil amendments. If your existing plants are failing, a good first step is to take samples to a garden centre that employs certified staff. If you need more information, many government and private labs can do a thorough plant diagnostic.

Goals

While goals are listed last, they are generally one of the first things you will consider. Something made you start thinking about developing your landscape, and quite often this is the goal itself.

After clearly establishing your goals, place them in order of priority. Not only will this make the installation of the landscape go more smoothly, you will get what you really want first and can then plan for the rest.

Equally important to establishing your goals is making sure they are really what you want. Many times we have heard people say they want a low-maintenance garden, only to end up with a lovely landscape that is lacking in colour. What they really had in mind was a colourful garden that gave them four seasons of interest and was as low maintenance as possible. Make sure your goals are detailed and accurately reflect your needs and wants.

Researching and Building an Idea Book

Once you have taken the time to analyze your needs, goals and the site, it's time to research your options. It is useful to have a working knowledge of the terminology of horticulture and landscaping. This is a vast subject and some people spend their lives learning about it, but your comprehension needn't be so sophisticated. We are fortunate to be living in an age when gardening is popular; magazines and books that deal with it are abundant and are focused on helping people to succeed. (In times past, many gardening periodicals were written purely to intimidate all but the most experienced.)

Perusing magazines and books can be both pleasurable and frustrating. Garden publications are full of neat ideas, tips and information; the challenge is narrowing down your options. I always suggest that people begin a portfolio of magazine clippings, newspaper articles and photographs. Include anything that piques your interest. It will help you narrow down what you like and it is also easier to keep track of this information in a binder, rather than trying to find it again in several magazines.

Don't limit yourself to just landscape and gardening sources. Inspiration can come from anywhere – home decorating magazines, architectural publications, travel magazines. If you are always thinking about your landscape, you will find ideas in some of the most obscure places.

DRAWING A PLAN

Before you put your plan on paper, there are a number of things that will make the process easier.

Large Graph Paper The bigger the better! The larger your scale drawing is, the easier it will be to work out your plan. When making site plans, make many copies so you can work out your ideas. An optional material is a product called "fade out." This is a special type of graph paper used by some in blueprinting. The graph is printed in blue, which won't reproduce. This will enable you to create a site plan and produce many copies without having to deal with the lines of the graph.

Tracing Paper When laid over your plan, this gives you the ability to have some fun playing with shapes and ideas without having to redo a whole new plan.

Sharp Pencils Good quality pencils that are not too hard or soft will make drawing easier. Try to create strong lines that will reproduce evenly. Optional items are mechanical pencils. Mechanical pencils let you buy one lead holder and change leads, depending on the weight of line you want.

Pencil Sharpener and Eraser Keeping your pencil sharp is critical to making the process work smoothly. A good eraser that doesn't smudge or leave marks behind is also important.

Architect's Scale Available at most office supply stores and all drafting suppliers, this is a three-sided ruler with gradations that allows you to draw your site to scale. When using a scale, ensure you are consistent with the scale you choose: ¼ inch or ⅛ inch are most commonly used. Of course this will depend on the size of your paper and your property. An option if you like to work in metric is an engineer's scale.

Ruler Use a long ruler for drawing straight lines. Another option is a bendable ruler, which lets you draw even curves for smooth, even lines.

Angle Square A set of squares will help you lay out angles and correctly create 90-degree, 45-degree and other angles. This is also available as an adjustable square, where you can change the angle , though this costs a bit more.

Drawing tools Many are available — visit your local drafting store and see what they have. Items such as circle templates will let you draw circles of various sizes, to represent trees and shrubs on landscape plans. For larger circles, a protractor is useful (if it doesn't bring back too many bad memories of high school geometry class).

Pictures of your site These are very useful. It may seem silly, as you live right there, but looking at pictures of the site while drawing is definitely helpful. Enlarging photographs and sketching trees and shrubs right on them is a great way to get a sense of what the site will look like.

Measuring and Laying Out Your Site

As with drawing, there are many things that will make measuring your property easier.

- A long tape measure (100 feet/30 m is often enough).
- A retractable tape for measuring the smaller areas (25 feet/7.5 m).
- A level. These come in many styles and shapes, all for different purposes. For getting a sense of slopes on your property and thus how you will deal with elevation changes, a line level can be useful. A laser level is also simple to use and now costs less than $30.
- Stakes will help you establish desired heights and enable you to mark where you measured.
- Spikes (large nails) can be used to fix one end of your long tape in one spot, which will allow you to measure many distances from one point (such as the diameter of a circle).

When making your site plan, remember to include as much information as possible. Indicate all buildings, water taps, gas lines (call the city for this information), water lines, city water shut off valves, gas meter, wet areas, dry areas, location of overhead wires and air conditioners (yours and those surrounding). The more information you include, the better. When you have a good basic site plan, make several copies.

Budget

Before you get too far along, take some time to evaluate your budget. This will have a significant impact on your design, although you can do a lot with a limited budget if you use a little creativity and imagination.

A new deck, patio, pool, hot tub, garden structure or large tree can be big-ticket items. Be aware that the costs include installation, maintenance and ongoing upkeep. Your budget may require that these features be added over time. In that case, you can design this option into your plan (a good example is installing a section of fence that is easy to remove for future access). Keep these things in mind and your plan will be implemented that much easier.

The Design Process

Here are some key steps that will help you get started on the design.

- Do bubble studies. Roughly lay out where all the elements of the landscape will go and how they will fit together, drawing circular shapes to help you visualize and determine the space needed for each activity and how they influence each other. Make many of these studies and include information about neighbouring influences.

- Start defining the spaces. Once you have a sense of where everything goes and how much room each area needs, you can begin to further define each area. The design should reflect the nature of the "room" (i.e. public or private space).
- Make cutouts, to scale, of items such as a table and chairs or swing set. Place them on the drawing and check if the room allotted is sufficient. You don't want to design a patio or other area that is too small for the activities it's intended for.
- Look at the environmental aspects of your design. Where is the water run-off going? Are the plantings accessible for maintenance?
- Are the trees and shrubs properly selected for their location? Putting the right plant in the right place will save you a lot of headaches in the future. To determine whether the plants will grow too big for their intended location, use scale-size cutouts to indicate their size at maturity.
- Start looking at materials. It's critical to select the right material for each area, whether it be patio or deck, arbour or water feature, shrub, flower or herb garden. Get to know the materials available by visiting garden centres and landscape supply stores for brochures and information.
- Finalize the design. I am always reluctant to call any landscape design final, for landscapes are dynamic places where change is ever-present. But at some time you need to stop planning and start planting.

The "Finished" Plan

After this process you should have a detailed landscape plan in front of you. Every bit of information should be on it, so you can proceed with confidence. Sometimes there is so much information on a drawing that you are better to have two or three of them. One might be the overall concept plan; another could be a detailed planting plan with little other information; a third might be the construction plan, where the decks and patios are shown with dimensions, but no plant material is included. This helps to illustrate the value of printing many copies of the site plan.

Throughout this process you should have been taking your plan outside and walking around with it. Use a garden hose, rope or other temporary line to see how your ideas translate into reality.

Now take your plan to the local garden centre and landscape supply yard, and start putting it into action.

Placing Trees in the Urban Landscape

KIM KAMSTRA, KAMSTRA LANDSCAPING, MAPLE RIDGE, B.C.

Urban landscapes have gone through dramatic changes over the last three decades. What was once called an average yard — that great space from your eavestrough to the neighbour's — has been greatly diminished as cities grow to accommodate an ever-increasing population. The large, stately trees that once adorned urban gardens are now found mainly in parks or botanical gardens.

In some cases trees that once complemented a landscape are being marred with chainsaws and hedge trimmers in order to restrain their normal growth patterns and prevent them from touching siding or blocking the light.

GROWTH HABITS AND PRUNING

A tree is an important visual element in the landscape, and if you know its growth habit and mature size before you purchase it, you will be able to let it grow naturally with as little intervention from secateurs or chainsaws as possible. Pruning should be restricted to removing dead, diseased, broken, crossing or tight parallel branches. On trees with single stems, the removal of secondary terminals should be done to encourage natural form. On multistem forms, watch for crossing or rubbing branches, and remove these when necessary. All new trees selected for your landscape should be able to grow to their mature height without topping them to maintain a certain size. Most deciduous trees develop frustrating water sprouts (small suckering branches) from large pruning cuts, so be very selective about removing or pruning large branches.

UNEXPECTED HAZARDS

Even if we take great pride in our home landscapes and the hard work we put in to maintain them, certain elements are beyond our control. Environmental factors, such as snow followed by a hard rain (which makes for heavy branch loads), strong winds that suddenly change direction, and flooding of a nearby stream may pose some problems. Other unexpected risks are innocent young children, armed with Dad's hammer, a fistful of nails and a burning desire to build the ultimate tree fort. Be on the lookout for neighbours who are constantly hoping to improve their view and always seem to be out there when you are pruning, encouraging you to take it down just a little more. And, of course, don't forget the enthusiastic family member with the new gas-powered line trimmer, who accidentally challenges the bark of every tree with grass growing around it. Depending on the amount of damage and its severity, you may be able to selectively prune out any bad cuts or damaged wood. If you are in doubt as to the extent of the damage or your ability to rectify it, seek the advice of a landscape professional or arborist.

10 TREES FOR URBAN LOTS

Here are my top 10 suggestions for trees that are appropriate for average urban lots, provided they are given the essentials of sunlight, moisture, fertile soil and a reasonable amount of space to grow in.

Abies koreana (**Korean fir**) This very slow-growing fir has striking early cone development (purple female cones) and quickly becomes the centre of attention in the landscape. The glossy green foliage (on top) and its symmetrical shape make it the perfect specimen conifer for an urban front yard. Height 20 to 30 feet (6 to 10 m). Zone 5.

Acer palmatum '**Villa Taranto**' (**threadleaf Japanese maple**) A member of the Linearilobum Group, this cultivar features thin-lobed, thread-like leaves that emerge with a reddish-pink hue. The soft green summer foliage is animate with the slightest breeze and is a good foil in a garden with many hard landscape features. Clear yellow autumn tones can be expected. Height 8 feet (2.5 m). Zone 5.

Chamaecyparis nootkatensis '**Pendula**' (**weeping yellow cedar**) An elegant specimen conifer with pendulous limbs and loosely hanging branches of coarse green foliage. Although it can grow fairly tall, the narrow profile makes it ideal for urban situations. A more slender selection, called *'Jubilee'*, is also available. Height 26 feet (8 m). Zone 5.

Cornus kousa (**Korean dogwood**) A flowering tree with white blooms in June-July, when most flowering trees have finished their display. The ascending branches allow for plenty of light below and this species also has brilliant autumn tones of scarlet and a multitude of strawberry-like fruits that the birds enjoy. Very disease resistant. Height 20 feet (6 m). Zone 5.

Fagus sylvatica '**Purple Fountain**' (**purple fountain beech**) A tall, slender form with deep purple foliage that cascades on descending branches held close to the trunk. The leaves are often a little late to emerge, but they can persist until early winter in milder regions. This cultivar works well near buildings, where its form and colour can both be admired. Height 26 feet (8 m). Zone 6.

Oxydendrum arboreum (**sourwood**) A small deciduous tree with fragrant blooms of pure white in late summer. Spectacular fall colours of orange and scarlet are often presented in layers. This native of eastern North America is quite slow growing in the Pacific Northwest. Height 20 feet (6 m). Zone 5.

Picea orientalis '**Aurea**' (**golden oriental spruce**) Absolutely amazing flushes of creamy-yellow to gold new growth make this conifer a real showpiece. This gold cultivar is also very slow growing, to an average height in 10 years of 10 feet (2–3 m), making it quite suitable for smaller urban gardens. Mature height 20 feet (6 m). Zone 5.

Stewartia pseudocamellia
bloom (Japanese stewartia)
(Photo: Kim Kamstra)
Colour photo p. 129

Picea pungens **'Baby Blue Eyes' (dwarf blue spruce)** 'Baby Blue Eyes' features brilliant steel-blue foliage and true conical form. It is one of the few conifers that fits comfortably within the confines of even the smallest urban landscape. Height 12 feet (3.5 m). Zone 3.

Stewartia pseudocamellia **(Japanese stewartia)** I had a hard time convincing myself to list this species as a small to medium-sized tree, but I have yet to see one exceed 25 feet (8 m) outside of its natural habitat, due to its reasonably slow growth habit. Consider this tree for a sheltered corner of the yard where the reddish flaking bark, brilliant autumn foliage and eye-catching winter seed pods can be appreciated. White, camellia-like blooms emerge in June and July, contrasting well against the deep green leaves. Mature height 50 feet (15 m). Zone 5.

Tsuga mertensiana **(mountain hemlock)** An alpine species that is very slow growing when young, allowing it to be enjoyed in urban landscapes. The bluish-green needles are very congested, giving this tree an almost bonsai-like appearance, without all of the intensive pruning. A good choice for naturalized gardens near the forest edge. Height 30 feet (10 m) or more. Zone 4.

PLANTING YOUR NEW TREE

Decisions have been made, the tree has been purchased and now it's time to plant. But before you plant, there are a few things to consider. Locate all underground services such as water, sewer, gas, electrical or irrigation lines before you dig. Contact your local gas company, city engineering or public works department to ensure that no damage will occur from the placement of your new tree.

Trees send out lateral roots in all directions, and these roots may interfere with adjacent sidewalks and driveways, whether they are made of cement, asphalt or paving stones. Using a little discretion during the planning stage will result in healthy trees that cause minimal disturbance to the surrounding elements. Planting is best done in the fall, when there is ample rain and the root system has time to become established before there is any flush of new growth. Do not prune trees after or before planting, as the removal of any branches can disrupt the growth relationships between root systems and the crown and may hinder proper development.

Digging a hole twice as wide as necessary will allow for lateral root growth. Digging too deep, however, will allow the tree to settle lower than the original soil level on the trunk and may cause stem rot or unwanted surface roots. Fertilize only with phosphorus (bone meal), to aid in root development rather than top growth.

Staking and tying trees can present some difficulty for the average home gardener. Many people tend to use whatever is on hand as a means of tree support — rope, wire, hose, zap straps, electrical tape or other equally ineffective or damaging materials. Most trees do not need to be supported as long as they are standing straight and are placed in well-structured soil. Sometimes, however, temporary wet conditions (common to new sites) or strong prevailing winds make it necessary to support the tree. Drive a stake (2 × 2 inches minimum) on each side of the tree, being careful not to damage any portion of the roots or root ball. Attach the tree to these stakes using a wide, soft strapping (similar in width to a car seatbelt) tied in a figure-eight fashion from the tree to a post on each side. The strapping is attached with nails to the post and simply loops around the stem of the tree for support. There should not be too much tension on these ties, as they are only meant to offer support in the case of heavy winds. Be sure to remove the stakes and ties after one year, by which time the tree should be well rooted.

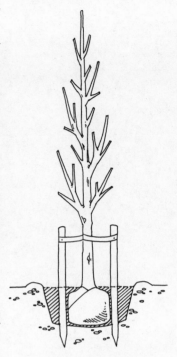

Proper staking and planting installation

Sustainable Horticultural Practice
TODD MAJOR, PARK & TILFORD GARDENS, NORTH VANCOUVER, B.C.

A farmer visiting Vancouver from Saskatchewan once stopped in our garden and asked if the garden was sustainable. The question startled me for a moment. I thought to myself, well of course it is. The farmer commented that he was facing a choice of continuing the practices taught to him by his father and grandfather or adopting modern agricultural methods of increasing crop yields. He was trapped between science and his intuitive belief in the system that had sustained three generations of his family for over 150 years on the same land. This encounter left quite an impression on me.

The following summary describes some of the horticultural practices I use at Park and Tilford Gardens and in my home garden. These practices have sustained and improved our gardens over the last 12 years — a short length of time in comparison to the farmer's account, but a good test of these methods nonetheless.

My approach to managing a garden has undergone a complete change in direction since I started my career. When I first began 19 years ago, the philosophy I followed was one based on using accepted gardening techniques to impose our expectations on the natural world. Techniques such as shearing plants into geometric forms, using chemical fertilizers or pesticides and creating the clean bed, or bare-earth, look were the standards driven by consumer demand. These standards involved constant maintenance or chemical sprays, which negatively affected the natural ecosystem.

Educators and the gardening public often misunderstand the ability of natural processes to transform matter to energy (such as turning rotting leaves into food). For example, a single, one-hundred-year-old Douglas fir (*Pseudotsuga menziesii*) tree grows in a symbiotic relationship with fungi in the forest soil, called mycorrhiza. The length of the fungi in association with the tree is estimated at half a mile (when all the strands are taken into consideration). This huge amount of fungi is helping to generate food for the tree and in return, the tree gives processed food (plant sugars) back to the fungi — a relationship that provides the elements of life for both organisms. By contrast, chemical fertilizers may last eight weeks and require continual reapplication. This is only one example of the many sustainable processes that I am taking advantage of at Park and Tilford Gardens.

THE H.E.L.P. SYSTEM

Our system of garden management is called Holistic Ecology Layering Program, or H.E.L.P. It is based on the understanding of how practical techniques (or inputs) affect the garden ecology and impact the quality of presentation and long-term sustainability of the garden.

Holistic simply means that the individual (and interrelated) parts of the ecology, such as soil, water, air, insects, fungi and plants, need to be healthy for the whole system to function well. If the soil has a problem, then plant and insect life may not thrive and may be unable to assist the rest of the garden. The soil problem could be poor drainage, an unacceptable pH or a soil structure not suited to the plants growing in it. This problem leads to a response from pests, as they are able to perceive a plant under stress and will move in to infest. The insect attack is not the problem; it is only a symptom of an underlying issue. Treatment of the pest (such as applying pesticide) does nothing to address the poor drainage, inappropriate pH or poorly situated plant. The garden system will not improve if only the pest is treated and not the cause of pest attack.

Ecology means understanding how the garden grows through the dynamic interrelationships of soil, air, water, plants, insects or microorganisms. Any intervention that affects one relationship will eventually affect the whole ecology. Plants have natural defense mechanisms in place to prevent infestation. To take advantage of these defenses, it's important to avoid applying substances that interfere with their environment. Plants exude chemicals that attract predatory insects to prey on potential pests, and pesticides interfere with these chemicals. Plants also exude substances that can kill or slow the digestion of an attacking pest. Pesticides and herbicides can interfere with this defense and kill the very predatory insects we are trying to encourage in the first place.

Ian Baldwin, of the Max Planck Institute in Jena, Germany, has found that domesticated or hybridized plants, designed for high yield, have lost much of their ability to utilize their natural chemical defense systems. These hybrids require more maintenance and more protection from pests and diseases. Chemical fertilizers further negate plant defense systems by causing plants to grow softer and larger tissue than is natural. Soft tissue is very prone to pest and disease attack or climate stress. These are just some examples of the ecological interrelationships occurring every day in your garden.

Layering refers to various horticultural techniques that are applied either simultaneously or sequentially to provide an overall benefit to the ecology. There are many different techniques that are seemingly unrelated, but when applied together they act as integrated layers. For example, the application of lime, followed by a deep watering and mulching, may seem unrelated. However, the lime allows nutrients to become available, the mulch allows a place for soil organisms to thrive and helps to retain the water that was applied.

These elements — holism, ecology and layering — are the focus of our H.E.L.P. program, which guides all of our decision-making in regards to the long-term sustainability of the garden. For nearly a decade, Park and Tilford Gardens and the adjacent shopping centre landscape have been free of pesticides and chemical fertilizers, as a result of using the program. One success story using this system was the renovation of our rose garden. The roses were increasingly subject to disease and pest attacks, and were producing fewer blooms. The soil in the rose beds was tested for nutrient levels, pH and drainage rates. The results revealed a thick layer of impermeable clay at a depth of 28 inches (40 cm), a pH of 5.9 and high levels of phosphorus. The remedy we devised involved a layered approach. First the soil was excavated down to 4 feet (1.2 m), including the removal of the clay layer. Then new drain tile was installed. Next, we adjusted the pH of all of the soil as it went back into the beds, creating a slight berm with the new soil grade. We then mixed 20 percent of the clay soil into the top 12 inches (30 cm) of the soil in the beds. The final step was destroying all the underperforming roses and planting ones selected for their disease resistance and fragrance.

SOME BASIC COMPONENTS OF THE H.E.L.P. SYSTEM

Many factors contribute to a healthy garden, but few are as important as preparing an adequate rooting depth in the soil. Deep soil will yield strong, healthy plants. In particular, trees exhibit an increased longevity where they can grow deeply into freely draining soil. The deeper the soil, the more nutrients and water are available. These are important to the plant's natural self-defense against pests and its ability to withstand frost or drought. Drainage is another important factor to consider when talking about soil depth. Always remove anything that prevents free drainage.

Irrigate infrequently and apply a large volume of water to promote deep root development. When water penetrates deeply into the soil, the more consistent soil moisture allows the plant longer access to a continuous water draw. Deep watering is also effective in counteracting temperature extremes. We check our watering effectiveness using custom-designed steel soil probes that pull a 1¾-inch (5-cm) core out of the soil in 8-inch (20-cm) increments. We check within 24 hours of watering to determine the percolation depth and saturation levels. It takes amazingly little time or effort and allows us to monitor the effectiveness of our watering program.

Pest and disease control is one of the most time-consuming tasks in the garden, and yet it does not have to be. Rather than trying to kill insects, we spend our time creating optimum conditions for plants and beneficial insects. Simple practices like choosing the right plant for the right place, applying mulch, never using pesticides and minimal (or no) use of chemical fertilizers create lasting benefits. We also provide the elements that will attract and sustain beneficial insects, instead of continually buying and releasing ladybugs or other commercially-raised predatory insects. This allows the plants to thrive without chemicals.

Plants require an optimal pH range (acidity or alkalinity) in order to obtain the mineral nutrients they need from the soil. If you want to fertilize your garden in a sustainable way, test the soil pH and, if needed, apply the appropriate amount of dolomite lime to adjust the pH. The acidity or alkalinity of the soil determines how much fertilizer will be available to the plant, regardless of how much is applied. Bone meal is a good example of fertilizer that is over-applied. When planting a 2-inch (5-cm) caliper (the width of the stem at 3 feet / 1 m) tree in soil prepared with compost or manure, no bone meal is required — the compost already supplies the phosphorus. If the same tree is planted with no organic amendments, one or two teaspoons (5 to 10 mL) of bone meal would be enough to last a decade.

Adding a layer of organic material to the surface of the garden protects and enriches the soil and soil organisms. Mulch benefits the soil both structurally and nutritionally. In addition, it affords protection for fungi, bacteria, worms, beetles and other soil organisms. These organisms consume (or modify) and release nutrients from decaying plant material, thereby

Ornamental mulching on dormant bulb beds at Park & Tilford Gardens, North Vancouver, B.C. (Photo: Todd Major)

enhancing the soil. They are the true food generators in the soil and the real secret of growing a healthy garden. Soil organisms work every day and when they finally die, their bodies become part of the soil.

No system is perfect, but we have seen some impressive results through the application of ecological principles and creative hard work. The H.E.L.P. program is simply our way of recognizing that nature has already provided a balanced ecology where people, plants and insect life can live in harmony. We just need to accept some limitations in regards to the cultural practices that many of us have used over the years, and learn to garden in a way that respects all life.

Botanical Garden Syndrome
MICHAEL LASCELLE, AMSTERDAM GARDEN CENTRE, PITT MEADOWS, B.C.

"Botanical garden syndrome" is a common malaise among serious plant collectors who have yet to gain the landscape design experience necessary to maintain their habit. Typically there is an extensive collection of rare plants (one of each) neatly stacked together, in their pots, on the edge of a back patio or balcony. Occasionally, there are actually more plants in containers than landscape to accommodate them, but the real problem here is that even if there was enough room, a one-of-each planting policy rarely results in a cohesive landscape design.

As a young garden designer, I was once guilty of creating one of these oddities. Despite my advice to the contrary, this particular homeowner envisioned a landscape design with as many hard features and plant specimens as the lot was capable of holding. As predicted, the resulting landscape looked busy and disorganized (despite the enormous amount of planning) simply because there were too many competing patios, arbours and plant textures. I have since learned that it is my responsibility as a designer to create an aesthetically pleasing landscape (with customer input). This may mean informing those with less palatial lots that sometimes there simply isn't enough room for an extensive plant collection.

SOLVING THE SYNDROME
While the solution is really quite simple, it can be difficult for an avid plant enthusiast. The average garden can only accommodate a limited number of specimen plants. However, there are always options. For instance, even a simple privacy hedge can be created with elegant fountain bamboo (*Fargesia nitida*) or a variegated conifer (*Cupressocyparis* x *leylandi* 'Castlewellan') rather than the usual emerald or western red cedars. Similarly, the shrub groupings, massed perennials and groundcovers (see list below for options) necessary for overall garden structure need not include the common spirea, potentilla and periwinkle that many seasoned gardeners find so dull. The standard shade tree in the middle of the front lawn can also be a great opportunity to feature an unusual specimen, such as *Davidia*

(dove tree) or *Catalpa speciosa* (Indian bean tree) — both of which exhibit exotic flowers (or bracts) and are very handsome street trees.

When incorporating mass plantings, always keep the old landscaper's rule in mind: use 3 to 5 plants per group. Using an odd number of shrubs is important, as even numbers tend to produce a very symmetrical or row-like pattern that looks unnatural. Also, don't be afraid to use several of the same plant groupings throughout the landscape to add some continuity. Foliage colour from a variety of plant sources (i.e. perennials, shrubs or conifers) can also be occasionally repeated in a mixed border. In particular, the use of gold or blue foliage can really help to draw the eye through the garden.

OUT-OF-THE-ORDINARY MASS PLANTING MATERIAL

Here are a few alternative plant choices to help inspire you and let you know that cotoneaster and mugho pines are not the only options waiting for you at your local garden centre.

Deciduous shrub — *Caryopteris* x *clandonensis* 'Worcester Gold'
Bright gold foliage contrasts with blue flowers in late summer.

Broadleaf evergreen — *Andromeda polifolia* 'Blue Ice'
Evergreen steel-blue foliage and pale pink heather-like blooms.

Conifer — *Podocarpus* 'Blue Gem'
Soft blue-green needles/horizontal growth habit. Tolerates shade or sun.

Groundcover — *Epimedium* x *versicolor* 'Sulphureum'
Semi-evergreen, heart-shaped foliage and profuse pale yellow blooms.

Ornamental grass — *Pennisetum orientale*
Pale pink to buff bottlebrush seed heads and fine-textured foliage.

Perennial — *Hosta* 'Sum & Substance'
Bright chartreuse foliage and huge leaves with deep, recessed veins.

A LAST WORD

If you are still not convinced that an average residential lot is the wrong place to house an extensive plant collection, I challenge you to have a good look around the next time you visit your local botanical garden or park. While you're enjoying the many rare plants, take a moment to ask yourself how many city lots would fit inside the garden, or try to envision your lot in one corner of the park. Most people soon realize that they are dealing with a completely different scale in their home garden, and that makes it easier to reign in their grandiose landscaping expectations.

CHAPTER 2
Tweaking the Seasons

Nature always wears the colors of the spirit.
   Ralph Waldo Emerson, "Nature"

One of the experiences that I really miss from my days as a
working gardener is moments of déjà vu. A good example of
this would find me up in the crown of a flowering cherry, doing
a little selective pruning…when suddenly I realize that I've done
this before. Quite literally, everything has been repeated exactly,
from the pruning cuts I make, to the prevailing weather, to the
time of day and even the fact that one of my co-workers will
show up with coffee in about 30 seconds. I have no reasonable
explanation for these bouts of déjà vu, but they were quite intense and all of them were triggered by marked seasonal events
such as autumn foliage, spring flowers or the lingering fragrance
of a nearby honeysuckle.

   The evidence of seasonal change in an urban landscape is
one of the hallmarks of a great garden design. The only exception here is the overemphasis that is often placed on spring-
flowering trees, shrubs and perennials. They provide a magnificent blaze of colour when in bloom, but once the show is over,
many of these spring landscapes can be quite boring. One of
the reasons for including a seasonal design section in this book
is so the other three seasons are not ignored.

   Seasons mark our years as gardeners, make us feel old or
young, remind us of good times and bad. But most of all, the
seasons bring us face to face with the years passing in our own
lives. The changing seasons offer us an opportunity to live life
to the fullest — don't make the mistake of leaving your garden
bare for even one of them.

Mixed tulip and forget-
me-not display designed
by Sharon Lawson
Colour photo p. 129

Designing with Spring Bulbs and Bedding

SHARON LAWSON, PARKS DEPARTMENT, BURNABY, B.C.

I have worked in the horticulture department of the city of Burnaby for the past 25 years. In those years of observing flower beds, I have come to believe that a combination of spring bulbs and bedding — of different types, colours and bloom times — is a lot more interesting than a solitary bulb planting. With careful planting, a bed can have several different looks over the period of a single spring season.

One year, I designed a bed where I combined 5 different types of tulip bulbs, each of a different colour. They were 'Monte Carlo' (early spring, double yellow), 'Apricot Beauty' (midseason, peach single), 'Daydream' (late flowering, yellow to orange), 'Blue Amiable' (late flowering, violet blue) and 'White Truimphator' (late flowering, lily type). I planted blue forget-me-nots (Myosotis sylvatica 'Victoria Blue') over the entire bed. The combination provided colour and texture over an extended period of time, starting off with one colour scheme, gradually changing through another and ending with a third.

DESIGNING WITH COLOUR

When picking colours for bulbs and spring bedding, there are a few standard combinations that work well.

- The primary colours: red, blue and yellow.
- Opposite, or complementary colours, such as blue and orange, or purple and yellow.
- Adjacent colours such as red, orange and yellow or blue, purple and red.

- A monochromatic scheme — different shades and hues of the same colour. (One of our gardeners once chose every red tulip available from our supplier and planted them in a patchwork-type pattern).
- White and, occasionally, black can be planted with any colour for contrast.

I find it best to use at least three colours in a bulb and spring bedding design. When using yellow and white, try adding a pale primrose yellow to make it more appealing. In large beds, group 3 to 5 plants of the same colour for a showier display.

BULB SELECTION

Several years ago one of our gardeners, Marie Jory, designed a bed where she alternated clumps of grape hyacinths *(Muscari armeniacum)* and *Tulipa* 'Abba' (early spring, red double). The different plant textures and the contrast of deep red and blue was quite dramatic.

When designing a bed, be sure the plants bloom at the same time for maximum impact (different cultivars of the same tulip type may bloom at different times). For example, the Darwin tulips (late-flowering, single-blooming tulips which include 'Blue Amiable', 'Queen of the Night' and 'Shirley') can bloom 2 to 3 weeks apart. You may be hoping for a rainbow effect, but you could end up with some portions of the bed in full bloom while others are just in bud, thus ruining the overall look. Observe and make notes on which bulbs bloom together, and if you are unsure, mix the bulbs randomly. If you have a large bed to work with, you can plant it like a patchwork quilt, with several different varieties of bulbs. This will look good as long as about ⅓ of them are blooming at the same time.

We have started to plant more daffodils over the last few years. Most of them naturalize quite well, which means they flower for several seasons. We have had great success with 'Dutchmaster', 'Ice Follies', 'Mount Hood', 'Quail', 'Rosy Sunrise', 'Fortissimo', 'King Alfred', 'Tahiti' and 'Jack Snipe'. (One cultivar that is listed as naturalizing, but in my experience does not, is 'Thalia'.) One year I designed a bed containing about 15 different types of daffodils with varying heights, colours and bloom times (the patchwork effect). It had interest for a much longer period of time than if the whole bed had been planted with just one variety of daffodil. But for the most part, we plant just one type of daffodil and add winter bedding to the border, changing the colour scheme or type of bedding each year.

Some tulips naturalize quite well, including 'Princess Irene', 'Oxford', 'Golden Oxford', 'Apeldoorn' and, of course, all of the botanical, or species, tulips. The bulbs of most cultivars divide up so much after the first season that they just produce leaves in the second year. However, we still plant some tulips, as few bulbs provide the colour range and impact that they have. This practice may not continue, as more and more areas seem to be ravaged by squirrels and other scavengers.

There are many other bulbs that naturalize quite well and should be considered for spring colour. Most like an exposure of sun to part shade. The following are some examples.

Bulb iris (including *Iris reticulata*) Blue, purple, yellow and white.
Crocus (cultivars and species) Many combinations of blue, mauve, purple ,white and yellow.
Dog-tooth violet *(Erythronium)* Pink, white or yellow.
Fritillaria (cultivars and species) Orange, purple, white or yellow.
Glory of the snow (*Chionodoxa* spp.) Blue, white or pink.
Hyacinth (these like sun) Burgundy, blue, orange, pink, purple, violet, white or yellow.
Siberian squill (*Scilla* spp.) Blue, pink or white.
Snowdrops (*Galanthus* spp.) White.
Spring star flower *(Triteleia)* A delightful little blue flower that spreads well once established.
Striped squill (*Puschkinia* spp.) Pale blue or white.
Windflowers (*Anemone* spp.) Blue, pink, red, violet or white.

Snowdrop *(Galanthus)* bulbs that are for sale in the fall don't generally have a great chance of survival. They do not like to dry out, and this usually occurs when they are sold this way. It is best to find someone who has some growing in their yard and ask if you can have a clump. For the best results, transplant when they are in bloom or just after, while they still have leaves.

SPRING BEDDING

Use bedding to extend the blooming season in beds or containers. Violas planted in autumn will bloom whenever they get some sunny weather over the winter. Pansies *(Viola* x *wittrockiana)* can also be planted in the fall if you live in a region with a mild winter climate. In some years, pansies do fine all winter in the Pacific Northwest, but gardeners in slightly colder regions would do better to plant them in mid-February. English daisies *(Bellis perennis),* forget-me-nots (*Myosotis* spp.) and wallflowers (*Cheiranthus* spp.) can be planted in the fall, but don't typically bloom until early to mid spring. In mild years, primroses (*Primula acaulis* varieties) will last through the winter and can bloom from October right into spring. The rain will spot the petals, but from a distance they still put on a good show of colour. Deadheading pansies, primula and English daisies will keep the plants looking tidier and encourage the development of more blooms.

BED PREPARATION AND PLANTING

We like to use a 6-8-6 organic fertilizer for most of our bedding plants. If we are just planting bulbs, we use a lower nitrogen/higher phosphorus formulation, such a 3-15-6 or 4-10-10. Daffodils that are left to naturalize in the beds are fertilized in spring and fall. Tulips grown for a single season are not fertilized, as the bulb contains everything it needs to produce leaves and flowers for that year. Wherever we plant wallflowers *(Cheiran-thus)* we always add dolomite lime to the bed, as it prefers a higher soil pH. Good drainage is important, especially here in the wet Pacific Northwest, to prevent rotting of the bulbs.

The most efficient way to plant large beds of bulbs is to have two people working together and using a heavy-duty long-handled bulb planter. One person removes a plug of soil, and the other person follows behind and places a bulb in the hole. For smaller beds, a hand trowel is sufficient. To plant clumps of bulbs, dig a small pit with a shovel. Arrange 11 or so bulbs in the hole and fill it in.

It's not the end of the world if the bulb is not placed with the pointed end up. The shoots will emerge from the bulb and then gradually turn and grow towards the surface. They often catch up to the ones that were correctly planted.

PESTS AND SCAVENGERS

Bulbs are not without a few problems. Several different creatures — such as squirrels, rats or voles — make a habit of stealing tulips for food. We have tried placing netting over the planting area, but these pests just dig holes in the netting (chicken wire also works but is very time consuming). We have had some success with spreading blood meal (an organic fertilizer) around the beds as a repellent, but it needs to be replenished as soon as the rain washes it in, which is not very practical in a large bed.

Watch out for crows, which will sometimes pull out bedding when you first install it. They find it an easy way to get at grubs and worms that are exposed when the root ball is torn out of the ground. One solution is to push a landscape fabric staple through the root ball into the soil.

DESIGN TIPS

When conditions make planting in the ground difficult, plant up containers with bulbs and disperse them throughout the garden. This works well if the ground is rootbound or is poorly drained, which will cause the bulbs to rot. Add small woody plants and ornamental grasses to your pots for more interest.

If you particularly like a combination of bulbs and bedding plants in a public park, don't hesitate to contact the local parks department and ask what was in the bed. Most staff will gladly find out for you, as it is a compliment to them that you enjoyed their design. There are also lots of great ideas in gardening magazines and books. If there is a small combination that you like, you can usually expand on it when designing a garden bed. Some retail garden centres also put together pots with interesting bulb and plant combinations, so drop by as many of them as you can and scout out new ideas.

Late Summer Colour

TONY MILBRADT & TINA LALONDE, RAIN FOREST NURSERIES, LANGLEY, B.C.

Spring is a period of intense activity in the garden, a time of growth and renewal. But many of us are frustrated when this short-lived burst of colour and freshness fades in the heat of summer. To me, it brings to mind Noel Coward, cocktails and laughter — but what comes after this riot of colour?

Flower colour during the garden doldrums of late summer can be elusive for many gardeners, particularly those who have forgone the cheap thrills, bright colours and impermanence of annuals. Fortunately, late summer is a period when the colour possibilities and plant selection can leap from the mundane to the unusual. It's an opportunity to focus on the artistry of foliage, plant form and flowers rather than relying on the bold splashes of colour common to summer flowers.

Perennials like *Cimicifuga* with its 4 to 5-foot (1.2 to 1.5-m) clumps of purple-black foliage, depending on the cultivar, can be used to illuminate late bloomers like *Rudbeckia, Echinacea* (purple coneflower), *Boltonia, Aster* and *Coreopsis. Hakonechloa macra* 'Aureola' (golden hakone grass), with its striking blades of green and gold, can enhance the spectacular, fall-blooming *Tricyrtis* (toad lily) for a tropical look in the shade garden. Shrubs like *Weigela* and *Sambucus* (elderberry) and red Japanese maples can be used for their foliar effect with late-blooming perennials such as *Schizostylis, Crocosmia, Phygelius* (Cape fuchsia), *Salvia, Verbascum, Alstromeria, Solidago* (golden rod) and *Penstemon.*

Late summer display of *Miscanthus* 'Morning Light,' *Phygelius* 'Moonraker' and *Sedum* 'Matrona' designed by Michael Lascelle
Colour photo p. 130

Nothing adds colour and texture quite like foliage. Foliage supports and enhances the star performers (the blooming plants). From lime green to black, foliage can be used to electrify a shady corner or make a bold statement in a mixed border. A personal favourite, *Cimicifuga* 'Brunette' (and the newer, darker 'Hillside Black Beauty') provides great plant partnerships all season. Not only is the plant itself spectacular with its black foliage, in late summer and autumn it sends up spikes of creamy white flowers whose fragrance never fails to send customers searching the nursery for its source.

Also worth noting is the annual (frost tender) grass *Pennisetum setaceum* 'Rubrum'. This outstanding ornamental grass supplies vibrant burgundy leaf blades and bottlebrush flowers right up to the first hard frost. This is a great choice for pairing with flowering perennials, such as Rudbeckia, for a rich contrast.

Structural plants such as *Phormium* (New Zealand flax) come in a host of colours. Other structural favorites, including *Agapanthus* (blue Nile lily), *Acanthus* and *Inula,* provide a late period of bloom as well. In the shade garden, *Thalictrum* and *Astilbe* bloom later, along with *Tricyrtis* and Japanese anemones (such as 'Whirlwind'). Another group of plants that liven up a late summer garden are the many forms of *Sedum*. They are completely bulletproof and actually thrive on neglect. A few other noteworthy filler plants include *Erigeron* (fleabane) and some tall *Campanula* species. Anthemis and the fall-blooming *Gentiana septemfida* (deep blue) also provide masses of colour.

For the avid gardener willing to experiment, the choices are limitless! Not only do traditional late bloomers fill the colour void, there are several species of earlier-flowering plants that will rebloom if cut back after the first flush of flowering. Examples include *Delphinium, Campanula* and some hardy geraniums, such as 'Johnson's Blue'. Let's also not forget such reliable plants as canna lilies and dahlias, which bloom until frost (they must be lifted and stored over winter). Some *Clematis* also flower until the hard frost hits, especially the Group C types, like 'Jackmanii'. Many warm-season grasses also start their inflorescence in late summer and some begin a vibrant foliage change in early autumn.

The garden challenges of late summer can provide you with limitless inspiration and spectacular foliage and flower colours. Just remember that gardening is a journey, not a destination!

Quintessential Fall Colour
MICHAEL LASCELLE, AMSTERDAM GARDEN CENTRE, PITT MEADOWS, B.C.

Forget the crisp morning air, the dew-laden spiderwebs or the silhouettes of barren trees disappearing in the fog — the quintessence of autumn is colour. While many gardeners are content with an incidental fall display, we do our landscapes a great disservice by concentrating on spring and summer and leaving them fallow for the balance of the year.

That said, even the most scrupulous garden designer will have some difficulty recreating an exact colour scheme, as autumn often seems to have a mind of its own. Some years it arrives resplendent in vivid foliage and fruit, yet in others it appears to be content with subtle earthen tones of sand, straw and umber.

Many consider autumn more a state of mind than a set period of time. Some gardeners, anxious for spring's arrival, usher in the season early with that first bouquet of cut tulips in late winter. If you consider yourself one of those gardeners who are eager for the glories of fall, this chapter will inspire you with a vision of colour for your own autumn landscape.

BALANCING YOUR DISPLAY
A balanced show of autumn colour is much like an elaborate fireworks display — it is best appreciated in layers or stages, where each feature can be admired individually but still contribute to the overall landscape. Clustering the entirety of your fall colour into too small an area is like setting off all your fireworks at once: the depth and intimacy are lost in a bright but garish display. Disperse autumn features throughout the garden, where their

Autumn foliage of
Hamamelis x *intermedia*
'Diane' (hybrid witch hazel)
Colour photo p. 131

brilliant hues will draw attention to portions of the landscape that might otherwise go unnoticed.

Case in point: it is often the crimson blaze of *Parthenocissus tricuspidata* (Boston ivy) that helps us appreciate the fine masonry it clings to. And the persistent blooms of *Pennisetum* 'Hameln' may stir us to look up and admire the setting sun, as it strikes the buff-coloured spikes and turns them to fire for a few fleeting moments. A background of decaying foliage in many shades and tones of brown often provides the best foil for bright autumn features, so leave these dormant plants intact until the fall display is over. A few late-season plants actually bear a contrasting palette of intense and dull colours at the same time. Some good examples include *Miscanthus purpurascens* with its blades of green, tan, red and burgundy, and one of my favorite trees, *Acer truncatum* x 'Pacific Sunset', a hybrid of *A. platanoides* and *A.truncatum* that features autumn foliage of russet, crimson, vermilion and green.

When planning, consider the varying height and form that plants provide, as well as autumn colour. The strong horizontal growth of *Euonymus alatus* 'Compacta' (compact burning bush) makes a bold statement in the foreground of columnar conifers, such as the upright *Juniperus scopulorum* 'Medora'. Similarly, the arching vase-shaped form of a singular *Hamamelis* (witch hazel) in full fall colour is striking when underplanted with a mass of low broadleaf evergreens, such as *Sarcococca hookeriana var. humilis.*

STRETCHING SEASONAL COLOUR

If you are like most garden enthusiasts, you probably have little space in your landscape to even consider making room for one-season wonders. The good news is that many trees and shrubs are attractive at more than one time of the year. To help inspire you along these lines, here is a select group of five trees or shrubs for you to consider.

Hamamelis x *intermedia* **'Diane'** (witch hazel) The coppery-red winter blooms of this hybrid witch hazel are only lightly fragrant and can be a little hard to see on those dull, overcast days, but the fall foliage colours are nothing short of spectacular. Depending on its exposure, you can expect leaves of green, yellow or amber ringed with a fiery red, slowly changing to a vivid scarlet as the season progresses. Height 8 to 13 feet (2.4 to 4 m). Zone 6.

Cornus kousa (Kousa dogwood) Abundant creamy white bracts in June are followed by large, strawberry-like fruit that usually persists after leaf drop (if the birds don't get it). This disease-resistant species is well-behaved and features deep red to burgundy autumn tones. Height 10 to 20 feet (3 to 6 m). Zone 5.

Rhododendron luteum A deciduous rhododendron species that is sought after for its fragrant yellow blooms, which appear in late spring. This tall shrub will produce rich red fall foliage when planted in an exposure with at least a half day of sun. Height 6 to 9 feet (1.8 to 3 m). Zone 5–6.

Cryptomeria japonica **'Elegans'** (Japanese plume cedar) Conifers are not often considered when it comes to fall colour, but this is the exception! The feathery foliage of 'Elegans' is generally a deep green in spring, summer and early fall, but as the cold winds of autumn arrive it changes to a coppery-red or purple-brown colour and remains that way until spring. First-time owners usually find this change a bit alarming, but once you get used to it, the winter hue will be as welcome as frost on the fallen leaves. Height 16 to 20 feet (5 to 6 m). Zone 6.

Enkianthus campanulatus **'Red Bells'** I can't figure out why more people aren't planting this shrub in their gardens as it seems to have something for every season. In late spring to early summer it produces prominent clusters of pale yellow urn-shaped blooms that are veined in red. In summer it exhibits its foliage proudly in unique terminal whorls, which turn a fiery rose-red before falling in autumn and revealing the bare winter framework with its distinctly tiered growth habit. It generally likes the same conditions as most rhododendrons. Height 6 to 9 feet (1.8 to 3 m). Zone 5.

THE ROLE OF TEXTURE

Texture also plays an important role in the autumn palette. It comes in many different forms, but dormant seed and flower heads are probably the most critical component. Many of these textures might easily go unnoticed without the presence of light and wind, which provide the subtle movement or luminescence that attracts our attention.

Ornamental grasses are an obvious source of textures. *Miscanthus, Pennisetum* and *Stipa* all persist well into the heavy frosts of winter. And don't ignore the dried flower heads of late-summer perennials. Prominent among these are the dark rose, broccoli-like heads of border sedums such as 'Autumn Joy', the cone-shaped seed heads of *Echinacea purpurea* and the remaining silvery spines of the ghostly *Eryngium giganteum* (sea holly).

Fallen leaves also create a tapestry of texture. The best example of this is *Ginkgo biloba*. I think the flaxen, fan-shaped leaves look better as a carpet on the ground than they do on the tree.

A FALL COLOUR CALENDAR

When designing a garden, remember the old cliché "timing is everything." To have the longest autumn season possible, you will have to be quite selective about the plant material you choose. This fall colour calendar will give you a start when considering the many options available from late summer through to early winter.

Late Summer

Brown **Calamagrostis** 'Karl Foerster' Prominent tan flower spikes. Zone 5.

Yellow **Phygelius** x 'Moonraker' Persistent blooms of pale yellow. Zone 7.

Orange **Crocosmia** 'Emberglow' Burnt orange flower spikes. Zone 6.

Red **Helenium autumnale** 'Bruno' Mahogany-red daisy blossoms. Zone 3.

Burgundy **Pennisetum s.** 'Rubrum' Deep wine-red foliage. Zone 9.

Early Fall

Brown **Sasa veitchii** Groundcover bamboo with buff leaf edges in fall. Zone 7.

Yellow **Rudbeckia fulgida** 'Goldsturm' Golden-yellow daisy, dark cones. Zone 3.

Orange **Pyracantha** 'Mohave' Clusters of deep orange berries. Zone 6.

Red **Geranium macrorrhizum** Bright red autumn foliage tones. Zone 2.

Burgundy **Parthenocissus henryana** Reddish-purple autumn leaves with veining. Zone 7.

Late Fall

Brown **Carex buchananii**
Upright, bronze evergreen
sedge. Zone 6.

Yellow **Hamamelis mollis**
Butter yellow fall foliage.
Zone 5.

Orange Acer palmatum
'**Katsura**' Prominent orange
autumn tones. Zone 5.

Red **Schizostylis coccinea**
Rich crimson gladioli blooms.
Zone 7.

Burgundy **Stewartia pseudoca-**
mellia Vivid purple-red fall
foliage. Zone 5.

Early Winter

Brown Miscanthus '**Strictus**'
Subtle dormant banding.
Zone 5.

Yellow **Cornus** '**Flaviramea**'
Bright yellow branches.
Zone 3.

Orange Rosa '**Kiftsgate**'
Masses of small orange hips.
Zone 5–6.

Red **Ilex verticillata** Bright red
berries on bare stems. Zone 3.

Burgundy **Acer griseum**
Reddish-brown exfoliating
bark. Zone 5.

Designing with Winter Garden Plants

GERALD GIBBENS, VANDUSEN BOTANICAL GARDEN, VANCOUVER, B.C.

During winter, when most of us have put our gardens to bed, it's really nice to settle down in front of the fireplace and enjoy those new nursery or seed catalogues. But don't ignore the garden at this time of year: although the flower displays are long gone, this time of year has its own form of beauty. The brightly coloured stems of many deciduous shrubs or the peeling mature bark of *Acer griseum* (paperbark maple), with its tints of glowing copper, stand out in the garden, and now is the best time to appreciate the silhouettes of larger trees, their bare branches accentuated by a background of grey skies.

There are a surprising number of plants that provide the sensory pleasures of sight, sound, touch and scent in the winter garden. Many landscapes are designed to create maximum interest from spring through to autumn, but a wide range of plant material can enhance those three seasons and also provide interest in winter.

Take, for instance, deciduous and evergreen trees. When all seems grey and misty, the branching skeletons of deciduous trees and the shape and texture of conifers are excellent backdrops in the landscape. These trees also provide environments that protect small bulbs, perennials and tender shrubs. An additional highlight of the winter garden is the variety of bird life attracted by the berries and seeds that many of these plants produce.

Many public gardens have developed their own winter gardens, where a wide range of plants are displayed solely for their winter interest. The dark texture of the bare soil and broadleaf evergreens or conifers are used to

The gnarled trunk of a mature dawn redwood (*Metasequoia glyptostroboides*)

accentuate the colour of ornamental bark, berries and flowers. The backdrop of trees creates an enclosed effect that allows the scents of fragrant plants to be appreciated. In the smaller residential landscape, it's important to choose winter plants that work in combination with plant material that is the focus during the rest of the year.

SOIL CONSIDERATIONS

Most plants require a rich loam — deeply dug soil with a pH from 5.5 to 6.5. The addition of light leaf mould in the fall further nurtures the plants and protects the roots from frost. Soils must be well drained. Too much moisture will interfere with the ability of the roots to exchange nutrients and it becomes an avenue for fungus and other diseases to attack the plant. Constant soil moisture should be maintained, as fluctuations can allow diseases to develop. Allow fallen leaves to remain on the beds, as they produce a light protective layer that reduces the effects of deep frosts. Proper soil conditions are critical for winter-flowering plants: soils that are too wet or dry at this time can result in premature blossom drop or the death of the tree or shrub.

LIGHT EXPOSURE

It's especially important to consider light exposure in the short days of winter. Sunlight and temperature are key factors in the development of early-flowering plants. Many plants can be severely damaged by a drastic increase in temperature. Situate your winter garden so it faces west and you will get the benefit of filtered sun from midday on. The most tender plants should face south and be planted close to larger plants or walls that will absorb heat during the day and release it in the evening.

PLANT SELECTION

Winter interest focuses on a few distinct areas: bark, flowering shrubs, herbaceous plants that flower from early winter through to spring and early-blooming bulbs (many are suitable for naturalizing in our gardens). The heaths and heathers included here require an acid soil with a pH between 4 and 5.5. They should have even moisture that readily drains away and do best in an open, meadow situation. Plant them in drifts or groupings of several plants (a minimum of 3 to 5) to create impact. Many of the Scotch heathers *(Calluna vulgaris)* have wonderful winter foliage (or growth tips), even though their prime blooming season is mid to late summer. The dormant foliage and plumes of many ornamental grasses make great additions to the winter garden (especially when coated with frost), and a few of the selections provide an evergreen display, which is why they have been included.

A WINTER SEASON COMPENDIUM

Ornamental Bark and Form

Acer davidii (snakebark maple) Green & white striped bark. Prefers open woodland. Zone 6.

Acer griseum (paperbark maple) Flaking copper bark. An understory tree. Zone 5.

Betula utilis var. *jacquemontii* (Himalayan birch) Brilliant white mature bark. Zone 5.

Cornus alba 'Elegantissima' (shrubby dogwood) Bright red stems. Zone 2.

Cornus sericea 'Flaviramea' (yellowtwig dogwood) Yellow stems. Zone 3.

Corylus avellana 'Contorta' (corkscrew hazel) Twisted branches with early yellow catkins. Zone 4.

Metasequoia glyptostroboides (dawn redwood) A deciduous conifer. Zone 5.

Parrotia persica (Persian ironwood) Mottled green, grey, brown bark. Zone 5.

Prunus serrula (willow leaf cherry) Deep copper, peeling bark. Zone 5.

Stewartia pseudocamellia (Japanese stewartia) Mottled grey, brown, red bark. Zone 5.

Flowering Trees and Shrubs

Abeliophyllum distichum (white forsythia) White scented blooms in February. Zone 5.

Camellia sasanqua (winter camellia) White, pink, red blooms from October–February. Zone 6.

Corylopsis pauciflora (winter hazel) Pale yellow flowers in March. Zone 6.

Daphne mezereum (February daphne) Fragrant pink blooms December–February. Zone 4.

Hamamelis mollis (witch hazel) Fragrant yellow flowers December–March. Zone 5.

Flowering Trees and Shrubs *continued*

Jasminum nudiflorum (winter jasmine) Yellow flowers in February–March. Zone 5.

Lonicera fragrantissima (winter honeysuckle) White fragrant blooms January–February. Zone 5.

Mahonia x 'Charity' (leatherleaf mahonia) Deep yellow blooms November–December. Zone 7.

Prunus mume (Japanese apricot) White, pink or red flowers February–March. Zone 6.

Rhododendron 'Christmas Cheer' (rhododendron) Blush pink blooms January–April. Zone 6–7.

Sarcococca hookeriana humuilis (sweet box) Scented white flowers. Zone 6.

Viburnum x *bodnantense* 'Dawn' (pink dawn) Scented pink blooms November–April. Zone 7.

Berried Plants

Callicarpa bodinieiri 'Profusion' (beautyberry) Purple berries October–January. Zone 5.

Gaultheria procumbens (wintergreen) Red berries September–March. Zone 3.

Ilex aquifolium hybrids (English holly) Red, yellow, amber berries October–February. Zone 6.

Ilex verticillata (winterberry) Red berries on bare stems October–January. Zone 3.

Sorbus 'Joseph Rock' (golden mountain ash) Amber berries October–December. Zone 5.

Symphoricarpos albus (snowberry) White berries September–January. Zone 3.

Flowering Bulbs and Perennials

Cyclamen coum (European cyclamen) Pink, crimson, white blooms December–March. Zone 6.

Eranthis hyemalis (winter aconite) Yellow flowers February–March. Zone 4.

Galanthus nivalis (snowdrop) Pure white blooms January–March. Zone 3.

Helleborus niger (Christmas rose) White flowers November–January. Zone 4.

Helleborus x *orientalis* or *H. hybridus* (lenten rose) White, pink, plum flowers January–March. Zone 5.

Leucojum vernum (snowflake) White with green blooms January–March. Zone 4.

Narcissus cyclamineus (dwarf daffodil) Yellow flowers February–April. Zone 6.

Ornamental Grasses

Carex oshimensis 'Evergold' (Japanese sedge grass) Yellow and green foliage. Zone 5.

Cortaderia 'Sunstripe' (variegated pampas grass) Gold variegation and plumes. Zone 7.

Helictotrichon sempervirens (blue oat grass) Arching blue foliage. Evergreen. Zone 3.

Miscanthus sinensis 'Strictus' (porcupine grass) Horizontal gold banding. Zone 5.

Pennisetum alopecuroides 'Hameln' (fountain grass) Persistent bottlebrush blooms. Zone 5.

Heaths and Heathers

Calluna vulgaris 'Aurea' (Scotch heather) Golden yellow foliage, turning bronze in winter. Zone 5.

Calluna vulgaris 'Orange Queen' (Scotch heather) Foliage turns yellow-orange in cold. Zone 5.

Erica carnea 'Pirbright Rose' (winter heather) Reddish-purple flowers December–February. Zone 6.

Erica carnea 'Springwood White' (winter heather) White blooms January–March. Zone 6.

Erica x *darleyensis* 'Jack Brummage' (winter heather) Gold foliage, pink blooms February–March. Zone 6.

Erica x *darleyensis* 'Jenny Porter' (winter heather) Purple-rose flowers December–April. Zone 6.

CHAPTER 3
Good Bones for the Garden

The squire was glad of any argument to defend his clipped
yew-trees and formal terraces, which had been occasionally
attacked by modern landscape-gardeners.
  Washington Irving, "Christmas Eve"

I can't tell you how many landscapes I've come across with wonderful specimen trees, rare shrubs and unique perennials all arranged in a cluttered mess — because little attention was paid to their context in the garden or their ultimate size. I have also seen landscapes with superb hard features, such as gazebos, sculpture, fine masonry and ponds, which were thrown together with little thought as to whether they complemented each other — or even more importantly, whether they suited the garden site (or neighbourhood). The problem with these endeavours was not a lack of money, it was an absence of overall direction in the basic design or garden layout.

A qualified garden designer or landscape architect can help homeowners assess their needs and provide the garden with the necessary bones, or hard landscaping. Giving thought to sidewalks, paths, lawn areas, fences, walls, lighting, irrigation or garden structures before you start the project saves you time and money in the long term.

As to Washington Irving's observations on the need to defend an old-fashioned landscape style…I wouldn't worry about that. A well designed (and installed) landscape transcends the passage of time and should survive the scrutiny of any future landscape-gardeners!

Left Hand-crafted wooden Asian gate by Jack Gunther of Maple Ridge, B.C. *Right* Intricate sheet metal gate in New Westminster, B.C.

The Garden Gate

MICHAEL LASCELLE, AMSTERDAM GARDEN CENTRE, PITT MEADOWS, B.C.

The garden gate has come a long way from the castle fortifications and estate entrances of its origins. Over the years it has been reduced and adapted and is now the property of everyone. Access to your garden may not entail a gate at all — it could be an arbour, an arched trellis or a passage through a tall hedge. But no matter what form or structure it takes, the garden entrance should be a reflection of the landscape beyond and the architecture of the residence.

As famous landscape designer Gertrude Jekyll (1843–1932) put it: "An honest relation must exist between the entry and what is entered." A gateway is more than an opening, it is the threshold between the outside world and your private space. As such, it is an extension of your personal taste. Among the suggestions that follow, you may be able to find something that appeals to your aesthetic and meets the practical needs of your garden.

GATE DESIGN

Recently there has been a lot of interest in wrought ironwork, in particular gates with stylized motifs and cast iron elements. Many of these patterns have been revived from centuries past and are being incorporated into the clean modern lines of contemporary architecture. Cast iron components range from simple fleurs-de-lis pickets to ornate medallions, while the wrought ironwork can reflect anything from floral to geometric forms. Quite often, the design is a combination of both, the only restriction being the skill and imagination of the manufacturer.

In contrast to much of the ironwork of the past, basic black is no longer the dominant gate colour. Other shades, such as teal blue and viridian, contrast with the earthen tones of coloured stucco and natural wood now popular. The wrought iron gate provides an enticing view of the garden within, which changes with the seasons. In winter, the architecture of the gate provides structure and colour. This effect is gradually diffused as the foliage and flowers of spring begin to dominate the garden beyond.

Wooden gates date back to medieval Europe, with parallel developments in the Far East. They were often designed in conjunction with fences, beginning with crude close board styles and later evolving into the elaborate treillage (latticework) of the French. The popularity of the wooden gate probably reached its zenith with the picket fences of colonial America and the subsequent opulence of the Victorian era. Rustic gates of the late nineteenth century retained the natural form and bark of selected tree limbs (such as hazel, willow and birch), whose branches were fashioned into detailed woven patterns or simply fitted together to form a crude arbour.

These are just a few of the more common elements of classic gateway construction. Modern gate designs also make use of tempered glass, sheet metal and aluminum — materials that are more durable than wood.

LIVING GATES

Many older homes in the Pacific Northwest have large established hedges of English laurel *(Prunus laurocerasus),* hemlock *(Tsuga canadensis* or *T. heterophylla)* or Western red cedar (*Thuja plicata* 'Excelsa'), which have been pruned to allow access to the garden. This type of entry can be further defined by placing a gate within the opening. The resulting contrast of dark foliage set against the profile of the gate is striking. A living archway of pleached conifers also makes an interesting garden entrance, particularly if your landscape places an emphasis on plant material rather than architectural features.

The pendulous branches of weeping spruce (*Picea abies* 'Pendula') or *Cedrus atlantica glauca* 'Pendula' (weeping blue atlas cedar) can be trained on a support framework that is hidden in the mature foliage. With this type of gate, limit the use of vines or climbing shrubs immediately around the archway — use only enough shrubbery to soften the appearance.

Formal entrances of wrought iron are best sparingly embellished, while the more colloquial arched trellis naturally lends itself to a climbing rose, clematis or a combination of both. Choosing what you want for your garden entrance may be as simple as taking a stroll in your neighbourhood to get some ideas from surrounding landscapes.

THE PRACTICAL GATE

When designing any gate or garden entrance, don't forget the practical concerns. Here are a few basic guidelines.

- Decide on the function of your gateway (security, privacy, ornamental) before designing an appropriate entrance.
- If adjacent stairs are necessary, make sure you allow for an adequate landing, where two people can stand side by side comfortably.
- Don't clutter the garden entrance with other objects such as a large mailbox or signs.
- The gate should be a minimum of 3 feet (90 cm) wide. A 4-foot (120-cm) width will provide wheelbarrow or machine access for the gardener.
- If the opening is larger than 4 feet (120 cm), consider a double gate to alleviate stress on the hinges.
- The size of the support posts is important to the overall effect. Large posts confer an imposing appearance.
- When selecting the entrance site, symmetry plays an important role. Balancing the landscape or architectural features around the framework of a gateway helps achieve a pleasing design.
- Don't restrict the use of arbours and trellises to the main entrance. They can also define a transition zone in the garden (such as the entrance to a vegetable garden).

The Garden Path

FRANK SCHORTINGHUIS, ALLGREEN LANDSCAPING LTD., LANTZVILLE, B.C.

Garden paths are an invitation to explore. Whether it is a front entrance, a side passageway, a formal promenade, or a meandering journey of discovery through shady fronds or scented herbs to the tranquility of a garden bench, a pathway increases the usefulness and accessibility of the spaces within a garden.

The materials used in constructing hard landscape features such as paths, patios and steps also add textures that accent and complement the soft landscaping of plants, lawn and water. A path provides secure footing in wet weather and access for garden maintenance, and helps one discover and appreciate all the beauty and varied perspectives that the landscape has to offer. A pathway that meanders back and forth increases the apparent size of the garden, slowing one's progress through the garden and allowing more time to see what is there.

Pathways may be of varying widths but should be appropriate to their function. Entrance and promenade pathways should be wide enough for two people to walk abreast, a minimum of 4 to 5 feet (1.2 to 1.5 m). Locate paths far enough away from walls and fences to allow comfortable pas-

Left A path of square patio slabs is cleverly masked with groundcovers, hosta, ferns and shrubs in this woodland garden
Right A curved path draws the viewer's eye into the garden (Photos: Frank Schortinghuis)
Colour photo p. 132

sage without scraping one's elbows when carrying bulky items to the front door. Informal paths leading through planted areas or from one part of the garden to another may be narrower, but should still be at least 2 to 3 feet (60 to 90 cm) wide, especially where plants encroach at the edges. Paths should lead to a destination — perhaps another part of the garden, a door, a patio, pond or bench. A path that ends abruptly at nowhere in particular is a disappointment and won't encourage a repeat visit.

Natural stone, clay brick, concrete pavers, gravel screenings, bark and even grass can be used in constructing pathways. Whatever the material, the surface should be level and have good traction to prevent tripping and slipping. Use durable materials, such as stone, brick or concrete pavers, in heavy traffic areas such as front entrances and well-used access pathways. Casual paths through wooded areas and planting beds are well suited to the use of gravel, bark or stepping stones.

When choosing materials for a pathway, consider the general theme and atmosphere of the garden, personal preference and budget. Quarried rock, bricks and pavers are more expensive to purchase and install, but they provide beautifully finished, clean surfaces appropriate for entrances, patios

Left A sturdy walkway of split basalt
Right Treated timbers and aggregate make a grade change very easy (Photos: Frank Schortinghuis)

and formal pathways. Bark, gravel and turf are less expensive and are well suited to informal parts of the garden.

Before you lay a path of stone, brick or pavers, it is essential to construct a compacted base of several inches of roadbase gravel topped with an inch (2.5 cm) of sand. This will ensure the pathway remains level. Bark and gravel may be placed directly on a regular graded surface. For gravel pathways, use fine gravel (½ inch/1.2 cm minimum), or better yet, gravel screenings, which provide a firmer and safer surface than larger stones, which tend to roll underfoot. Grass pathways have a nice informal appearance, but do not stand up well to heavy traffic. One solution is to embed stepping stones. Set them level with the grass to allow for mowing. Grass grows more vigorously in the open than in shady or wooded areas, so grass pathways are most successful in open areas with light to moderate traffic.

There are many creepers and groundcovers that do an excellent job of filling in around stepping stones, though some do better than others due to their growth habits and durability. *Isotoma* or *Laurentia* (blue star creeper), *Helxine soleirolii* (baby tears) and mosses work particularly well as fill-in plants. In very dry or shady areas, stepping stones can be set into a bed of

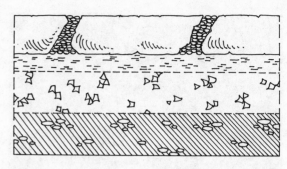

Proper stepping stone installation: profile of an informal path with split basalt and pea gravel on a base of 1 inch (2.5 cm) sand, with 2 to 3 inches (5 to 7.5 cm) road base gravel over the subsoil.

gravel or drainrock for a durable, attractive and relatively inexpensive pathway. Stepping stones should be set close enough together to accommodate easy steps and be embedded deep enough so that there are no protruding edges to trip over.

Consider also the treatment of the pathway edges. They can be defined and regular, or staggered and blended with the plant material that grows beside it. A distinct edge or support can be made with stone, brick or treated lumber, but avoid the use of plastic and metal edgings, which look unnatural.

Whatever type of path you choose, it will undoubtedly add a dimension of style and mystery to your garden and help you move around with ease to enjoy the beauty of your landscape.

LOW-PROFILE PERENNIALS

Here is a short list of low-profile perennials that may be used between stepping stones and random pieces of slate. Please keep in mind that they vary in their tolerance of foot traffic. A plus sign (+) indicates those groundcovers that tolerate medium to high traffic well.

Acaena microphylla (New Zealand burr) Height 2 inches (5 cm). Zone 3. +

Leptinella 'Platt's Black' (black brass buttons) Height 2 inches (5 cm). Zone 7. +

Mazus reptans (creeping mazus) Height 2 inches (5 cm). Zone 5.

Mentha requienii (Corsican mint) Height ½ inch (1 cm). Zone 7.

Sagina subulata (Irish moss) Height 1 inch (2.5 cm). Zone 3.

Sedum acre 'Aureum' (golden mossy stonecrop) Height 1 to 2 inches (2.5 to 5 cm). Zone 2.

Thymus praecox 'Coccineus' (red creeping thyme) Height 1 inch (2.5 cm). Zone 3. +

Thymus pseudolanuginosus (woolly thyme) Height 1 inch (2.5 cm). Zone 3. +

Irrigation Made Simple

NICK HARRIS, HARRIS IRRIGATION LTD., VANCOUVER, B.C.

New residents in Vancouver or the Lower Mainland might be forgiven for thinking that it never stops raining. The winter months can be unrelentingly grey and wet, and sometimes it seems that summer will never come. When the clouds dissipate and the sun shines, however, Vancouver is spectacular — and that is when our plants, shrubs and lawns can begin to suffer. It's not long before the hoses and oscillating sprinklers are hauled out of the garage, but hauling hoses can present challenges. "How few places can I move this sprinkler?" "How do I water the flowerbed along the sidewalk without soaking everybody that walks by?" Or even "Do I really want to get up at 4 a.m. to turn the hose on?"

A well-installed, well-designed automatic sprinkler system can be programmed to water different areas at different times, but it can and should be far more efficient than using the scattergun approach of a moveable sprinkler. No more water on the sidewalks, the neighbours or the front of the house. And no more dragging unwieldy hoses through the flower beds.

A good sprinkler system starts with the connection to the house water line, usually close to the municipal shut-off to optimize pressure and minimize the sound of water running in the house. To keep polluted water from the garden sprinklers from entering the common drinking water system, a backflow prevention device must be installed. Permits are required and each municipality requires the installation to be done correctly and to be tested. The protection of drinking water is of paramount importance.

When designing the sprinkler system, divide the garden into sunny or shady areas. Areas with different watering requirements need different sprinkler heads. How you use the garden is important. Do you have a vegetable garden that you tend daily? Do you plant annuals in some areas? There are a lot of things to consider in order to achieve a successful watering system. Use pop-up heads for the lawn areas and, whenever possible, the shrub areas or use heads on ½-inch-wide (1-cm) pipe supports (you choose the stem height) behind large shrub areas. Pots and planters can be watered with small misting or drip irrigation heads, which are separately controlled.

Nowadays, controllers are computerized and are able to handle the requirements of different zones at different times — including separate programming for various days or lengths of watering time. A good system should optimize the capacity of the controllers — in other words, use a simple controller for a basic irrigation system and a more complicated controller only when necessary.

A sprinkler system should be invisible. Sprinkler heads should pop up only when needed (and be hidden the rest of the time), with valves conveniently and discreetly located underground in fibreglass valve boxes, and pipe buried under walls.

In new gardens, some preparation is always a good thing. Put sleeves under new driveways — not the ½-inch poly pipe on special at the local hardware store, but a 4-inch (10-cm) PVC drain pipe large enough to accommodate several future irrigation lines (or electrical lighting conduits). Plan for the future by laying in extra wire for possible additions or changes to the valves. Install a controller with a spare zone or two, and for people who will be away for long periods each year during the summer, a rain sensor is a great idea. It will prevent the system from watering day after day when it is raining — good both for security and for the environment.

Don't forget that a sprinkler system needs to be winterized. Even though winters in the Pacific Northwest are usually mild, the occasional hard frost can cause considerable damage to a system under pressure. There are two ways to insure against winter damage. The most effective is blowing the lines out by means of a compressor, a service offered by some installation companies. Like insurance, it is good when needed. Another method is the use of automatic drains, which are small, plastic, pressure-operated devices installed at the low points of the system. It is not a bad alternative, provided there are enough installed and none of them fail, either open or closed.

It is possible to install a sprinkler system yourself, but don't underestimate the value of good professional advice. Talk to the parts suppliers and provide them with an accurate plan of your garden, with measurements, slopes, shady areas and the types of flowers or shrubs growing there. (For example, roses and azaleas need different types of heads.)

The mechanics of an irrigation system are deceptively simple. A PVC pipe cutter, a small container of PVC cement, a few hundred feet of pipe and a mixed bag of fittings and sprinkler heads — and you are ready to go. But a poorly installed and/or designed system can cause endless headaches. There is nothing worse than coming home after a long weekend away to find that a fitting has given way in the flowerbed near the house. Apart from the small deluge of mud and the possible flooded basement, it is bound to cause a certain amount of anxiety every time you go on vacation.

A poor design can leave you in a situation where in order to water some areas adequately, other areas are permanently saturated. After investing in a system, you don't want to be dragging a hose to the rhododendron at the far end of the garden on a regular basis, or watching those petunias swimming for their lives every morning. If you are not handy with tools and your budget allows for it, you may want to opt for having a system professionally installed.

A well installed, carefully thought out sprinkler system can seem like magic. The garden is well watered on a regular basis whether you're at home or away, it is easy to adjust and it does what you want. Simple irrigation can truly be a great labour-saving device and it is always a good long-term garden investment.

Installing a Healthy Lawn

NICK BROAD, ENGLISH LAWNS LTD., NORTH VANCOUVER, B.C.

A well-manicured lawn can make the difference between a great landscape and a garden that few people even bother to look at. Tufts of pale green moss or bare patches choked with weeds reflect very poorly on the rest of the landscape, no matter how well the trees, shrubs and perennials are maintained. Consider that your lawn is the first impression of the garden and remember that first impressions are lasting!

Some gardeners have concerns about the environmental impact of turf maintenance, but a properly installed lawn requires less fertilizer than a lawn laid on poor soil, and weeds generally don't get the chance to establish themselves in thick, healthy lawns (which greatly reduces the use of selective herbicide). Water consumption can be reduced through the use of deep, infrequent waterings, which helps to develop strong, drought-resistant root systems. A well-installed lawn can be healthy and low maintenance — you just have to choose the right grass for your site and prepare the site properly.

The long-term health of your lawn is dependent on two major factors, good soil drainage and adequate sunlight. You will need a minimum of 4 hours of direct sun for turf and 2 hours for a seeded lawn (using a shade grass seed blend). More sunlight is better, but these are the absolute minimums. The best time to consider installing lawn drainage is when you are dealing with the sub-grade, and not after the lawn has been laid or seeded.

PREPARING THE SUB-GRADE

In lawn areas located at the base of a slope or adjacent to extensive patio surfaces, a drainage system may be necessary. Perforated 4-inch (10-cm) PVC pipe is one of the better choices for drainage. It can be placed in a 14-inch-deep (35-cm) trench, with a minimum of 3 inches (8 cm) of crushed gravel on the bottom and sides. The pipe should be oriented with the holes facing down, so that as the water fills the gravel trench, it percolates into the pipe and drains down the grade to the catch-basin or ditch. (Note that most bylaws prohibit you from diverting your drainage water onto a neighbour's property.) The drain pipe should always be sloped — 1 inch (2.5 cm) slope for every 4 feet (1.2 m) away from the residence or the periphery of the yard — to prevent water from pooling in these areas. We sometimes cover just the top of the pipe with a strip of landscape fabric (do not use landscape fabric on the bottom and sides of the trench, as it tends to silt up very quickly) and cover it with 6 inches (15 cm) of gravel or a blend of 50 percent topsoil and 50 percent coarse sand, as this drains well and still allows the grass to root properly.

Make sure that the subsoil in the rest of the lawn area is graded roughly level, with a slight slope for surface water drainage. This is also the best time in the design process to consider an in-ground irrigation system

— especially if you have an exposed, full-sun site. If you have a heavy clay subsoil, you may want to try to amend it by adding 2 to 3 inches (5 to 8 cm) of coarse sand and 1 inch (2.5 cm) of organic matter (such as mushroom manure, fine compost or peat moss). Rototill it into the subsoil to create a consistent blend. Don't use sand alone as an amendment. The mix of sand and heavy clay (without the organic content) compacts very quickly and packs like concrete. In any case, you want to avoid creating layers in your soil base, as this will cause inconsistent moisture levels in each of the strata. For example, 6 inches (15 cm) of a blended sandy soil is a better lawn base than 3 inches (8 cm) of coarse sand layered over 3 inches (8 cm) of topsoil. A mixture of 50 percent blended topsoil and 50 percent coarse sand is an ideal medium for growing both turf and seed. Be sure to incorporate some dolomite lime (at twice the suggested rate) into this soil blend, as most grasses prefer a higher pH and many parent soils in the Pacific Northwest are slightly acidic. Apply turf starter fertilizer (6-20-15) to the prepared soil bed (at rates indicated) prior to sodding.

Once the rough grading and soil amending has been completed, you are ready to fine-tune the levelling. Use a wide aluminum rake and a water-filled hand roller to help firm the soil surface. If you are not sure how your grading skills measure up, just get on your knees and look across the grade right after you roll it — any dips will be quite apparent and can be corrected. You are now ready to decide whether you will be using turf or seed.

LAYING TURF

If you are a person who likes instant gratification or if you need a reasonably durable lawn surface in short order, then turf is for you.

Most turf in the Pacific Northwest comes in rolls approximately 18 inches (45 cm) wide and 6 feet (2 m) long, equalling 1 square yard in area (larger commercial rolls are also available). This is why lawns are measured out by the square yard. Most people are unaware that there are different types of turf available, including shade, sports, full sun and standard grades (among others). It is important to consider what conditions exist in your yard. Turf is also grown on different mediums, ranging from sand to clay soils, and it is crucial to match the turf base to the soil that exists in your prepared area to prevent the layered effect discussed earlier.

When you roll the turf out, stagger the ends, and make sure there are no gaps or overlaps between the sides or the ends of the rolls. Patches should be limited to pieces no less than 1 foot (30 cm) long, as smaller portions of sod are prone to drying out or slipping. Once the turf is laid out, you can use a garden hose to help determine what shape to cut the edges. A coarse serrated or carpet knife can be used for this purpose. When the lawn has been laid out, edges cut and remnants removed, go over it with a half-filled hand roller to firm it, running it over the joints along the length of the roll.

Keep the sod well watered for the first two weeks, averaging 1 inch (2.5 cm) of water a day when sunny. After 2 weeks the lawn should be lightly

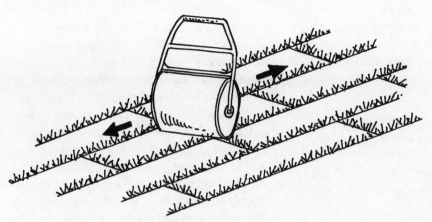

Firming a recently laid turf lawn with a water-filled hand roller

rooted and you can water only as needed. Less frequent, deep waterings are better than daily sprinkles — which promotes a shallow root system that is vulnerable to even mild drought conditions. Try to keep everyone off the new lawn for at least three weeks and begin cutting the grass when it reaches 2½ inches (6 cm) and no higher!

SEEDING A LAWN

Just like turf, there are different grass varieties and/or blends to choose from in the the Pacific Northwest, each with its own specific cultural needs. Fine fescues are often the dominant grass in shade mixes, as they grow well in shade, but they dislike heavy foot traffic. **Kentucky blue grass** is more common in full sun mixes, as it thrives in full sun and tolerates foot traffic rather well. **Perennial ryegrass** also prefers sunny exposures, germinates quickly and is often used for overseeding lawns. However, it is not very cold tolerant and should not be used in interior climates. As with turf, take the time to determine your needs and then purchase an appropriate seed or mix.

Start the seeding process by taking a leaf rake and gently scratching the surface of your prepared lawn bed. This will create shallow furrows to receive the seed. Evenly spread your seed with a cyclone spreader (a hand-held or push model) and then roll it with a light hand-roller. Make sure it is dry or the seed will stick to the roller surface. This will gently press the seed approximately ⅛ inch (3 mm) below the soil level and will help with the germination process.

After this, you need only keep the seed constantly moist with a fine mist or sprinkler (too strong a spray will wash the seed out), but be careful not to waterlog the seed bed. During this period, keep people and pets off the area. Once the seed has germinated, water twice a week if necessary. When it is long enough to cut it is very important that you pick a dry day for cutting and be sure that your mower is sharp, as newly germinated grass can be pulled up very easily. Also, you should anticipate reseeding several times, as germination is rarely perfect and small washouts are quite common.

TAKING CARE OF YOUR NEW LAWN

Once your lawn has been installed, it will require some regular maintenance to keep it strong and healthy. Here are a few simple tips to keep you on track.

Mowing

- Never cut more than ⅓ of the total grass height (less on the first cut), as this causes shock.
- The height at which you cut the grass should not vary a great deal during the growing season.
- Never cut the grass less than 1 inch (2.5 cm) high; a height of 1¼ to 2 inches (3 to 5 cm) is recommended for most lawns.
- Never let the grass grow taller than 2½ inches (6 cm), especially in the case of a seeded lawn.
- The grass should be dry for the first 2 cuts, but it's better to cut it damp than let it get over 3 inches (8 cm) tall.
- Never leave the grass clippings on the lawn and always remove the leaves in fall.
- A healthy lawn should be cut once a week when actively growing and always cut at right angles to the previous cut.
- Use a well-maintained lawnmower with a *sharp* blade.

Fertilizing

- Overfertilizing is as bad as not fertilizing. Always measure your lawn to determine how much fertilizer is necessary.
- Even distribution of fertilizer is essential to prevent burning. Use a cyclone or drop spreader.
- Divide the fertilizer needed into 2 equal portions and apply in two different directions.
- If rain does not fall for 2 days after application, water the fertilized lawn thoroughly.

- Fertilizing builds up resistance to drought and disease, and dense turf resists weeds and moss.
- Avoid fertilizing during hot summer months or during periods of drought.
- A new lawn should be fertilized 3 to 4 weeks after it has been installed.
- Slow-release fertilizers are best (many nitrogen/phosphorus/potash formulations exist, 23-3-23 being one type). These can be used in spring or late spring and early summer (i.e. at the end of May and mid-June, possibly once again in early September).
- Shade turf requires less fertilizer (specifically, nitrogen) and water than other grass types.
- Organic-based fertilizers are more environmentally friendly and somewhat safer for children and pets who may come in contact with the grass.
- A new lawn should be de-thatched in spring to prevent any buildup of grass clippings.
- Aerate the lawn in either spring or fall, but only when the soil is moist. Aerating improves drainage, relieves compaction and stimulates root growth. A ¼-inch (5-mm) layer of top dressing mix after aeration is beneficial.
- Deal with weeds and moss as soon as they appear, before they get out of hand.
- Spread dolomite lime (at the rate indicated on the bag) in early spring and late fall to raise the pH.
- During the winter, keep off the lawn as much as possible, as walking on it can cause fungal problems.

A FINAL WORD

Some gardeners are quite capable of installing their own lawn, but many people will find the grading, rolling and installation process to be very physically demanding (a moist roll of turf is quite heavy). You may want to consider hiring a landscaper to handle this for you.

If you follow this route, the information here will give you a good idea of what you can expect from any landscape professional you might hire. In either case, a well-installed lawn will provide years of pleasure and need not be a constant source of visual annoyance or endless work. It can be your low-maintenance pride and joy!

Painting the Garden with Light
GERALD CUPIDO, EXCEL LANDSCAPING & DESIGN, SURREY, B.C.

Do you take pride in the beautiful flower combinations, the architectural shrub forms and the striking foliage found in your garden? Maybe you have a dramatic arbour, or perhaps a lovely waterfall, or even a specimen tree or prominent piece of statuary. Why not enjoy this landscape in the evening, as well as during the day? By installing the right kind of outdoor night lighting you will reap the visual benefits from your garden even after the sun sets — not to mention the added incentive of safety and security. After all, why invest time and money on landscaping, only to have it disappear at night when you are most likely to be at home?

By planning your outdoor lighting project carefully, you can create a dramatic landscape that has the look of a luxurious estate. The lighting should not be noticeable during the day, other than the fixtures that are used to light the pathways. At night, all that should be visible is the effect of the light, not the actual source.

Although there are many light kits available on the market, most give what I call a "runway" or "birthday cake" effect. After the sun sets, all that is evident is a straight row of dim lights running up and down the driveway (or sidewalk), or a ring of plastic fixtures arranged in circle around the beds. These inexpensive kits don't light up anything in particular, other than the small fixtures they come with.

LIGHTING CALCULATIONS

The first task is to make a lighting plan. Some areas to consider include steps and walks, architectural features, trees and· shrubs, garden paths, patios and decks, and statuary. Using graph paper, draw a scale plan of the outside of your home and the surrounding landscape. Be sure to include the above-mentioned features, along with the wattage size required for each light. This is important, because it will determine the size of transformer you need to buy. For example, if you have 3 spotlights of 50 watts, 3 spotlights of 20 watts and 4 path lights of 50 watts, you will have a total of 410 watts. You will need a transformer that can handle 450 watts, plus any lights you may consider adding later. I suggest that you initially buy a transformer with 20 to 30 percent more capacity than you need, in case you want to add more fixtures as the plants and trees grow (or decide to increase the lamp wattage). In the example above, a suitable transformer size would be a 600-watt unit (make sure you do not exceed the wattage of the transformer). Plug the transformer directly into the socket (do not use an extension cord) and always be sure to use a GFI (ground fault interrupter) receptacle. Check the proper circuit load size for the outlet and do not exceed it.

LIGHTING TECHNIQUES

When choosing light fixtures, be creative and use a mixture of techniques to create drama in your landscape. Here are a few techniques for highlighting the garden at night.

Moon or Downlighting Light fixtures are placed above eye level and high up in tree canopies to simulate the effect of the moonlight shining through the branches. Shadows from the branches make intricate patterns on the ground. Downlighting provides security and safety lighting in large areas where it might otherwise be dark.

Path Lighting Fixtures are set close to the path to light pedestrian areas. These lights are approximately 18 inches (45 cm) to 2 feet (60 cm) high, with the fixture directing the light down. It is important to illuminate a path with steps, stepping stones or uneven surfaces to prevent accidents. These fixtures should be decorative, since they will be in view night and day. When positioned properly, they can also light up the surrounding flower beds, groundcovers and perennials planted along the path.

Uplighting The lights are positioned at ground level, facing up to provide a dramatic effect. Try this technique on multi-stemmed shrubs, weeping trees or even a textured wall surface. Be careful to not position the fixture so that it creates a glare, and try to hide the fixture by using natural rock, shrouds or even shrubs. The fixture should be aimed away from the primary viewing angles.

Shadowing or Silhouetting This technique allows you to create dramatic effects. Light the plant from in front at a low angle, to project the shadows upwards against a wall or other surface. Placing the fixture behind the plant creates a bold silhouette. The silhouette technique also gives the effect of a plant sitting up on a ridge, outlined against the sky at dusk.

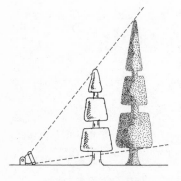

Creating a silhouette using a shadowing technique

LIGHT FIXTURES AND BULBS

Another key to successful landscape lighting is choosing the appropriate lamp. Too much light or a misplaced beam will cause unwanted glare. Not enough light can make for a very ineffective display. Consider using lower-wattage lamps and more fixtures; at night a little light goes a long way.

Many fixtures that come packaged together include a lamp that works best for that particular selection. If they do not include a lamp you will have to choose one. MR lamps require a luminaire with a lens to protect the lamps from weather conditions. PAR lamps are made with their own tempered glass lens and need no extra protection. PAR lamps give an oval beam of light in which the horizontal beam is wider than the vertical beam. MR-16 lamps are available with a permanent lens cover to protect people (or pets) from accidentally touching the halogen bulb (and also to protect it from the elements).

INSTALLATION CONCERNS

When designing wire runs to your landscape lights, try to avoid straight runs. In this scenario the first light on the run will receive the most voltage and each subsequent feature receives less, providing a very unbalanced effect. The best configuration is a centre-fed T run. This type of run allows almost equal voltage to all fixtures and prolongs individual lamp life.

Proper wire size is also very important — short runs and long runs use different gauge wire. The best way to connect your fixtures to the main line

Night lighting greatly enhances this elaborate arbour planter and water feature created and designed by Pink Lotus Inc. (Photo: Pink Lotus Inc.)

is by using a "quick connect." These can be purchased separately or may come packaged with your fixtures. The connectors make it easy to fasten a fixture to the power cable and are flexible enough to move as the landscape changes.

Low-voltage lighting can be buried without a conduit. It is a good practice to seal the connector with some silicone caulking, but check to see that the connection is actually working first. At the ends of the runs, be sure to seal the wire with electrical tape to stop voltage draw that will result from the oxidation of the copper wire. When installing lamps, spray the base of the lamp with a silicone compound to help prevent corrosion in the socket. This should be done once a year, as preventative maintenance.

A FINAL WORD

Night lighting adds another dimension to any landscape, a dimension of bold texture and form, rather than flower colour or the overall garden layout. The effect of night lighting is also quite intimate in nature, as each shadow or silhouette is appreciated in isolation. And while light and shadow have no substance, they can often become the most elaborate features of the landscape.

Using Structures in the Garden

SHARON & PAUL GOUGH, PINK LOTUS INC., (WWW.PINKLOTUS.CA), COQUITLAM, B.C.

Garden structures add visual interest, providing depth and dimension to the landscape. A carefully placed pergola or arbour can create a focal point, help define the style of the garden and lead visitors from one area to another. To create a harmonious effect, it's important to consider the architecture of the house when designing outdoor structures. The new structure should nestle into the landscape, rather than appearing to be an afterthought.

A GARDEN STRUCTURE SAMPLER

Pergolas Pergolas are usually a primary focal point in the landscape due to their size. A pergola is basically an arbour that you can walk through. It adds a vertical element that encourages visitors to look upwards. The roof structure can be an open framework and the crosspieces should be positioned from east to west, in order to maximize shading. For a more intimate feeling, the roof can be covered with vines, which also helps to cool the area. The roof can also be composed of a number of arches, placed to create a tunnel effect. Pergolas situated at the end of a path or at the back of the garden become a destination point, encouraging traffic flow through the landscape. When built as an extension to the patio or entertaining space, they function as a garden room.

An outdoor entertainment area complete with hot tub, outdoor kitchen, pergola and night lighting (Photo and design: Pink Lotus Inc.)

Gazebos Gazebos are functional garden shelters, offering protection from the elements in all seasons. Some are completed with fine screening to keep out insects, so you can entertain well into the evening. With minor changes, they can be designed to complement almost any garden style. Simply altering the roof can change a gazebo from a Victorian style to a West Coast contemporary or Asian-influenced design.

Trellises A blank wall in the garden can be transformed simply by installing a trellis and covering it with flowering vines. A trellis can also be freestanding, although it must have sturdy legs to support its own weight as well as the plant material. We recommend that the supports extend 12 to 18 inches (30 to 45 cm) into the ground. Other functions of a simple trellis are to divide the garden into rooms, offer a privacy screen and create a wind barrier.

Outdoor Kitchens Outdoor kitchens are being used more frequently in modern landscapes and allow the cook to enjoy outdoor festivities while preparing the meal. An outdoor kitchen might include a grilling area, preparation and serving area, storage cabinets, sink and/or wet bar, and a refrigerator. For easy maintenance, consider installing tile countertops, as these can be easily wiped and sanitized. It's always a good idea to provide some shelter from the sun (or you may end up with a cook that is a little more well done than the meal). Outdoor directional lighting in the cooking area serves a practical purpose and also creates night-time ambience. All outdoor electrical outlets, light fixtures and switches must be watertight and protected by a ground fault interrupter (GFI). A fireplace or fire pit built nearby can extend the entertaining into the late evening. It's hard to imagine a more perfect ending to a day than sitting around a fire, enjoying the flickering flames and some great conversation.

Children's Play Areas Don't forget about the little ones when considering structures in the landscape. When children are young, locate the play area close to the house, where it's easy to monitor them. To offer shelter from the sun, locate the play area on the north side of the property, incorporate a screen or roof, or plant shade trees in the area. When considering play structures, choose a unit that the children will not easily outgrow. Many of the prefabricated units offer pieces that can be added as needed. Reflective surfaces, such as slides, should be positioned facing north, to reduce the likelihood of overheating and potential burns. The play surface should be soft to cushion any falls. Sand, bark mulch or grass provide a good buffer. If you decide to build a custom structure, you will only be limited by your imagination and your budget. Planning a play area can bring out the child in just about anyone, so have fun with this project — it's not often that we get to revisit our childhood.

CHOOSING YOUR STYLE

Before you purchase building materials, consider the type of structure and the weather conditions. Cedar posts, rough timbers and river rock are common west coast features. Bamboo, granite and Malaysian pottery are a few elements of an Asian style. If a Roman or Grecian effect is desired, marble, concrete and stucco are popular choices. The delicate Victorian landscape will feature latticework, spindles, intricately carved woodwork and the wrought iron common to that period. For a Southwest flavour, include terra cotta, mosaic tiles, stucco and coarse wrought iron. Building bylaws vary from district to district and will help to determine the building materials suitable for your region.

DRESSING YOUR GARDEN STRUCTURE

Vines and climbing shrubs are traditionally used to soften garden structures. But before you plant, consider carefully the type of structure and the ultimate size of the planting. For instance, wisteria can quickly destroy fine latticework and should only be used with a substantial structure. On the other hand, the fine stems of some clematis might not suit heavy beams or posts. The following are a few examples of common vines and climbing shrubs, along with their basic cultural needs. They were all chosen for their reliability and ease of care.

Clematis (hybrids and species) Part to full sun with good soil drainage.
C. armandii Fast-growing evergreen vine with fragrant white blooms in spring. Height 20 feet (6 m). Zone 7.
C. 'Ville de Lyon' Produces crimson blooms with yellow stamens all summer long. Height 10 feet (3 m). Zone 3–4.

Honeysuckle *(Lonicera)* Part to full sun with good air circulation, to avoid fungal problems.
L. 'Dropmore Scarlet' A hardy, deciduous vine with scarlet blooms for hummingbirds. Height 12 feet (4 m). Zone 3.
L. henryi An evergreen species with fragrant purple-red flowers. Height 12 feet (4 m). Zone 5.

Jasmine *(Jasminum)* Part to full sun with protection from cold winter winds.
J. officinale A semi-evergreen vine with fragrant white summer blooms. Height 12 feet (4 m). Zone 7.
J. nudiflorum A winter species with bright yellow flowers (not fragrant). Height 9 feet (3 m). Zone 6.

Wisteria (hybrids) Part to full sun; avoid very fertile soils if you want young plants to bloom.
W. floribunda 'Rosea' Fragrant, pale pink blooms on a vigorous plant. Height 24 feet (8 m). Zone 5–6.
W. 'Issai' White and lilac flowers on short trusses. Blooms at a young age. Height 24 feet (8 m). Zone 5–6.

Climbing Roses *(Rosa)* Part to full sun with good soil drainage and air circulation.
R. 'Dublin Bay' (Climber) A short plant with fully double, deep red blooms. Height 8 feet (2.5 m).
R. 'New Dawn' (Rambler) Fragrant, pale pink flowers that repeat bloom. Disease resistant. Height 12 feet (4 m).

Ivy *(Hedera)* Shade to full sun. Tolerant of many soil conditions.
H. colchica 'Dentata Variegata' Large, evergreen leaves with pale yellow variegation. Height 18 feet (6 m). Zone 7.
H. helix 'Gold Heart' A delicate form with gold inset variegation. Good for a trellis. Height 9 feet (3 m). Zone 6.

Grapes *(Vitis)* Full sun exposure with excellent soil drainage and air circulation.
V. vinifera 'Purpurea' An ornamental form with deep burgundy autumn foliage. Height 15 feet (5 m). Zone 5.
V. 'Himrod' A white, seedless table grape that crops well in cooler coastal summers. Height 15 feet (5 m). Zone 5.

CHAPTER 4
Contained Landscape Features

There is a garden in her face,
Where roses and white lilies grow;
A heav'nly paradise in that place,
Wherein all pleasant fruits do flow.
　　Thomas Campion, *Fourth Book of Airs*

How do you define a garden? Are gardens only found in large public parks or around residential homes? Is it possible that a garden can transcend a plot of soil and exist in other forms? This section of the book explores gardens in containers, which can be placed anywhere you can find room for a pot.

Plants in containers are often used by businesses and individuals who live or work in high-density urban settings or people who find themselves in high-rise buildings, looking down at the landscapes below. Try telling them they can't have a garden and many will respond by flaunting their spectacular hanging baskets, alpine troughs and mixed planters.

It takes only a fertile imagination and a dedication to regular watering and fertilizing to create and maintain a containerized landscape. After reading this chapter, you will likely be looking in some very unusual places to find those inspirational plant combinations and the many containers used to showcase them.

Magnolia stellata blooms
(star magnolia)
Colour photo p. 133

Balconies to Brag About

DAVID TARRANT, UBC BOTANICAL GARDEN, VANCOUVER, B.C.

Balcony gardening is just plain fun! It fulfills the apartment dweller's basic desire to be in touch with the green world without all the chores of a larger landscape, such as mowing the lawn and trimming hedges. It is a chance to get your hands dirty and do some light maintenance, such as weeding, without bending over for hours and getting an aching back. Perhaps the best fringe benefit is that all your favourite plants can be arranged and rearranged in their containers as many times as you like.

Of course, you will have to follow some guidelines if you want to have a successful balcony garden. First and foremost, check with the building management and enquire as to whether gardening is allowed on the balconies and if there are any weight restrictions. Each building will have its own rules, but I am always reminded of an amazing apartment building I saw in Adelaide, Australia, which actually had large planters built into every balcony. This is something to look forward to, here in North America.

CHOOSING THE CONTAINER

Gardening containers have come a long way over the years. For overall ease of use, I recommend plastic over ceramic pots. They have the advantage of being lightweight and they generally do not split during winter freezes. There are some fabulous faux terra cotta pots on the market today with superb detail and even pitted surfaces — the only way to really tell them apart from the real thing is to actually touch them!

While ornamental pots are lovely to look at, the truth is that plants will grow in almost any container. Recycled plastic buckets with drainage holes drilled in the bottom make excellent containers. They can be made more aesthetically pleasing by slipping them inside baskets for that "Martha Stewart" effect. Many years ago, when I first started teaching balcony gardening, I met an amazing gardener who lived in Vancouver's West End. Each summer he had an open-house tea party at his fourteenth-floor rooftop garden. Everything he grew was planted in old recycled boxes in which cheese had been imported! He grew roses, dahlias, marigolds, petunias, strawberries, pole beans and corn to name just a few — it was truly inspirational.

Size is important. Containers should be at least 12 inches by 12 inches (30 × 30 cm). Anything smaller will dry out far too quickly during the heat of summer, and maintenance will become a real headache. Pots must have drainage holes in the bottom. Without drainage, pots placed in an open situation can become instant bogs during heavy rains. And don't forget to place trays or saucers under your containers — one of the worst ways to meet your downstairs neighbour is while they are sunbathing and your excess water drips on them!

SOIL MEDIUMS

Potting mixes or container soils are readily available at most garden centres, and they vary from source to source. Peat is the main component of most purchased mixes and can be problematic. In rainy seasons it can stay wet for too long, in dry seasons it can dry out quickly and shrink away from the inside pot surface, making it a challenge to moisten it again.

I prefer a planter mix with some topsoil and well-rotted manure incorporated in it. Back in the old days when I made up my own container soil, I mixed it at a ratio of two parts good topsoil, 1 part well-rotted manure or compost, 1 part peat and one part sand or perlite.

Before planting a container, try to put a layer of drainage material in the bottom of the pot — at least enough to cover the drainage holes. All kinds of recycled household objects make great drainage materials, including broken pieces of styrofoam cups, plastic pill bottles, empty dental floss containers and scrunched-up plastic six-pack trays used for bedding plants.

PLANT SELECTION

When potting up summer bedding plants, fill your containers with potting mix to within 6 inches (15 cm) of the rim. Firm the mix gently, then place your plants on it, arranging them in a design or any free-form fashion you like. Firmly fill in the gaps between the root balls with potting mix, making sure to leave a 4-inch (10-cm) space at the top of the pot (this makes for easier watering). When working with summer flowers, always plant them close together, so the root balls are touching each other. This will give you immediate impact and with a careful feeding program, they will provide a good show all summer long.

If traditional bedding plants are not your style, try using perennials (see the list below). As far as selection is concerned, the sky is the limit. The root balls of perennials tend to be larger, so the key is to use fewer plants per pot, even if you want that full-looking effect.

Shrubs or small trees grow well in containers and can add height to a balcony garden. But with this plant group, one shrub or tree per pot is the best approach. For example, I have a *Magnolia stellata* (star magnolia) that has been in a 2-foot (60-cm) pot for over 7 years now. An *Acer circinatum* (vine maple) in a similarly sized container is also doing just fine.

FEEDING AND WATERING

Feeding and watering balcony planters is the key to their long-term success. Amounts will vary, depending on the plants. If the planter mix contains some manure or compost, feeding won't be required for the first month or so (based on a spring planting, about April).

For established annual planters that are well rooted, use light liquid feedings (such as 15-30-15 or 20-20-20) every second day. From July on, feed daily with diluted fertilizer. Use one-third of the amount of fertilizer recommended by the manufacturer. The plants get less fertilizer with each watering, but receive it more often. The reason for this is that when a container is root-bound it generally requires daily watering, and that leaches the nutrients out, making daily replenishing essential.

With perennials, not as much fertilizer is required, although in the peak of summer I feed mine twice weekly with a weak solution. For trees and shrubs during the active growing season (May through mid-September), once a week is the key.

BALCONY DESIGN

Arranging pots with various plants and textural forms can be great fun and, as mentioned above, they can be rearranged as often as you like. Trees or shrubs make good background plants and, to some degree, will act as windbreaks. Wind can be a major problem on taller high-rise buildings.

When arranging pots, try not to have them all at the same level. If all the containers are exactly the same size, raise some on blocks or upturned pots to add a bit of interest. When purchasing containers, imagine groupings of three containers of different sizes. The varied heights will make for a more interesting grouping.

Strong shelves or racks for holding pots can also add interest. If you have the right building conditions, trellises can be attached to the wall or pots to provide yet another dimension. For example, a golden hops (*Humulus lupulus* 'Aureus') happily climbs on a trellis in a shady corner of my balcony during summer.

SUITABLE PLANTS FOR BALCONY PLANTERS

Annuals — Sun

Cerinthe major **'Purpurascens'** Easy from seed. Wonderful purple-blue foliage.

Felicia Delicate daisy blooms of blue or pink.

Gazania **hybrids** Large, starry blooms of yellow, orange, purple, red and cream.

Heliotropium arborescens (heliotrope) Very fragrant.

Nemesia Many forms are distinctly bicoloured.

Portulaca Very drought resistant; good in shallow bowls.

Annuals — Shade

Begonia Both fibrous and tuberous.

Fuchsia Pendulous and upright cultivars.

Lobelia Upright and trailing cultivars available.

Torenia Exotic-looking blooms of pink, white and purple.

Perennials — Sun

Coreopsis Durable perennial; many cultivars are yellow. Zone 4.

Lavatera Tall woody perennial with mallow-like blooms. Zone 6.

Limonium latifolium (sea lavender) Lavender blooms good for drying. Zone 2.

Salvia Flowering forms and edible sage (*S. officinalis*). Zones 3 to 6.

Perennials — Shade

Astilbe Bright plumes of white, pink, red, purple and salmon. Zones 3 to 4.

Ferns Both herbaceous and evergreen. Zones 2 to 7.

Hosta Brightly variegated forms such as 'Frances Williams.' Zone 2.

Liriope Member of the lily family. Lilac to purple blooms. Zones 4 to 6.

Vinca (periwinkle) Variegated forms such as 'Illumination.' Zone 3.

Shrubs

Chamaecyparis obtusa (Hinoki false cypress) Many dwarf forms available. Zone 5.

Kerria japonica (Japanese rose) Bright green stems in winter. Zone 5.

Mahonia aquifolium (Oregon grape) Leaves turn burgundy in winter. Zone 5.

Pieris japonica (lily-of-the-valley shrub) Dwarf forms available. Zone 6.

Syringa vulgaris (French lilac) Very fragrant blooms. Zone 3.

Trees

Acer palmatum (Japanese maples) Both weeping and upright forms. Zone 5.

Magnolia stellata (star magnolia) White, star-shaped flowers. Zone 5.

Salix discolor (pussy willow) A shrub-like tree with grey pussy willows. Zone 3.

Styrax japonica (Japanese snowbell) Delicate fragrant white flowers. Zone 5.

Cast iron trough with *Chrysanthemum* 'Road Runner'

The Beauty of Container Planting

SHELLEY SORENSEN, BRAMBLES & BLOOMS ORGANIC GARDEN CARE,
WEST VANCOUVER, B.C.

A well-placed container planting can be an effective feature in any landscape design. It can be as simple as setting a terra cotta pot by the entrance gate, placing a brightly glazed container as a bit of interest in front of a drab green hedge, or assembling a tasteful planting to create some ambience by the front step. By adding seasonal plant treasures to your pots, you can provide ever-changing pleasure from spring through to winter. Creating exciting container gardens is one of my favourite jobs as a gardener, and I always enjoy the entire process of designing a container, from start to finish.

DRAINAGE AND SOIL

Before any potting takes place, I always check to see that the container's drainage holes are large enough. Holes can be drilled (or made larger) in ceramic or terra cotta pots by the careful use of a masonry drill bit. I like to fill the bottom quarter of the pot with coarse styrofoam chips; gravel or pieces of broken terra cotta also work well. Make sure the drainage material is larger than the drain holes themselves, so the holes don't get plugged up. To separate the drainage material from the potting soil, I lay a piece of landscape fabric on top of the styrofoam or gravel.

I prefer to use a potting soil with a high organic content and I usually mix my own blend of two parts potting or container soil, one part well-rotted organic hog manure and one part compost or worm castings. I also add a custom fertilizer blend to enhance the mineral content of the potting soil. For this I mix one part bone meal, two parts blood meal, one part sulfate of potash and one part treble superphosphate. I usually add two or three cups

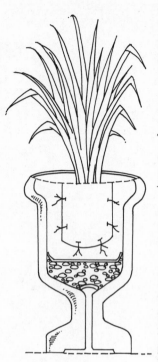

Profile of urn planting

(500 to 750 mL) of this fertilizer mixture to 20 gallons (80 L) of the soil mix. Use 1 cup (250 mL) of this mix for a small pot, 2 cups (500 mL) for a large container. This combination of organic soil mix with added fertilizer really makes for phenomenal plant growth during the summer. If I am planting mostly drought-resistant plants or succulents, I modify the soil mixture by adding 30 percent sand or grit and using less compost or worm castings.

CHOOSING THE RIGHT CONTAINER

There are a wide variety of pots available on the market today, but when choosing a container for a specific location, I always look at the surroundings. The architecture of the house or building will influence your choices. You may want an elegant, formal look, a heavily textured cottage style, a customized wooden planter or a bold exposed aggregate container. Where there is a colourful painted door or stained glass window in view, the use of a glazed ceramic pot to complement these colours can be quite effective.

Positioning ceramic containers against a wall or under an overhang will provide enough residual warmth to protect the glaze from chipping or cracking in winter. These locations also create nice microclimates for tender plants, which will help them to bloom longer. The types of plants you intend to use in the pot and the soil necessary to accommodate their root growth will be a factor in the size of container you choose. Ask yourself how often the pot will be maintained. If the waterings are going to be few and far between, choose a larger container to provide more soil volume (and water capacity).

When creating designs for clients, the theme of the landscape is an important factor in my choice of containers. I always consider a person's interior decorating and colour preferences when designing their garden and container plantings. A formal setting of clipped boxwood hedges and perfectly edged pathways would be a great place to introduce a more carefree planting in a large cement or terra cotta pot, just to lighten things up a bit. Or perhaps in keeping with the style, I would make use of a smaller, textured pot with a centred columnar yew and a subdued annual planting — because sometimes simple is best.

For a formal setting in larger areas, a topiary privet *(Ligustrum)* or shaped boxwood in a large urn or cement pot makes a suitable statement. Where bricks are used in the landscaping, I lean towards terra cotta pots, to complement the earthen tones of the brick. Terra cotta containers also work well on cement pathways and patios, adding a little contrast and interest to the area. Terra cotta works well for the plant's cultural needs, as it offers reasonable air circulation (for the roots) through its porous walls, provided the pots have not been sealed.

USING COLOUR AND TEXTURE

My planting style in containers is much the same as it is in the landscape — I like to use a combination of texture and colour to please the eye. Plants with different flowering periods keep the container or feature interesting.

Texture and leaf colour also provide interest during periods when flowers are not present.

The colour combinations I choose cover a wide range. I might make a mixed planting of pinks, blues and burgundy, with some grey and white. Or I'll use primary colours with a strong palette of yellows, reds, purples, blues and some green foliage for contrast. I often add grey, chartreuse and deep wine reds to these primary plantings. Some of the plants I enjoy using include black violas ('Sawyer's Black'), chartreuse flowering tobacco (*Nicotiana* 'Lime Green') and coleus varieties (such as the sun tolerant 'Solar' series) in all their glorious colour combinations.

Grey- or silver-leafed plants usually find a home in my more colourful plantings. The colour and texture of plants such as *Artemisia* 'Silver Brocade' or *Senecio greyii* complement bright colours and add softness to the overall appearance of the display. Mixing plant colours is a lot like painting — sometimes a wide variety of colour is necessary to create that beautiful blend. A trip to your favourite garden centre can be a great place to get your creative energy flowing and discover new plants, colours and textures to work with.

Left A fall display of *Molinia* 'Variegata,' lingonberry (*Vaccinium vitis-idaea*) and *Rudbeckia* 'Toto'
Right A winter planting of *Carex buchananii,* winter pansies, variegated English ivy and lingonberry
Colour photo p. 133

PLANT ELEMENTS TO WORK WITH

Consider the location of the pot and the surrounding landscape before choosing the plants. It's important to think about where the container will be in relation to sun or shade, wind and water. To get you started, here are a few plant suggestions for specific sites or exposures.

Low Light or Shade Exposures

Buxus (boxwood) (evergreen)
    Buxus sempervirens 'Suffruticosa'
      True dwarf boxwood. Zone 5.
    Buxus microphylla 'Winter Gem'
      Retains green winter colour. Zone 5.

Ferns (evergreen)
    Polystichum tsus-simense
      (Korean rock fern). Zone 6.
    Dryopteris erythrosora (autumn fern)
      Red new growth. Zone 5.

Heuchera (evergreen perennial)
    H. 'Black Beauty'
      Dark purple, ruffled foliage. Zone 4.
    H. 'Amber Waves'
      Golden yellow with tan highlights. Zone 4.

Hosta (perennial)
    H. 'Patriot'
      Bold white marginal variegation. Zone 2.
    H. 'Queen Josephine'
      Glossy leaves with gold margins. Zone 2.

Hedera (ivy) (evergreen)
    H. helix 'Glacier'
      Dark green foliage with cream margins. Zone 6.
    H. helix 'Needlepoint'
      Very fine textured foliage. Zone 5.

Taxus (yew) (conifer)
    T. baccata 'Fastigiata' (Irish yew)
      Very thin profile. Zone 6.
    T. x *media* 'Hicksii'
      Narrow, upright form. Zone 5.

Colour for Full Sun Exposures

Echeveria (tender) Evergreen rosettes which resemble hens and chicks.

Heliotrope 'Royal Marine' (tender) Sweetly scented purple flowers.

Lantana (tender) Yellow, pink and purple blooms. ('Sunburst' — bright yellow)

Phormium tenax 'Rubrum' (evergreen) Dramatic spikes of deep burgundy-red. Zone 8.

Rhodochiton atrosanguineum (annual) Cascading purple bells.

Sedum (perennial)
    S. spurium 'Roseum'
      Low form with bright pink blooms. Zone 2
    S. telephium 'Matrona'
      Upright form with purple-grey foliage. Zone 2.

Plants for Windy Exposures/Full Sun

Arctostaphylos 'Vancouver Jade' (evergreen groundcover) Red berries. Zone 4.

Juniperus virginiana 'Skyrocket' (conifer) Upright form with steel-blue foliage. Zone 3.

Lavandula (lavender) (broadleaf evergreen)
    L. angustifolia 'Hidcote'
      Lavender-blue. Zone 4.
    L. angustifolia 'Hidcote Blue'
      Rich purple. Zone 4.

Salvia (sage) (evergreen herb)
    S. officinalis 'Tricolor'
      Variegated foliage. Zone 4.
    S. officinalis 'Icterina'
      Bold gold margins. Zone 4.

Santolina chamaecyparissus (lavender cotton) (evergreen perennial) Silver foliage. Zone 6.

Thymus (thyme) (evergreen herb)
    T. praecox 'Coccineus'
      Magenta-red blooms. Zone 2.

A Few Favourite Annuals

Bacopa 'Snowflake' (sun) Cascading white flowers all summer long.

Browallia 'Blue & White Troll' (shade) Small blue or white bells.

Coleus 'Carefree Mix' (shade) Brightly coloured foliage; violet blooms.

Heliotrope 'Mini Marine' (sun) Compact; scented deep purple flowers.

Illumination begonias 'Apricot & White' (shade) Cascading colour forms.

Plectranthus argentatus (sun) Very large, glaucous-grey foliage.

Salvia hormineum 'Tricolor' (sun) Mixed purple, white and pink bracts.

Verbena 'Lanai Lavender' (sun) Dainty, cascading blooms of light mauve.

Hanging Baskets — The Versatile Planters

CLAUDE LEDOUX, NEW WESTMINSTER PARKS, NEW WESTMINSTER, B.C.

Hanging baskets afford a wonderful opportunity for both home and professional gardeners to express their creative ideas. Many gardening enthusiasts have limited space and hanging baskets help fill that niche. The main limiting factor is the volume of soil available for the plant roots, which means constant watering and fertilizing.

The suspended format is the best opportunity to use a wide variety of plants. Annuals, biennials, perennials, or any combination of these plants all work well. And don't exclude vegetables, fruits and herbs. They are easily grown and the plants generally receive more light in their elevated location. One great example — almost a salad in a pot! — is a 'Tumbler' tomato with parsley and oregano as side plantings.

THE PLANTER AND FRAME

A hanging basket can be made from any type of container as long as it can retain soil and moisture. Traditionally, wire baskets have been used with sphagnum moss as the liner. Liners can also be plastic, paper, burlap, coco fibre, wood fibre or even wool mats, to name a few. The wire basket frames come in various sizes: choose the largest size you can, as this will reduce water needs and allow more soil for root growth. On the other hand, the larger the size, the heavier the planter, and you will have to determine if the hanger can support the weight. Watering the planter will increase its weight, so make sure to include this in your calculations. Always use the best quality materials (i.e. chains and wire) for hanging and double-check to make sure that the bracket or hook can support the weight prior to hanging.

GROWING MEDIA

The growing medium is the single most important component of your hanging basket. Knowing the soil requirements of the plants you are using will help you make an educated decision on the soil blend. There are many

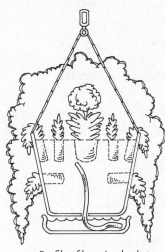

Profile of hanging basket
assembly

premixed planter box soils (primarily peat moss-based) on the market. They have a tendency to dry out quickly between waterings and I suggest adding ⅓ weed-free compost, well-rotted manure or a composted bark to ⅔ soil mix by volume.

WATER AND FERTILIZER REQUIREMENTS

With any container planting, it's critical to water and fertilize regularly. Monitoring the soil moisture and plant health is the first step. Super-absorbent water crystals have proven to be fairly reliable in retaining soil moisture; this product should be mixed into the soil prior to planting. A simple micro-irrigation system (a series of small irrigation tubes that supply water) goes a long way when you consider that it is a rather small investment. I would recommend this type of system and an internal wick. The wick is a ⅝-inch (1.5-cm) double-braided polyester rope. You will need approximately 18 inches (45 cm), half of which is embedded in the soil medium. The remainder feeds into a plastic pan that is wired to the bottom of the frame. The pan collects excess water, which can be reabsorbed by the soil via the wick.

Fertilizers can be water-soluble and/or slow-release types. Inconsistent fertilizing will produce unhealthy plants that are less attractive and more vulnerable to insect infestations. A combination of slow-release fertilizers and water-soluble types is the best way to supply constant nutrients.

PLANTING YOUR HANGING BASKET

The assembling of the hanging basket is the easiest and most rewarding step. After you have designed the basket, purchase all the components: plants, soil mixture (including slow-release fertilizer), basket frame, liner material, wick and pan. Make sure all the plants are well watered, as it is most important not to transplant a dry or stressed plant. The two-layer planting process is a quick and easy method to use. Place the liner halfway up the container and pull the wick through the planter base. Add the soil mixture and level it with the wick in place. Half the wick should be inside the basket and the remainder sticking out the bottom (this portion of the wick will be hidden inside the pan). The lower level plants are then placed as close as possible to the edge of the basket, in a horizontal position. Make sure the wick is still upright and stops just below the surface as the soil is added. Then add the top layer of plants, starting with the outer edge. These will be planted on a 45-degree angle, close to the edge, so they can cascade over the rim. Place the remaining plants upright in the centre.

Hanging the basket is a two-person job. Once the basket is secured and stable, attach the pan to the bottom of the basket, making sure the wick is inside. A simple way to do this is with plastic cable ties, strung from the second rung of the wire basket through small holes in the pan (be sure to allow for a small gap between the pan and the basket base). Once the pan is level and secure, slowly add water to the basket from the top — making sure the entire soil mass is thoroughly moistened. The excess water will fill the pan and be absorbed again by the watering wick. Keep the pan full of water at all times. If your plants are watered and well maintained, a beautiful summer-long display will be your reward.

SOME HANGING BASKET PLANT COMBINATIONS

Herbs

Artemisia dracunculus (tarragon) Top layer.

Petroselinum crispum (parsley) Top or side layer.

Origanum (oregano; dwarf or golden cultivars) Side layer.

Salvia officinalis (dwarf, purple, golden or tricolor) Top layer.

Rosmarinum officinalis (rosemary/trailing) Side layer.

Thymus vulgaris or *T. citriodorus* (thyme; common or lemon) Side layer.

West Coast Native Plants

Camassia 'Blue Melody' (blue camus lily; variegated) Top layer.

Blechnum spicant (deer fern) Top layer.

Cornus canadensis (bunchberry) Side layer.

Penstemon cardwellii (Cardwell's penstemon) Top layer.

Fritillaria pudica (yellow bell lily) Top layer.

Sedum spathulifolium (stonecrop) Side layer.

Perennials

Salvia nemerosa 'Blue Queen' Top layer.

Festuca glauca 'Golden Toupee' (golden fescue) Side layer.

Artemisia stelleriana 'Silver Brocade' (artemesia) Side layer.

Bergenia 'Bressingham Ruby' Top or side layer.

Carex oshimensis 'Evergold' (golden sedge) Top or side layer.

Mixed Media Planters

Erica carnea 'Springwood Pink & White' (winter heather) Top or side layer.

Brassica oleracea (ornamental kale) Top layer.

Hedera helix 'Mini Adam' (variegated ivy) Side layer.

Annuals

Nierembergia 'Purple Robe' Top or side layer.

Pelargonium 'Frank Headley' (variegated geranium) Top layer.

Helichrysum 'Limelight' Side layer.

Pelargonium 'Maverick White' (geranium) Top layer.

Thunbergia alata (black-eyed susan vine) Top layer.

Fuchsia 'Golden Anniversary' Side layer.

Bacopa speciosa 'Snowflake' Side layer.

Begonia 'Pink Dragon Wings' Top layer.

Lobelia erinus 'Regatta Blue' Side layer.

Dicondra argentea 'Silver Falls' Side layer.

CHAPTER 5
Gardens by Design

If Nature had been comfortable, mankind would never have created architecture....
Oscar Wilde, *The Decay of Lying*

Oscar Wilde was in the habit of making outrageous comments on just about any subject. Here Mr. Wilde succinctly assesses the basis of garden design: essentially, all landscaping is an attempt to make our surroundings more comfortable or aesthetically pleasing (a form of cerebral comfort) by one means or another.

This is the philosophical portion of the book, the one that asks the questions: what constitutes a good garden design and do the rules or guidelines change from place to place? You'll find that the opinions vary, just as the writers' cultural influences, horticultural backgrounds and life experience varies. Some advocate a "site-generated" design, others suggest a return to more natural forms and one examines landscapes created primarily around leisure needs — a garden that is an extension of the home.

There is no definitive answer here, just differing opinions among professionals — which is really nothing new in the horticulture business. The pieces in this chapter may have a philosophical tone, but they are certainly not esoteric, as all present very practical landscape advice from some of British Columbia's most successful garden designers and landscape architects.

Formal arrangement of herbaceous perennials on an English estate (Photo: Clare Philips)

Lessons From the Estate — Gardening in Large Spaces

MICHAEL LASCELLE, AMSTERDAM GARDEN CENTRE, PITT MEADOWS, B.C.

If you had asked me when I was about 10 years old what I wanted to be when I grew up, I am quite sure that the word "gardener" would have never crossed my lips — marine biologist or astronaut maybe, but not gardener. I began my career in horticulture quite by mistake, but I couldn't have started with a better garden if I had planned it.

The position was on a 40-acre estate, with about three acres of cultivated garden and several in lawn. It was perched on a southwest slope with a perfect view of Mount Baker from the top. The owner was on the board of governors for VanDusen Botanical Garden in Vancouver, so rhododendrons abounded in his established ravine garden.

LESSON #1: LOOKING GOOD FROM A DISTANCE

The first thing the head gardener taught me was to always keep the sides of the garden beds well-edged and weeded to about 18 inches (45 cm). His theory was that no matter what the state of the remainder of the bed, if the edges were clearly cut and kept clear of weeds, the garden would always appear to be tidy from a distance. I was a little skeptical at first, but I have to admit that we rarely received a complaint about a bed unless the periphery was neglected and it caught the attention of the owner.

Owing to the size of the property and the limited number of staff (2 full-time gardeners), the estate was maintained in shifts. That meant that a bed was weeded, lightly pruned and raked clean about once a month, unless an emergency occurred. This allowed us to divide the cultivated garden into about 20 different sections, with each section being maintained one after another.

Lawns were cut once a week when in growth and great care was taken to ensure that the lines of the gang-reels (5 pulled behind a tractor) were perfectly straight and crossed at a right angle to ensure a consistent cut and an attractive pattern. Moles were diligently trapped — trapping being the only effective control — not only for the unsightly mounds of soil they left behind, which dulled the gang-reels, but also because if enough tunnels were present in a limited area, the tractors or heavy machinery would literally sink into the lawn, even with wide turf tires.

LESSON #2: AVOIDING MONOCULTURES

Another common problem was frequent pest or disease outbreaks in the mass shrub plantings. In designing a garden with large banks of rhododendrons or hardy fuchsia, we were actually creating small monocultures that were highly susceptible to pests and diseases. The large bed of *Rhododendron* 'Elizabeth Hobbie' (dwarf red) was absolutely spectacular when in bloom and was well frequented by the hummingbirds, but it was nearly impossible to control the regular outbreaks of whitefly due to the dense canopy. The damage was only superficial and did not affect the vigour of the plants, so pesticides were not used in this case. However, more severe measures had to be used on a large bank of Japanese azaleas (80 to 100 plants). They eventually had to be removed due to a severe outbreak of azalea leaf gall which threatened more established azaleas in other portions of the garden. Similarly, the deciduous azalea bed should have been renamed the powdery mildew bed every fall. Fortunately, this was a temporary condition that was best dealt with by removing the fallen leaves.

LESSON #3: GRADE RETENTION

Much of the cultivated garden was built around a steep ravine, so retaining walls were part of the landscape design on this portion of the estate. At the time, we used short sections of remnant telephone poles — probably because the manufacturing mill was just down the hill, a few miles away. The pole segments were installed vertically, with 2 feet (60 cm) of the length buried into the grade for support. All fresh cuts were treated with a wood preservative which has since been taken off the market. A layer of tar paper was placed on the grade side and the wall was carefully backfilled with 8 inches (20 cm) of crushed gravel against the paper. It was common for the base of a pole to rot out after several years, but replacement of an individual piece was relatively easy using this method of grade retention.

My time spent on the estate gave me the opportunity to learn installation techniques and how to determine the appropriate retaining-wall structure for a specific site. There are many different means of managing grade retention and they vary from site to site, but there are a few basic principles to be aware of.

First of all, whenever you build a wall on a slope, you are creating a dam of sorts, and you will have to consider how to manage the subsequent drainage. Most contractors install a 4-inch (10-cm) drain behind the wall (near the base of the gravel backfill), which is hooked into a weeping pipe or a proper catch basin that eventually links into the storm sewer.

Secondly, a wall is only as strong as its base. Build it on soft, unstable soil and it will probably shift or tilt before you have finished it. All walls used for grade retention must be built on a stable base, preferably 6 inches (15 cm) of a compacted crushed aggregate. You may also have to bury a portion of the wood tie or block, depending on the height of the wall.

Third, be very careful who you hire to build retaining walls. When you consider the enormous costs of removing and rebuilding defective retaining walls, it is simply not worth the few dollars you might save by automatically hiring the lowest bidder. Choose a landscape contractor who designs and builds retaining walls on a regular basis, then be diligent about checking their references and ask to see their portfolio.

Lastly, be aware of local bylaws before you build your wall and, if permits are necessary, be sure to get them. Most municipalities restrict the height of retaining walls to 3 feet (90 cm) before a deep setback of 6 feet (2 m) is required, where the next 3-foot-high (90-cm) wall can be built (The profile of these setbacks is much like a set of stairs with treads twice as deep as the height of the step.) Many require substantial walls to be designed by an engineer before a permit is granted. Bylaws and bylaw officers are never a problem until someone complains, and then you can expect to hear and see a lot of them until the project is completed to their satisfaction. A better route is to simply comply with the rules — remembering that they have been created with safety in mind.

Here are some of the building materials available and their relative strengths and weaknesses.

Segmented concrete units are stackable, manufactured concrete blocks with built-in setbacks. They are versatile and can be arranged into taller (over 3 feet/90 cm) walls using geogrids, a synthetic mesh which is buried into the grade.

Treated wooden ties come in various lengths and sizes, with the most common sizes being 4 × 4 inches (10 × 10 cm) and 6 × 6 inches (15 × 15 cm). The arsenic used as the wood preservative in some of these ties can be an environmental concern and their lifespan averages only 15 to 20 years in our wet coastal climate. Extensive tiebacks (which are buried in the grade) are also necessary.

Poured concrete walls often require extensive footings and form work, making them expensive, relative to other wall systems. They are also subject to cracking over time.

Mortared stone walls can vary in quality, depending on the mortar mix and the skill of the mason involved. This is a versatile option for custom work and the stone can often be found on site.

A dry stack stone wall can be very aesthetically pleasing, and perennials can be planted between the joints. The initial cost can be high when you consider that most of the stone is buried in the grade. Dry stack walls drain freely and can be rebuilt if necessary.

Brick walls require a poured footing and possibly the backing of a concrete or cement block wall. They are expensive and used brick may begin to weather rather quickly.

LESSON #4: PLANTING ON SLOPES

Once the walls were built and the grades stabilized, it was time to plant the sloped sections of the estate garden. Many people make the initial mistake of planting slopes too sparsely, which usually leads to months of weeding the empty patches and subsequent difficulty trying to match the original shrubs, so they can plant a little more densely. We chose several dwarf shrubs to plant in mass, and kept our plant material low near the wall's edge, building height further up the slope.

Sun-tolerant rhododendrons, such as 'Moerheim,' 'Ramapo,' 'Purple Gem' and the species *R. impeditum* (all violet-blue in colour) make an impressive show when planted in groups of 7 to 9. Similarly, large banks of winter heather *(Erica carnea* or *E. darleyensis)* will quickly stabilize your soil and provide massive displays of white, pink and deep rose ('Kramer's Red') blooms. Several cultivars even provide additional foliar interest of fine gold leaves ('Golden Starlet') or pale yellow new growth tips ('J.W. Porter').

There are a few spreading conifers that also work well in mass plantings. *Taxus baccata* 'Repandens' with its deep green foliage, dwarf forms of golden threadleaf cypress (*Chamaecyparis pisifera filifera* 'Aurea') and a relative newcomer, *Podocarpus* 'Blue Gem', with soft blue-green needles, all work well. For full sun exposures where a low-profile groundcover is required, I highly recommend two University of British Columbia plant introductions — *Arctostaphylos uva-ursi* 'Vancouver Jade' (evergreen, pale pink heather bells, red berries) and *Genista pilosa* 'Vancouver Gold,' a low-growing broom that is an absolute carpet of deep yellow when in bloom.

Single specimens of red weeping Japanese maple (such as *Acer palmatum dissectum* 'Crimson Queen') or *Tsuga canadensis* 'Pendula' (weeping eastern hemlock) cascading over the edge of the wall will provide a textural contrast for the mass plantings. They can also serve as a focal point, suitable for placement near stairs or the corner of a wall.

Small groupings of upright conifers (*Juniperus* 'Skyrocket' or *Taxus baccata* 'Fastigiata Aurea') or pendulous trees with narrow profiles (*Fagus sylvatica* 'Purple Fountain') will help add a vertical element without shading the surrounding plant material.

In any case, make sure that there is a balance of seasonal interest, as well as evergreen versus deciduous (or herbaceous) plant material, so your terraced display will look good all year round. And never plant a single plant species (or members of a single plant family) on a bank, in order to avoid pests and diseases associated with monocultures.

The West Coast Garden

REINIER VAN DE POLL, VAN DE POLL GARDEN DESIGN, MAPLE RIDGE, B.C.

A controversial, yet illuminating, story among local gardeners involves the famous English garden designer John Brookes and his recent visit to British Columbia. Local garden experts were keen to show Mr. Brookes all the best that our regional landscapes had to offer. However, after a day of touring, Mr. Brookes sadly commented that he did not come all the way from England to look at British gardens. Where, he inquired, are your gardens? Where is an example of a West Coast landscape?

A West Coast garden is what John Brookes travelled here to see. What would this garden look like and does such a landscape design even exist?

Over the centuries, styles in fashion, architecture and gardens have emerged and developed. English gardeners, during the eighteenth century, would have been proud to show off their finely groomed gardens to visiting Italian tourists. The Italian visitor might well have made a comment similar to that of John Brookes: "Where is your style? Where is an example of the English garden?" After all, eighteenth-century British gardens were largely inspired by Italian art, architecture and even landscape design.

This is not the forum for an analysis of the history of garden design and its influences. And in the end, it might not lead us to our topic: creating our own style. Defining a current style is as futile as chasing the wind...by the time you catch it, it has already changed directions.

Perhaps what is required is an operating philosophy that guides the design process, thereby allowing an indigenous style to emerge. One of our most famous artists from the past, Emily Carr, was able to reflect the spirit of the west coast on her canvas without ever trying to define its style. She simply allowed all of her senses to open up to its unique beauty...and then she began to paint.

A helpful approach may be borrowed from the garden philosophers Guy Cooper and Gordon Taylor, authors of *Gardens for the Future: Gestures Against the Wild.* They maintain that the most successful gardens of the past 20 years have been inspired by "the intrinsic nature of the site," thus becoming true site-generated expressions. With this guiding principle, the garden design is drawn from a site's physical attributes, its environs and other details, such as the geology and history of the area. Such landscape designs would be, as a rule, completely unique and innovative — reminiscent of Alexander Pope's call to "consult the genius of the place in all."

All this grand talk about landscape design may seem a bit lofty, and I have to admit that even writing about it makes me feel a little presumptuous. After all, isn't a quiet stroll across the lawn, past a mixed border of flowering shrubs and perennials, to a secluded patio with its own reflecting pool just the setting that most of us long for in our backyard retreats? Perhaps, but let me ask this question. Should we have stopped the develop-

Machine placed boulders were used to soften the lines of necessary retaining walls (Photo: Reinier van de Poll)

ment of fine art with the Impressionists? Was that period of artistic expression not soothing and comforting enough to console our weary minds? Surely the wealth of pleasant images created by Monet, Van Gogh and Renoir which currently adorn our calendars, coffee mugs and wall prints is enough to satisfy all of our aesthetic needs. Thankfully, no. And while most of us can look back and still savour the "breath of fresh air" that Emily Carr left on her canvases, that doesn't preclude us from appreciating the artists of today. Our society's well-being is forever linked with its artists — and the garden designer, as many would say, is the artist with the largest palette.

The site-generated approach to developing a West Coast design begins with a site analysis. The analysis includes the property's history, its climatic conditions and its natural elements. The evaluation precedes designing the space.

Let's look at an example of residential acreage in the Fraser valley of British Columbia, which I had the privilege of developing. The clients purchased and cleared the property about 12 years ago in order to build a family home with a driveway, garden areas and outbuildings. The couple asked me to design a rear landscape suitable for their family use. They presented me with a list of their needs and wishes: a large entertaining area, intimate seating areas, integrated hot tub and water feature, bridge access to forested trails, privacy from neighbouring development, seasonal interest plantings with low-maintenance requirements, night lighting and irrigation systems. Such a list is quite the norm for large residential landscapes, but the challenge for a designer is to satisfy the client's needs while developing a design inspired by the intrinsic nature of the site.

The clients were also interested in preserving the natural setting of their property. Mature cedars, Douglas firs and bigleaf maples were the background for our landscape palette. The mysterious, ancient character of old Douglas firs evoked the wild romance that one might associate with a West Coast garden style, and several of these were carefully integrated into the site layout. The preservation of these mature trees posed a challenge when planning a privacy planting to screen their neighbour's new development. This portion of the landscape needed to appear as natural as possible, so the usual pyramid cedar or laurel hedging would not suffice. An informal, mixed planting of mature rhododendrons, conifers and ferns led to a very successful and effective screen. When this planting was completed, the client made a comment that was the best compliment a West Coast designer could hope for. He said, "It doesn't look like the forest has changed! When are the privacy plantings going to be done?" This is the essence of a West Coast design: a seamless integration of new plantings with existing native vegetation.

The slope of the site needed to be retained in order to provide useable seating and planting areas. In previous discussions the owners and I agreed that terraced rows of stacked concrete wall blocks would completely distract from the site's natural features. The challenge was to provide the practical results of grade retention, while using natural materials. Massive moss-encrusted boulders on the site gave us our direction. Off-site boulders that looked true to the site's own geology were acquired. Backbreaking labour and a very skillful excavator operator were key to the craftsmanship of placing about 30 tons of moss- and lichen-covered boulders. These large stones created irregular, undulating retaining walls that were softened with planting pockets and crevices.

The main patio off the house also required a large retaining wall to contain about 3 feet (90 cm) of grade change. To remain true to the site's geological make-up, the same boulders were cut into various sizes suitable for a mortared stone wall. Five separate patio seating areas were located at various levels. The surface material was not a natural material such as stone, due to budgetary restraints. Instead, we chose a manufactured product that would best complement the boulders; warm beige and grey tones of tumbled paving stones were used to echo the site's geology. The backdrop of the upper patio was framed with a rustic post-and-beam cedar structure that serves as an entrance gateway into the forest.

The tranquility that comes from the sound of running water is reminiscent of the many creeks and waterfalls that can be found on local mountain trails. Recreated within a garden setting, the effect is truly transforming. This particular landscape site did not have natural running water, but the forest setting and nearby surroundings supported this feature. In nature, clear water flows over moss-covered rocks and the stream gravel, and is naturally filtered. The water feature constructed on the site relied on the latest technology of filters, pumps and skimmers and the craftsmanship of well-positioned, hand-selected boulders. Ideally, a water feature is positioned for its visual appeal and the tranquil sounds it creates, which can be enjoyed from windows and outdoor seating areas. Yet, careful attention needed to be paid to the various sloping grades of the site.

This example is a brief look at the design challenges and the process of receiving inspiration from "the intrinsic nature of the site." In theory, a designer can achieve this goal without compromise. In practice, the designer must balance the nature of the site and the needs of the home-owner. Success and satisfaction result in blending the two. Visitors perceive the landscape as a marriage of design and the natural environs, and thus we reach our goal of a distinct West Coast garden style — so that we may one day be able to tell Mr. Brookes with confidence that there is such a thing as a West Coast garden style in British Columbia.

The Colour of Passion
ELKE & KEN KNECHTEL, PERENNIAL GARDENS, MAPLE RIDGE, B.C.

Red is a strong colour that affects people in many different ways. Some get a romantic image of red geraniums spilling out of window boxes on the front of an old-fashioned cottage, others a row of bright red salvias planted along a white picket fence. Those who have travelled to tropical regions may conjure up warm nights and exotic, lush landscapes. Red is often associated with royalty or warfare, but it can also be sultry and passionate, as expressed by the satins and silks evident around Valentine's Day. However you feel about this colour, you can be sure that it will directly affect the way you use red in your landscape.

For many gardeners, red is not an easy colour to work with, so it is helpful to know a little about it before you begin to use it. Its complementary colour is green, the most common hue in the landscape, so you really can't go wrong with placing red in a predominantly green garden. The harmonious colours for red are violet (on one side of the colour wheel) and orange (on the other). These closely aligned colours are the ones red can most easily blend with. Red cannot be seen in low light conditions, so it should be placed in areas of the garden that are enjoyed during the day. This is definitely not a colour you should use in a landscape where you entertain primarily in the evening. Red is an active colour, jumping out at you and making the garden seem smaller, or more intimate.

The various tones of red need to be used in different ways in the garden. Reds on the cooler side, such as violet reds, tend to be easier to blend with pastel colours, such as pinks, lavenders, blues and whites. Many roses tend to be in this colour range, especially the shrub roses like 'Scarlet Pavement', and perennials such as *Knautia macedonica*, which is often used to visually

Astrantia 'Ruby Wedding'
(Photo: Elke Knechtel)
Colour photo p. 134

tie a garden together. Reds on the orange side are considered "hot" colours. These blend better with yellow, gold or orange but can look equally good with rich purple and vivid blue. *Crocosmia* 'Lucifer' and *Lychnis chalcedonica* (Maltese cross) are strong orange-reds that show well when backed by *Sambucus* 'Sutherland Gold' (golden elderberry) or the lustrous purple-flowered *Campanula* 'Kent Belle'. "Hot" reds can help you create those tropical looks that are much in vogue these days.

Also popular today are plants with dark foliage. Most bear leaves in mahogany to maroon tones, or regal reds on the purple side. Use these plants as you would use red in the garden. They are great accents for green but in the evening can disappear like black holes. These incredible foliage plants can go with everything in the garden. Hold them against any colour and you will soon find that nothing clashes. The classic red-leafed plants are Japanese maples (such as 'Bloodgood' or 'Red Pygmy'), used frequently by garden designers as accents to liven a typically green landscape. Degrees of red are also found on new growth, from the warm reds of *Pieris japonica* 'Forest Flame' to the deep mahogany red foliage of some of the *phormiums* (New Zealand flax), such as 'Dusky Chief'. Use these foliage plants as container specimens to tie colours together or provide year-round interest. Most gardeners find that foliage provides a much longer period of interest than the relatively short lifespan of a flower display.

Autumn tones also heighten interest. Colour may last for a week or even a month (depending on the plant) and adds interest when the garden is usually not looking its best. *Liquidambar styraciflua* (sweet gum) provides brilliant red and orange fall colour for a long time, holding its leaves well into winter. *Aronia* 'Autumn Magic' and *Euonymus alatus* (burning bush) are absolutely brilliant in the fall and are a perfect foil for evergreen shrubs such as cotoneaster and rhododendron.

In North America there is another reason to garden with red, and that is to attract a form of wildlife found only in North and South America — the hummingbird. Many plants in the Americas actually have a partnership with this little bird and are coloured red for this purpose. One example is honeysuckle — not fragrant here in North America as in Europe but nonetheless richly coloured with red and orange blooms to attract hummingbirds for pollination. *Monarda didyma* (bee balm) is another North American plant available in vivid reds, including the cultivars 'Gardenview Scarlet' and 'Feuerschopf'.

While the idea of using red in the garden may alarm some people, for others it evokes feelings of warmth or even power. So give it a try — you will never be bored when designing with the colour of passion.

The Plants of Passion

Aquilegia vulgaris 'Ruby Port' (columbine) Herbaceous perennial. Zone 2.

Bergenia 'Bressingham Ruby' Evergreen perennial with red winter foliage. Zone 3.

Cotinus coggygria 'Royal Purple' (purple smoke bush) Deciduous shrub. Zone 4–5.

Euphorbia amygdaloides 'Purpurea' Evergreen perennial with mahogany-red foliage. Zone 5.

Monarda didyma 'Jacob Kline' or 'Feuerschopf' (bee balm) Herbaceous perennial. Zone 3

Paeonia 'Nippon Beauty' (garden peony) Herbaceous perennial. Zone 2.

Papaver orientale 'Turkenlouis' (oriental poppy) Herbaceous perennial. Zone 2.

Phygelius 'Winchester Fanfare' (Cape fuchsia) Evergreen perennial. Zone 7.

Physocarpus opulifolius 'Diabolo' Deciduous shrub with burgundy foliage. Zone 3.

Rosa 'Eddie's Jewel' (Rosa moyesii hybrid) Single rose-red blooms. Zone 5.

Sambucus nigra 'Black Beauty' Deciduous shrub with deep maroon foliage. Zone 4.

Sempervivum 'Rogin' (hens and chicks) Evergreen perennial. Zone 2.

Garden Rooms
RUTH OLDE, BLASIG LANDSCAPE DESIGN, MAPLE RIDGE, B.C.

Gardens are for people and their enjoyment. They offer additional living space and a quiet haven to ease some of the stresses of modern life. You can actually enjoy a vacation at home — with no vaccinations, no delays at airports, no bumper-to-bumper traffic and no disappointment when your hotel room falls considerably short of the one pictured in the brochure.

You may be thinking to yourself, "that's easy for her to say." Perhaps you have spent countless hours staring at that confusing space outside the walls of your home, wondering where to begin. It should have so much potential — but no matter how long you stare outside, it offers no solution to the dilemma of how to make it look like the gardens in the magazines. In that case, you might just need a new perspective. As Leonardo da Vinci said, "You don't have to learn how to draw, you have to learn how to see."

Approach your outside space in much the same way you would if you were making changes to your house. Think of your garden as rooms. Simple, isn't it? Ask yourself what rooms you would like to have outdoors. Think about a living room, a dining room, storage room, family room, kitchen, bathroom, playroom, reading room, foyer…even a room for meditation. Don't restrict the possibilities yet — constraints and reality will be a part of the process all too soon.

What would you fill these dream rooms with? What would add pleasure and joy to your life? A swimming pool, a hot tub, a cozy seat to curl up in and read, some cupboards and counter space, a tennis or bocci court, a dining or living room with a fireplace, a pond and waterfall to add a sense of peace and quiet? Now that you have your wish list, it's time to think about where those rooms can go and how many you can actually accommodate.

Start with the front of your house, as the garden room potential here is far too often ignored. The first impression anyone has of your home is not when you open the front door, it's when your guests park their car.

While the scale of the entry and pathway to your home needs to maintain a balance between hard and soft landscaping, the house tends to dominate the landscape, so think big. A 4-foot-wide (1.2-m) pathway is the minimum to allow two people to walk side by side. Wider is better, and flaring it out at the street will put out the welcome mat. The path can meander and still lead directly to the front door. People will take the path of least resistance. A worn-down lawn or trampled plants are evidence of an unsuccessful informal approach. Add an arbour or a gate to establish the street entry to your home and you begin to create an outdoor room. Building walls, fences or other structures beyond your property line is generally not a good idea. But in the no-man's land between the sidewalk and the street (the area that never looks good and tracks dirt and chewed up lawn into your yard), you could add paving stones on a sand base, so they can be lifted and relaid if necessary. Remember to think big, as a wider pathway will visually extend your garden, and welcome people sooner.

Think about which portion of the front yard gets early morning or late afternoon sun in seasons when we don't need shelter from the sun's rays. There may be an overlooked corner that would be a perfect place to sit when you get home from work, or to enjoy your coffee first thing in the morning. It can be enclosed and secluded or open to the neighbourhood, depending on your personality. A planted berm, hedge or screen no taller than 4 feet (1.2 m) will provide privacy when you are sitting down, but won't block out light or create a security concern.

When planning outside rooms, always be aware of the impact they will have on the inside rooms. While romantic covered porches have wonderful eye appeal and offer protection from the weather, they can darken the

An intimate garden room (Photo: Blasig Landscape Design)

inside of the house. Consider putting a glass roof over the porch, or adding skylights, to make it and the house a little brighter. Another option is to cover only a part of the porch. Or move that room away from the house and enjoy a view of the home you work so hard to keep beautiful — a view that is seldom incorporated into a garden design.

The hallway connecting the front and back of your property is often the skeleton in the closet of landscaping. It is usually paved in a narrow, straight line — just a connection from back to front — often ignored, dark and damp, and used as a catch-all for things you will someday get rid of. It does provide the necessary access for wheelbarrows, other tools and perhaps garden furniture, so it needs to be practical, but it doesn't have to look bad. Concrete stepping stones, paving stones or poured concrete (brushed or stamped) make access easy. Allow the path to meander down the side of the house with plantings on either side, reducing the tunnel effect. If there are windows along the side of the house, think about raising the planting beds beside the pathway to make the plants visible from the inside. When well-thought-out, views from the house can be as satisfying as being outside. Depending on the space available, a storage shed can be built against the wall of the house. Finish the shed with the same surface as the house, and you will have an outdoor closet, as easy to use as the inside ones.

A more familiar space, the back garden, is easier to divide into rooms. Wherever possible, the outdoor rooms should flow out from the house at the same level. This extends the view from the inside to the outside, or vice versa, making both spaces appear larger. If possible, eliminate steps that lead directly into the house. It is easier to move in and out without them. However, if steps are required, make sure there is a large landing, a minimum of 4 feet deep (1.2 m), in front of a door before the first step.

A gazebo with a glass roof makes a distinct outdoor room, especially if you have to go up a few steps to get inside. Elevation changes add a sense of separation, but having only one step should be avoided, as it tends to be a tripping hazard. (When planning, always add a few extra square feet to the size of any outdoor room.) Hard surfaces, when constructed properly, require less long-term maintenance than flower beds or lawn. Adding lights and heaters prevents darkness or cool air from driving you indoors when you are cuddled up outside with your favorite book or person.

No matter what type of room or where it is located, be sure to add water. It's irresistible and brings life to any garden, regardless of size. It masks unpleasant noises with its own sounds and rhythms. Whether tucked away in a forgotten corner or shared with other garden rooms, like a fireplace that is open to the kitchen and family room, it has a calming influence.

I can just hear you thinking, "What about the work to take care of all this? Designers are always creating nightmares for the rest of us to take care of." I know…I know. The amount of long-term care required to maintain your newfound haven needs to be a part of the initial design considerations. It will be "Paradise Lost" if every spare moment is spent weeding or staking or pruning. These suggestions should help you minimize maintenance.

- Consider hard-surface materials carefully. Do not just look at the budget but consider longevity in the outdoors and the amount of work required to keep them looking good.
- Use plants that suit the soil, light and water conditions you have to offer.
- Be aware of the mature size of plants so they won't outgrow their welcome and need to be hacked back. (Pardon me…pruned.)
- Put annuals in pots for focal points or dividers, and plant perennials in the garden beds.
- Space plants, allowing for 2 to 3 years' growth. In that time they should grow in and cover the ground, drastically reducing the open area that is a magnet for weeds.
- Put a 2- to 3-inch (5- to 8-cm) layer of garden mulch in newly planted areas.

Start the process with the end in mind and have a plan. Having a clear vision and being sure it is the same vision as those who will share your space makes the process much easier and saves time, energy and money.

Heated debates about how big the patio will be, whether you will use concrete or paving stones, if you will really use a hot tub and how much lawn is too much are inevitable. But they are better to have on a piece of paper that you can discuss over a cup of coffee, rather than in the garden, with workers waiting for instructions.

Now…look outside again. Envision your future hideaway with new energy and resolve. Lush greenery, an arbour that creates a doorway, fragrance, warmth, light, a comfortable place to sit (or lie)…whatever makes you feel like you are wrapped up in your favourite blanket. Welcoming, enclosed and private are the keys to success. Now make those rooms come true!

Interior Landscape Design

ANN CASSIDY, BOTANY BAY LANDSCAPE SERVICES INC., SURREY, B.C.

Interior landscape design is a relatively new profession. While growing plants in containers dates back more than 4,000 years, the Roman atrium of 2,000 years ago was the first use of plants within an enclosed environment. The reintroduction of the atrium in modern hotel design in the 1960s was quite an advancement, as it established the use of large-scale plants as a planned component of a building's public spaces. The Hyatt Regency in Atlanta, with its 22-story atrium, opened in 1967 and was an instant success. Other atriums used as architectural focal points quickly followed. Their grandiose size was both thrilling and intimidating. Plant material, especially large trees and palms, provided a human scale in these vast interior spaces, adding texture to mitigate the starkness of the open areas.

The use of plants in the interior of both public and private spaces has now been shown to provide a low-tech option for purifying indoor air. Plants in the workplace have been shown to enhance productivity by 12 percent. They have a positive effect on employees' dispositions, decrease employee turnover, reduce overall stress and cut down on distractions due to office noise.

Dr. Virginia Lohr of Washington State University conducted a study where participants reacted to randomized computer symbols. Plants present in the space or a lack of plants were the only variables that the study participants experienced. The study indicated that participants in the presence of plants were less stressed and reacted 12 percent more quickly to computer symbols than those placed in an area with no plant material.

Dr. Bill Wolverton and his aids in the Environmental Research Laboratory at John C. Stennis Space Centre have been conducting research on the natural air purification process for nearly 20 years and have proved that indoor plants work constantly to clean the air. By absorbing pollutants into their leaves and emitting oxygen, interior plants can drastically improve indoor air quality. And plant-filled rooms actually contain 50 to 60 percent fewer airborne moulds and bacteria than rooms without plants.

When purchasing tropical plants for your home, do your research before you buy. Plants that fail are most often an impulse purchase of the wrong plant for the location. Know where you want to place the plant, and how it will grow. Do you want the plant to trail down, grow up to fill the corner, or fill a window and create privacy? Will the plant be in front of the window or in the corner away from the light? Be aware of the natural light levels, and you will be much better equipped to select a species that will thrive. Think ahead to what the plant will look like in two years, and make sure you allow for future growth. Remember that not all plants can be pruned as they mature. For example, kentia palms are as wide as they are high when they reach maturity. Less is often best. Rather than having a lot of small pots, invest in one or two large, dramatic plants that will provide more impact with less effort. Place a few flowering cyclamen and ferns at the base and you will have created a mixed visual delight.

The quality and quantity of your light dictates the selection of plants. The more light, the more choice you will have. Beware of glossy leaves and very bushy plants, as this is a sign that they may be field grown and not acclimatized to interior light.

Don't kill plants with kindness by putting them outside; sun and wind may burn them to a crisp, and they may even pick up insects. If you ever feel compelled to drag your plants outside, please do so on a rainy day when they can at least get a good cleaning.

The only way to really know what is going on in your pots is to probe the soil. Use a chopstick to measure the moisture level before you water a plant. Ideally, the soil should feel slightly dry on top, moist in the middle and not soggy on the bottom. Cut back on the watering as winter approaches and increase as spring arrives. The one-cup-every-Monday watering pattern is the kiss of death! Plants do not drink at the same rate all year, and each week the light they receive is different. Avoid the dreaded "puddle water-ing," whereby the water creates a depression, exposing the roots to air and possibly bacterial or fungal infections. Water evenly with tepid water, over all the soil surface and stir the top ¼ inch (5 mm) of the soil a few times a year.

Only fertilize your plants when the soil is moist. A weekly application of 10-10-10 from April to September will make a major difference to a plant's health. Do not use slow-release fertilizers indoors, as this can result in too much salt in the soil. In containers this can prove to be fatal.

These are just a few of the simple cultural practices necessary to main-tain the long-term health of your indoor garden. Take the time to care for your plants and they will return the favour with fresh air, not to men-tion the deep sense of satisfaction you will get from nurturing these living things.

This Is My Backyard — The Boundaries of the Yard
PAWEL GRADOWSKI, LANDSCAPE ARCHITECT, M.BCSLA/M.CSLA

Consider an apartment balcony on the thirty-fifth floor with a few plants in a clay pot, a wicker chair and a magnificent view of the mountains on the horizon. Some would consider this the best backyard in the world. Others might disagree — wanting the experience of planting in their own yard. Still others just want to look at nature without getting dirty. For some, privacy is the key element of the backyard; for a select few, being together with other people in a public park is more enjoyable.

As you can see, *my backyard* can be understood in many different ways. A great view of a lake is an integral part of a small garden located on its shore, even if the legal property line does not touch the water. For both private owners and those in the business of designing gardens, it's important to understand how landscapes impact on the surrounding areas, whether privately owned or not. Many designers and developers think only within the legal boundaries of the developed lot, but it's good to be aware of how considerable changes in the landscape, even if made on privately owned land, will affect the neighbourhood, the needs of the entire community or the environment.

Regardless of the main purpose of a garden, its immediate neighborhood has an important influence on the quality of its environment. Adjoining areas affect wind patterns, sunlight, temperature or may cause changes in ground water levels or water quality that could have a significant impact on plant growth. Intrusions such as noise, smells and traffic can easily destroy the tranquility of any refuge.

Coordination of garden design with the surrounding landscape has been done for thousands of years. At the time when Egyptian pharaohs were building elaborate water channels to irrigate their gardens, the Chinese were incorporating the idea of a "borrowed landscape" into their gardens. This was usually done by creating a special viewing area, which allowed visitors to appreciate the features within the garden and at the same time enjoy a view of a mountain, an island or another significant piece of landscape located far away. The view was an integral part of the design.

The concept of looking far beyond the boundaries of the garden was gradually absorbed by many western civilizations. A fascination with Asian culture began in Europe in the seventeenth and eighteenth centuries after the first successful expeditions to the Far East. It significantly influenced European garden design. The new style, which became known as the English Garden, broke away from established French garden traditions with their focus on elaborate human creations such as topiaries, complex parterres, water features and sculptures. The English Garden was a radical departure that focussed on naturalistic landscapes. View lines of natural or man-made features located within the estate or beyond its boundaries became one of the tenets of this new gardening style.

View through the moon
gate screen at Sun Yat-Sen
Classical Chinese Garden in
Vancouver, B.C.

Views played a significant role in the design of these landscapes, but
even these had to be balanced with the necessities of a working estate. Farm
animals would often wander in pastures around the gardens and there was
a need to protect the carefully groomed grounds from potential damage.
The solution was the ha-ha — a series of barriers or fences hidden in the
bottom of wide ditches or behind tall earthen berms. The ha-ha was prac-
tically invisible unless seen from a short distance and it in no way marred
the intended views.

English Garden traditions are a significant part of many landscapes
today. We still have big open lawns, plant trees and shrubs in complex
groups and use borrowed landscapes wherever it is appropriate. We also
have large public parks and planted boulevards to provide us with some
relief from the noise and pollution common to urban areas.

Almost everyone needs their own private place. People generally create
these spaces in their backyard to provide a refuge from everyday stress. In
cities, the limited lot size does not allow for the creation of spacious buffers
like those available in large suburban estates. To protect their privacy, some
people plant hedges to provide visual isolation — others build fences (or
use a combination of methods) to partially screen themselves from noise.

Considering that the general population in North America comes from
every possible ethnic and cultural background, it is not surprising that

everyone has a different concept of the private space. One neighbour may want to open up views, while another builds visual barriers on his property. Incompatible garden designs can create tension and local planning departments try to reduce the number of conflicts between neighbours by creating bylaws and design guidelines. These guide any new development in the area and are used as the basis for legal help when negotiating between neighbours. The rules are often revised and updated to reflect the evolving needs of people and changes in the environment.

There are a growing number of commercial sites that exhibit a lack of coordination between developers. For example, there might be two adjacent projects where the designers did not coordinate their efforts or the city did not compare the two designs during the approval process. The finished project could have two identical chain link fences at a common property line, as well as a double row of specimen trees just a few feet apart on both sides of the double fence. Not only is doubling the fence and the trees a waste of money and materials, but when these trees mature, the competition for nutrients, sun, water and space will probably weaken them and eventually cause most to decline.

From the landscape architect's point of view, it is very important to step outside the box and think about the kind of impact a development might have on the local environment. As gardeners, we should never forget that adding or eliminating elements in the landscape may affect many animals and plants that coexist with us and use our gardens as a place of refuge. Others affected by development may be local residents or distant neighbours who lose their view because of our actions. So whether I am designing a large commercial site, a tiny high-rise balcony or an elaborate residential landscape — I am always thinking a little beyond the legal property lines, to the many *backyards* that will coexist with the garden I am about to create.

The Power of Perennials — Building Herbaceous Borders
CLARE PHILIPS, PHOENIX PERENNIALS, VANCOUVER, B.C.

At the beginning of the twentieth century, perennial borders became an essential component of an established garden. As the name implies, they were usually used to edge or border a garden area and were often backed by stone or brick walls or by hedging, with the front of the border meeting wide paths or lawn. The key to the borders' success lay in the arrangements of groups of herbaceous perennials.

Usually the gardens were large enough to provide other areas of interest at times when the perennials were less colourful or had died down for winter. The windows of the grand houses seldom looked out directly upon perennial borders, as they were often found a good stroll away from the house. The flowering displays would be in their prime in May and June, when the stalwarts of the classical perennial borders — roses, delphiniums, lupines and peonies — come into flower. The development and maintenance of border plantings were often costly and time consuming. The expertise of a head gardener was needed throughout the year, along with the foreman gardeners, who directed a group of "garden boys."

In order to keep a succession of interest in the beds, "fill-ins" were recommended. Gertrude Jekyll — one of the originators of the classic herbaceous border — encouraged the addition of lilies, hydrangeas and chrysanthemums that were started in pots and transferred into the border at times when it needed extra interest. She also devised ways of staking down taller plants, such as aster and rudbeckia, forcing them to develop shorter side-shoots that would cover earlier-flowering plants that were no longer performing.

Above all else, the borders were carefully designed to provide drifts of colour and tapestries of plant associations in flower and foliage that would create a changing vista of interest. It is to Gertrude Jekyll, perhaps more than anyone else, that we owe the inspiration and amazing complexity of planned perennial plantings.

THE WORK OF GERTRUDE JEKYLL

This rather severe, myopic, middle-aged woman paradoxically designed and planted borders manifesting a profound sensitivity to colour and the beauty of individual plants. Together with a younger landscape architect, Edwin Lutyens, she was responsible for designing well over 100 gardens in England.

The garden she developed in her beloved home at Munstead Wood had a border 200 feet long by 14 feet wide (60 × 4 m), edged in front by lawn and backed by an 11-foot-high (3.3-m) wall. In this long border she experimented with color runs. Blue, green and grey were used at the two ends, moving to the centre with a crescendo of crimson, red and orange. It seems possible that her impaired eyesight may have helped her evolve the impressionistic effects that she wished to produce. Her planting plans show a method of plant positioning that worked roughly parallel to the grass edge, with increasing plant heights as the border deepened towards the back wall.

Inevitably, borders of this size that evolved at the turn of the twentieth century were costly to keep, though competitively developed by the great houses of the time. Labour was relatively cheap, especially at the "garden boy" level. These supervised apprentices received the equivalent of about $10 a day while garden laborers got about $19. Usually, they were given food and lodgings as a part of their wages, living in a separate cottage on the estate. The head gardener, who was often trained in places such as Kew

Jekyll garden in Hestercombe, Somerset, U.K. (Photo: Clare Philips)
Colour photo p. 136

Colour photo p. 136

Gardens, could receive as much as $305 a week in today's money. Gardens such as Hestercombe, Somerset, a Jekyll/Lutyens project, had in its prime as many as 16 gardeners who worked full-time to keep up the grounds. A rough calculation of the salaries of the day suggests it would cost an equivalent today of approximately $100,000 a year to maintain. (Wage calculations are based on John J. McCusker, "Comparing the Purchasing Power of Money in Great Britain from 1600 to any year, including the present." Economic History Services, 2001, http:/www.eh.net/hmit/ppowerbp.)

Few have the space, finances or dedication to build perennial borders in the manner that Jekyll recommended. Labour costs have spiralled upwards since World War II and most gardens have become relatively small urban plots. Hestercombe barely manages today with a staff of one full-time gardener and a part-time assistant. However, many of Gertrude Jekyll's ideas and approaches are firmly established in gardens large or small, public or private, that have been built in the last 100 years.

Perennials are planted in patches or drifts, usually in odd numbers (3, 5 or 7), in order to achieve a naturalistic effect. Concern for plant form, or architecture, has joined other dimensions (foliage, flower colour, height, spread, etc.) in planning plant positions. For the most part, the plants are arranged in drifts that roughly run parallel to the front edge of the bed, though the recommended use of drifts prevents this from becoming rigid. Pulling forward a taller group of plants into the mid-border, or even to the front, is now a recognized way to encourage the sense of movement and provide intriguing effects. Increasingly, "transparent" perennials such as grasses have been used in this way, allowing the viewer to see through a veil to blooms beyond. This increases the sense of depth in the narrower borders of today's urban gardens. But it is the inspiration that comes from Jekyll's colour games that, above all else, has inspired gardeners and designers.

The changing colour combinations and unpredictable seasonal interest of perennials has played a large role in making gardens. Even in the smallest space, colour can be manipulated to get different effects. Mixed borders are also the best solution for smaller gardens; flower beds are visible for 12 months of the year and privacy screening is a matter of great importance in their planning. Small trees (deciduous or evergreen), as well as flowering shrubs, vine-clad fences or arbours work well with perennial plantings.

The balance between large evergreen shrubs and trees, and the planting space at their feet is a major concern for garden planning. The need for hard or soft landscaping (the "bones" of the garden) can sometimes dominate, resulting in perennial borders that are too narrow to allow cross-seasonal colour effects. Often perennials are just popped in as fillers and lose their impact. Possibly the biggest mistake in planning is the tendency to cut meagre borders that cling to the edge of the plot. Bold, wide borders make smaller gardens feel larger.

Jekyll's genius was to arrange and order perennials in a naturalistic way markedly different from the rigid, controlled plantings of the nineteeth century. Her ideas have inspired gardeners ever since. Interestingly, in the last decade, exponents of new approaches to perennial borders are emerging.

Piet Oudolf's double herbaceous border at Wisley, Surrey, U.K. (Photo: Clare Philips)

MODERN BORDER INTERPRETATIONS

Currently, a Canadian couple from Vancouver Island working in Somerset, England, and a Dutch designer are evolving two different approaches to perennial plantings.

Nori and Sandra Pope are deeply committed to the development of what they have called monochrome borders, an idea detailed in their book, *Color By Design*. They have been undertaking this work at Hadspen Manor Gardens, the old Hobhouse family home in England.

In the former kitchen garden of the estate, they are developing perennial beds that run for over half a mile (1 km) along the base of an old brick wall in a D-shape. The Popes have a knowledge of plant material and a sensitivity to colour only matched by their humour and inventiveness. Drawing from their own nursery (much as Jekyll did), they focus on an exploration of each major colour through hue, tone and colour echoes. Sometimes a comparative foliage or flower colour is introduced to further explore a colour group (such as using bronze fennel in a yellow border). Occasionally, a colour extension may almost carry the primary colour into another colour group (for instance, crimson *Geranium psilostemon* straddles the red/purple to pink border). The overall drive, however, is to keep within the colour quadrant being explored and to follow it as far and as deeply as possible.

The consequence has been the development of one of the most interesting modern colour experiments to date. Sometimes you find yourself excited as you look into the complex textures and effects, or laughing to yourself at the humour presented by some of the plant echos. At other times you just find yourself melting into the beauty of the wide, meandering colourscape. Anyone who has the opportunity to see Hadspen will be inspired to play with these ideas in their own garden, following the colours wherever they may lead.

Another visionary has appeared in the form of a modest Dutchman: Piet Oudolf. He has produced a number of original perennial plantings and borders; the most relevant for this discussion is his double herbaceous border in R.H.S. Wisley, Surrey, UK. It replicates in shape and size the traditional double perennial border in this garden — each border is 14 by 420 feet (4.5 by 140 m) — but dramatically breaks the mould.

Oudolf has been deeply influenced by the patterns and flow of flowers in the wild. He emulates the scattered runs of wild flowers as they self-seed in alpine meadows. In contrast to the Popes, he sees colour as the least important component when planning the border. Primarily, he considers plant structure: spires (such as *Cimicifuga*), buttons and globes *(Sanguisorba* and *Echinops)*, plumes *(Filipendula)*, umbels *(Achillea)*, daisies *(Aster)* and screens or curtains *(Stipa)*. Next, he considers form — the shape and texture of the plants, especially foliage. Finally, he contemplates the colour of the flower or foliage, almost as an afterthought.

He writes in his book, *Designing With Plants,* that colours found in nature will all work together without problem. However, he carefully selects perennials for their natural look and ease of growing — preferring species to overbred cultivars — in order to avoid top-heavy appearances and high maintenance requirements. He chooses garden-worthy plants with long season effects, which are self-sustaining and retain interesting structure even as they go to seed. Running a nursery himself, he has been closely in touch with the plant material and is a critic worth hearing. In his recent book, *Dream Plants for the Natural Garden,* he goes so far as to define troublesome border perennials using several categories, including "invasive," "capricious" and "demanding plants to be avoided."

Oudolf's double perennial border at Wisley is startlingly original, both in concept and planning. Perennials (3 or 4 species in each of the approximately 35 "rivers") flow from the outer edge towards the middle grass path in a natural, meandering manner. Across the path on the opposite border, the same 3 or 4 species flow on towards the outer edge. Walking along the central path, the viewer looks through one river of texture into a different grouping flowing behind it. Looking back at the facing border, the same species are now mingled with a different river of texture. Looking vertically into the planting as it reaches the centre provides yet another view. Heights are not carefully considered. Movement is constant as the restless grass plumes catch the breeze.

The result is a unique sense of being within a plant display. Yet we are able to gain a perspective of it from many different vantage points. The plants are left to evolve with minimal interference or maintenance. In many ways, his concept is simple when compared to the more complex plant associations planned by the Popes or by Jekyll's methods. But the shift in focus is startlingly original. Instead of horizontal planting tiered back from the front, the vertical dimension is exploited right from the edge of the border, and naturalistic rivers of plants take over from clumps or drifts.

Interestingly, both the Popes and Oudolf are working exclusively with soft landscaping in their design work. They are bringing us back to the key component of perennial borders: the arrangement of the groups of herbaceous perennials. The development of landscape architecture has tended to take the emphasis from plant material and placed it on hard architectural features — often to the detriment of garden development.

These new designers seek to redress this imbalance, encouraging every gardener to explore the power of perennials, be it by plant structure, form or colour. Gertrude Jekyll would have been thrilled by the influence she has had, and the new developments that are occurring 100 years after her seminal work.

Overcoming Zone Envy

MICHAEL LASCELLE, AMSTERDAM GARDEN CENTRE, PITT MEADOWS, B.C.

We are a well-travelled people and perhaps more than any generation before us, highly mobile in our living habits, frequently moving from one place to another. As a nursery manager in coastal British Columbia, I have customers who have lived or still live across this country or even further afield. I encounter local gardeners returning from holidays in Hawaii or New Zealand, hoping to find a few of those tree ferns or hardy gingers they admired while away on vacation. I have expatriate South Africans looking for their native blue Nile lily *(Agapanthus)* or red-hot pokers *(Kniphofia)*; at the other end of the spectrum, former Winnipeg residents are searching for a saskatoonberry bush.

Whether it is a small remembrance of home or just something out of the ordinary, these plants are important to the people who seek them out. The problems often begin after finding the plants they want. It is then that the gap between expectation and what can be realistically achieved with our temperature extremes, rainfall and local soils becomes obvious. The information here is meant to reduce that gap, so you can create a landscape designed for your yard and the conditions that exist there.

Zone envy also works both ways — which is why I have divided this into three separate sections. "A Taste of the Tropics" is primarily for Zone 7–9 gardeners looking to create an exotic landscape, with a few marginally hardy plants included. "A Piece of the Prairies" is for those gardeners in Zones 5–9 who miss some of their prairie favourites from Alberta, Saskatchewan and Manitoba. "The Hardy Exotics" is geared towards Zone 4–6 gardeners who are also looking for hardy plant material to create a landscape with a tropical feel.

A TASTE OF THE TROPICS

All tropical landscapes are essentially plant-based. Without the bold textures, brightly coloured blooms and unusual foliage, there is no exotic garden, and no amount of hard landscaping, residential architecture or garden bric-a-brac will create this unique effect. They may complement the design, but they can't replace the organic component.

When designing an exotic garden, you also have to consider what your landscape is going to look like during the winter. Once the tree ferns are put away in the greenhouse, the hardy bananas are bundled up for frost protection and the hardy gingers are mulched…what's left? There may be a cluster of palms, a few clumps of bamboo and maybe a yucca or two, but is that enough to keep you content from late fall until early spring?

One option is to include strategic groupings of exotic-looking broadleaf evergreens such as *Ceanothus* 'Victoria', *Escallonia* 'Newport Dwarf' or even a refined cultivar of Portuguese laurel (*Prunus lusitanica* 'Lolita'), with its smaller foliage. Many gardeners with tropical landscapes simply resign themselves to the bundled plants and empty garden space during the

Passiflora incarnata
(Maypop passionflower)
Colour photo p. 136

winter — but they usually limit themselves to the backyard, where these seasonal interruptions are less obvious.

Whether you are planning a full tropical look or a combination of designs, the following list should help. These are some of the more reliable trees, shrubs and perennials that have been an intricate part of exotic landscapes in the Pacific Northwest for decades now.

Brugmansia (angel trumpet) A group of species and hybrid shrub-like perennials with large, trumpet-shaped, pendulous blooms. Includes *B. sanguinea* (orange trumpet/red flare), *B. arborea* (scented white blooms) and *B. aurea* (fragrant golden blooms). Average height 8 feet (2.4 m). Frost tender. Native to South America.

Cynara cardunculus (cardoon) A bold specimen perennial with silver-grey foliage and prominent purple thistle flower heads. Height 6 feet (2 m). Zone 7. Native to the Mediterranean region and Morocco.

Dicksonia antarctica (Tasmanian tree fern) A bold specimen fern that eventually develops a tall, shaggy stalk or trunk. Evergreen in tropical climates but best overwintered in a greenhouse in temperate regions. Height 10 feet+ (3 m+). Zone 9–10. Native to eastern Australia and Tasmania.

Diospyros khaki (persimmon) An ornamental fruit tree with foliage that flushes a bright lime green in spring and changes to orange or gold in the fall. The fruit resembles a tomato; the best cultivar is 'Fuyu'. Height 20 feet+ (6 m+). Zone 7. Native to Japan and China.

Eriobotrya japonica (loquat) A tropical fruit tree with large, lance-shaped leaves, fragrant white flowers and small orange-yellow fruit. Primarily grown for its exotic foliage. Height 20 feet (6 m). Zone 7. Native to China and Japan.

Fatsia japonica (Japanese aralia) An exotic broadleaf evergreen shrub with glossy, palmate foliage and spherical white flowers. Height 10 feet (3 m). Zone 7. Native to Japan.

Ficus carica (common fig) A self-fertile, deciduous fruit tree with glossy, deeply lobed leaves and fruit that develops right on the stem. Some of the more hardy cultivars include 'Brown Turkey' (strawberry flesh), 'Latturula' (amber flesh) and 'Desert King' (green with strawberry flesh). Height 12 feet (4 m). Zone 6. Native to the eastern Mediterranean.

Gunnera manicata (giant rhubarb) A huge, herbaceous perennial with 6-foot-wide (2-m) leaves on mature specimens. Reddish flowers are held on bizarre 3-foot-tall (90-cm) cone-shaped panicles. Height 8 feet (2.4 m). Zone 7 with mulch. Native to Colombia and Brazil.

Hedychium (hardy ginger) A group of herbaceous perennials with prominent flower spikes (often fragrant) resembling orchids. Includes *H. coronarium* (white), *H. gardnerianum* (yellow with orange stamens) and *H. greenii* (purple reverse on foliage). Average height 4 feet (1.2 m). Zone 8 with mulch. Native to India and the Himalayas.

Magnolia grandiflora (evergreen magnolia) A reliably evergreen tree with large, glossy foliage (rust-coloured hairs on the underside) and fragrant, creamy-white flowers. Height 20 feet+ (7 m+). Zone 7. Native to the southeast United States.

Miscanthus floridulus (giant miscanthus) An ornamental grass with bamboo proportions. Rarely blooms in regions with cool summers. Height to 10 feet (3 m). Zone 6. Native to China.

Musa 'Basjoo' (Japanese fibre banana) A bold foliage plant with typical banana form on tall stems (once mature). It readily suckers and produces small, unpalatable bananas on 4- to 5-year-old stalks. Height 10 feet+ (3 m+). Zone 7–8 with winter protection. Native to Japan.

Passiflora spp. (passion flower) The two hardiest species to choose from are *P. incarnata* (pink blooms) and *P. caerulea* (blue passion flower). *P. incarnata* is generally herbaceous in colder climates, while *P. caerulea* is evergreen. Height to 15 feet (5 m). Zone 7. Native to Central America and Brazil.

Phormium (New Zealand flax) A group of evergreen perennials composed of two species *(P. tenax* and *P. cookianum)* and many cultivars. The broad, yucca-like foliage comes in bronze, green, yellow, pink, red and blends of these colours. Height to 6 feet (2 m). Zone 8. Native to New Zealand.

Phyllostachys **spp.** (bamboo) A large genus of bamboo with ornamental culms, or canes, and evergreen foliage. A sampling would include *P. nigra* (black bamboo), *P. vivax* (Chinese timber bamboo) and *P. bambusoides* (giant timber bamboo). Height 20 feet+ (6 m+). Zones 7–8. Native to China and Japan.

Spartium junceum (Spanish broom) A shrub with fragrant, yellow, pea-like blooms and deep green rush-like stems. Height 10 feet (3 m). Zone 8. Native to Turkey, Syria and Africa.

Tibouchina urvilleana (princess flower) A tall bush or small containerized tree with velvety, deeply ribbed foliage and purple blooms throughout the summer. Height to 10 feet (3 m). Frost tender. Native to Brazil.

Trachycarpus fortunei (hardy windmill palm) A large, single-stemmed palm with bold fan-shaped leaves and bluish-black fruit on the female specimens. Height 15 feet (5 m). Zone 8.

A PIECE OF THE PRAIRIES

The first thing to accept when trying to establish prairie favourites in the warmer coastal climate is that they will never be exactly the same. It is not a trick of your memory that the peonies, saskatoonberries, rugosa roses and French lilacs seemed bigger, better, tastier or more fragrant back home (but you can console yourself with the fact that you will never again have to shovel the snow off of the driveway or donate a pint of blood to the mosquitos every time you go out to garden in the summer).

In fact, some prairie plants do too poorly to even consider growing them here. Some that I have found to languish in our wet springs and cool summers include Russian olive *(Elaeagnus angustifolia),* red honeysuckle *(Lonicera tartarica)* and double-flowering almond (*Prunus triloba* 'Multiplex'). But other prairie-hardy plants can be grown quite satisfactorily in coastal climes and a select few seem to thrive equally well here. Here are a few perennials, shrubs and trees commonly grown on the prairies that can be successfully incorporated into a coastal landscape — along with a few relevant cultural notes.

Euonymus alata '**Compacta**' (dwarf burning bush) A reliable deciduous shrub in almost any climate zone — with the same deep rose autumn colour in Winnipeg and Vancouver. Height 6 feet (2 m). Zone 4.

Malus (flowering crabapple) These small flowering trees are a mixed bag as far as resistance to scab or fireblight is concerned. But their spectacular spring displays and persistent ornamental fruit make them excellent choices for urban landscapes. Choose 'Prairie Fire' (new growth red) or 'Louisa' (weeping form) for coastal regions. For edible crabapples, try 'Dolgo', as it performs equally well in coastal and interior climates and is a good universal pollinator. Average height 15 feet (5 m). Zone 2–4, depending on cultivar.

Paeonia (herbaceous peonies) There is such a thing as a fabulous coastal peony and David Jack of Ferncliff Gardens in Mission, British Columbia, has fields of them to prove it. But for average gardeners with a desire to grow the peonies of their prairie child-hood, growing them here can be a bit of a challenge. The trick is to choose a well-drained site with fertile soil, full sun and good air circulation where the dreaded grey mould or botrytis blight can be kept to a minimum, should our usual wet spring conditions prevail. Height 3 feet (90 cm). Zone 2.

Rosa rugosa (*R. rugosa* hybrids) Rugosa roses are surprisingly tolerant shrubs and are even quite disease resistant in cool coastal climates, where many hybrid teas really struggle with black spot. A slightly more intense fragrance can be expected in areas with warmer summers. Height 6 feet (2 m). Zone 3.

Syringa vulgaris (French lilacs) Resist the urge to add a little peat moss to every planting hole (like you do for those rhododendrons and pieris), as this shrub dislikes acid soils and will often sulk for quite some time. They are also a little more susceptible to lilac leafminer and bacterial blight in the Pacific Northwest. Despite the few cultural idiosyncrasies, it only takes one bouquet of their intensely fragrant blooms to make it all worth it! Height 10 feet (3 m). Zone 3.

THE HARDY EXOTICS

Somewhere between the two extremes of the coast and the prairies are many interior valleys with moderate zone 5 growing conditions. While this middle ground of garden hardiness will allow you to grow a wider variety of plant material than may be available in prairie regions, it isn't quite warm enough for many of the exotics that will grow in zones 7–9 on the coast. That doesn't mean that an exotic or tropical-theme landscape cannot be achieved in zone 5, it just means that you have to be a little more selective about the plants you choose. So here's a short list of perennials, trees and shrubs that combine an exotic flare with the attribute of cold hardiness.

Aralia spinosa (angelica tree) This small, generally multistem tree branches very sparingly along the trunk. Most of the finely divided leaves are held near the top, giving it a very palm-like appearance. Best in full sun. Height 15 feet+ (5 m+). Zone 4.

Caryopteris x *clandonensis* 'Worcester Gold' (blue spirea) A fabulous cultivar with a brilliant contrast of gold foliage and deep blue, late-summer blooms. The foliage also emits a pleasantly pungent odour when brushed. Height 3 feet (1 m). Zone 5.

Delosperma nubigenum (yellow ice plant) Creates a low carpet of thick, succulent foliage with bright yellow star blooms in late spring. Tolerates drought. Height 4 inches (10 cm). Zone 3.

Festuca glauca 'Skinner's Blue' (blue fescue grass) Ornamental grasses add a Mediterranean flare to any landscape and 'Skinner's Blue' is perhaps one of the hardiest fescues. The fine-textured clumps are turquoise-blue in colour and are best used in mass plantings at the front of the border. Height 12 inches (30 cm). Zone 3.

Hydrangea paniculata 'Unique' (unique hydrangea) A bold specimen shrub with huge cone-shaped blooms of creamy-white (fading to a bronze-pink) from late summer right up to frost. Plant in partial shade in interior gardens. Height 6 feet+ (2 m+). Zone 4.

Physocarpus opulifolius 'Diabolo' (ninebark) The deep burgundy foliage of 'Diabolo' is a great foil for shrubs and perennials with white or yellow flowers. Try pairing this deciduous shrub with Physocarpus 'Dart's Gold' for a fantastic display! Height 6 feet (2 m). Zone 3.

Rhododendron impeditum (species rhododendron) A low-growing species with bluish-grey foliage and vibrant, bright purple flowers that often cover the entire plant. It should be grown in partial shade in interior gardens. Height 18 inches (45 cm). Zone 5.

Sedum x 'Bertram Anderson' (stonecrop) Unusual foliage of deep burgundy to black provides a great backdrop for the bright rose flowers that appear from July to August. Works well in combination with blue fescue grass. Height 6 inches (15 cm). Zone 3.

Sempervivum hybrids (hens and chicks) Ordinary hens and chicks come in many colours (Including green, red, bronze, grey, bluish and bicolour), as well as cobweb types with fine white hairs strung between the leaf tips. They are low maintenance and drought resistant, only requiring sharp drainage. Height 4 inches (10 cm). Zone 2.

Yucca glauca (soapweed) Narrow ½-inch-wide (1.2 cm) grey-green leaves extend to about 2 feet (60 cm) in very dense clusters. While the blooms are a bit small, the overall form is quite dramatic and very desert-like in appearance. Height 3 feet (1 m). Zone 3.

CHAPTER 6
The Liquid Landscape

Except in the case of Water-lilies I have often noticed that the smaller the pool or pond in which ornamental water-plants are grown the better one is able to enjoy them.
Gertrude Jekyll, *Wall & Water Gardens*

Water gardens come in many shapes and sizes, and often come about through unique circumstances. Some gardeners with acreage inherit natural ponds, while others are so enamoured with water gardening that they are willing to go to great expense to create a water feature from scratch. No matter what the circumstances, there is a place in any landscape for a fountain, reflecting pool, water bowl or perhaps even a full-sized pond — complete with waterfall, filtration system, plants and fish.

Water features breathe life into the garden with their relaxing sounds, soothing reflections and the unpredictable antics of their inhabitants (both those that are intended and those that seem to arrive by themselves, such as blue herons, raccoons, dragonflies and frogs). Whether you like it or not, nature will eventually come calling.

This section covers almost every aspect of water gardening. Whether you're thinking about a large water bowl with a clump of papyrus, an artificial stream threading through the backyard or a koi pond, this chapter will get you started. And as Gertrude Jekyll pointed out, a water feature need not be large — so those living in urban areas should also find some inspiration here.

Water lettuce *(Pistia stratiotes)*, a floating plant
Colour photo p. 137

An Aquatic Plant Primer

MICHAEL LASCELLE, AMSTERDAM GARDEN CENTRE, PITT MEADOWS, B.C.

Why bother spending thousands of dollars to have a professional create beautiful waterfalls and streams if you are only going to leave them bare, with the occasional iris tucked here or there? Look at a natural pond or stream during the summer, and you will find a wild landscape resplendent with lush ferns, sedges and numerous aquatic perennials thriving in the shallows, so why should a constructed water feature be any different? Aquatic plants are an essential component of any water garden design, and it seems unnatural to throw them in as a mere afterthought.

Of course, there are more attractive alternatives than some of the plants indigenous to our wet ecosystems, and these aquatics are becoming easier to obtain. Unfortunately, many gardeners are unfamiliar with the specific roles that these plants fulfill in the pond environment; understanding these roles will help you choose the right plants for your needs. Here is a description of each plant group and its purpose, along with a few of the better selections available in the Pacific Northwest.

FLOATERS

Floaters do not require any soil — they simply float on the surface and live off the dissolved nutrients in the water. These are important plants in the control of algae, as they compete for light and available nutrients. Many floaters also provide ideal surfaces for goldfish spawn, and their vast root systems offer protection to baby fish. Most floaters are tropical (flown in from Asia or the southern United States) and they should not be put into the pond until the water is reasonably warm or they will simply go into shock and languish for the rest of the summer. Also, many of the fine-tex-

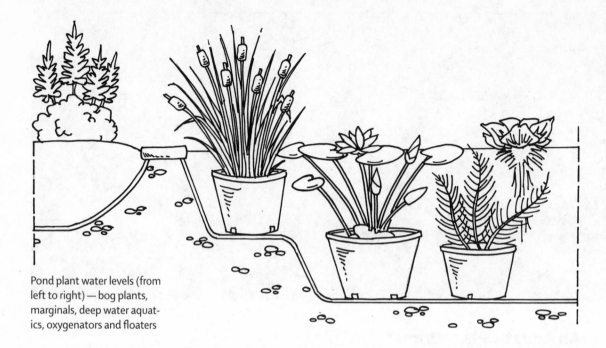

Pond plant water levels (from left to right) — bog plants, marginals, deep water aquatics, oxygenators and floaters

tured floaters (such as *Azolla,* or duckweed) multiply very aggressively and can quickly cover a pond. This can easily be remedied by scooping out the excess with a fine net and throwing it on the compost. As a plant group, floaters are relatively inexpensive and many water gardeners consider them as aquatic bedding plants. Be sure that you don't gather floating plants from the wild, as that handful of duckweed may also bring with it pond snails, which will quickly start defoliating your waterlily leaves (there are also beneficial snails that do not eat plants).

Azolla caroliniana (fairy moss) A member of the fern family that forms dense mats of richly textured foliage, much resembling club moss. A rapid spreader that sometimes turns a brick red colour during the summer. It will occasionally overwinter on its own, but it can be kept in a small jar with water and soil and reintroduced to the pond the following spring.

Eichornia crassipes (water hyacinth) Large, deep green leaves, each with its own swollen flotation device at the stem base. They multiply very quickly and produce lovely lavender blooms during warm summers. Frost tender.

Hydrocharis morsus-ranae (frogbit) A wonderful floater with leaves reminiscent of a small waterlily; small white flowers are also occasionally produced. May overwinter as a dormant bud on the bottom of the pond.

Lemna minor (duckweed) A very aggressive floater not recommended for natural ponds, as it can quickly become invasive. It is, however,

useful for its fast growth and you can always control it in a lined
pond by skimming it out. Hardy.

Pistia stratiotes (water lettuce) Very unusual scalloped foliage, with
deep ribs and a velvety texture. Tolerates partial shade well but prefers warm water temperatures. Frost tender.

OXYGENATORS

Oxygenators are, for the most part, submerged plants that help with water
clarity, absorbing excess nutrients or minerals and providing shelter and
spawning grounds for fish. As the name implies, they also absorb carbon
dioxide and release oxygen directly into the water during the day. As with
any other water garden component, oxygenators should be used in balanced proportions and should not be allowed to exceed more than ⅓ of the
water volume, as they consume oxygen at night and may end up depriving
your fish. By competing for available nutrients and light, oxygenators also
help to control algae.

Ceratophyllum demersum (hornwort) A shade or sun-tolerant oxygenator generally sold as bundled cuttings in the spring; simply
drop them into your pond. This finely textured plant will overwinter as a stem on the pond's bottom and will regrow in spring.

Elodea canadensis (Canadian pondweed) A hardy and very rapid-
growing oxygenator that is often not recommended due to its
aggressive nature. As a potted specimen, it can work just fine in
smaller ponds, where it can be controlled.

Myriophyllum **species** (parrot's feather) This is sometimes classi-
fied as a marginal plant, as the submerged leaves will grow to the
pond's surface and rise to about 6 inches (15 cm) above the water. It
is rather tender but when potted and left in the pond (rather than
leaving loose stems to float on the surface), the stems below the ice
not exposed to the air will generally survive through winter in the
Pacific Northwest.

MARGINALS

Marginals have their roots submerged anywhere from 1 to 8 inches (2.5 to
20 cm) deep, but the foliage is generally above the water's surface. These
plants help to soften the edges of a pond and many people design their
water features with shallow water shelves to accommodate them. Most
marginal plants are robust herbaceous perennials and are best grown in
large plastic pots, where their growth can be contained. These plants also
help to absorb excess nutrients or minerals in the water, but only those
with larger foliage volume, such as yellow flag iris or large cattails, are really
effective in this regard.

Acorus gramineus 'Variegatus' (variegated sweet flag) An evergreen
perennial with spikes of green and creamy-white variegated foliage,
which grow to a height of 12 inches (30 cm) on average. Quite iris-

like in appearance. Tolerates a crown depth of 1 to 2 inches (2.5 to 5 cm) below the water.

Caltha palustris (marsh marigold) Spectacular early spring blooms of bright yellow with rounded, glossy green foliage. White ('Alba') and double forms ('Plena') are also available. Tolerates a crown depth of 1 to 2 inches (2.5 to 5 cm) below the water.

Houttuynia cordata **'Chameleon'** (chameleon plant) The bane of terrestrial gardens actually makes a great aquatic plant when potted up. The brilliant red, green and yellow heart-shaped foliage is a wonderful contrast against dark waters, and the delicate white blooms are also appreciated. Tolerates a crown depth of 1 to 3 inches (2.5 to 8 cm) below the water.

Iris pseudacorus **'Variegata'** (variegated yellow flag iris) The species is often considered too aggressive for large ponds, as it has naturalized over a wide area in the Pacific Northwest. The variegated form features more restrained growth, cream variegation and the standard yellow blooms. Tolerates a crown depth of 2 to 12 inches (5 to 30 cm) below the water.

Juncus effusus **'Spiralis'** (corkscrew rush) Fantastically twisted, cylindrical leaves of deep green make a bold living sculpture for a small pond feature. Grows to 18 inches (45 cm) tall and is semi-evergreen in mild regions. Tolerates a crown depth of 1 inch (2.5 cm) below the water.

Saururus cernuus (lizard's tail) Elegant stems from 1½ to 2 feet (45 to 60 cm) tall with elongated, heart-shaped foliage. Unusual, fragrant white blooms that look like whips or lizard's tails appear midsummer. Tolerates a crown depth of 1 to 4 inches (2.5 to 10 cm) below the water.

Typha minima (miniature cattail) This is a great feature for smaller ponds or even aquatic containers. It features reed-like foliage and small, rounded 1-inch-long (2.5-cm) cattails. Tolerates a crown depth of 1 to 6 inches (2.5 to 15 cm) below the water.

Typha latifolia **'Variegatus'** (variegated cattail) A very attractive, ornamental form of cattail with prominent creamy-white variegation, which grows to a height of 4 to 5 feet (1.2 to 1.5 m). Tolerates a crown depth of 4 to 12 inches (10 to 30 cm) below the water.

TROPICAL MARGINAL PLANTS

This group of water plants is comprised mainly of taro, papyrus, tropical waterlilies and lotus *(Nelumbo)*. The latter is hardy in the Pacific Northwest with the proper care. Tropical waterlilies are a rather rare commodity here. They require warm waters during the summer and the protection of a greenhouse over the winter, but the spectacular fragrant blooms of purple and blue (among other colours) are hard to find in any aquatic plant and some of the tropical waterlilies actually bloom at night. Papyrus and taro are commonly available, but not enough people are informed of their tender nature at the time of purchase, and they are subsequently lost over the winter. The shame is that they make fine houseplants and can easily be kept in a shallow saucer of water. Even common canna lilies are good marginal aquatic plants — just be sure to overwinter those dormant rhizomes in a frost-free location, just as you do for the ones in your garden.

Colocasia esculenta **'Illustris'** (imperial taro) Bold, heart-shaped leaves of green and violet-black on graceful stems that can reach 5 feet (1.5 m) over time. 'Black Magic', the deep purple taro, is also occasionally available. Tolerates a crown depth of 1 to 4 inches (2.5 to 10 cm) below the water.

Cyperus haspan **'Viviparus'** (dwarf papyrus) A great focal point for a tub or a small water feature. Ultimate size is usually about 2 feet (60 cm) tall. Tolerates a crown depth of 1 to 6 inches (2.5 to 15 cm) below the water.

Cyperus papyrus (Egyptian papyrus) A bold specimen with tall, triangular stalks ending in wispy leaf clusters. Fast growing and easily capable of reaching average heights of 6 to 7 feet (2 to 2.3 m). Tolerates a crown depth of 4 to 10 inches (10 to 25 cm) below the water.

HARDY WATERLILIES (NYMPHAEA)

Hardy waterlilies come in all sizes and, except for purple and blue, they also come in every colour including pink, salmon, orange, red, white, burgundy and yellow. The water depth required will vary from 6 inches to 4 feet (15 cm to 1.2 m), depending on the size and vigour of the particular cultivar, although most waterlilies on the market require a depth of 18 to 24 inches (45 to 60 cm). The cultural requirements are simple: they should be grown in containers (2 to 5 gallons), fertilized once a month when in bloom (use an aquatic fertilizer tablet with a 10-14-8 ratio), divided every 2 to 3 years and given a sunny growing location (although some cultivars will tolerate partial shade). There are hundreds of varieties on the market and space does not allow me to list even a small portion of the better cultivars, so I will leave you with a few of my personal favourites.

'Chromatella' An old reliable with marbled dark green and reddish-brown foliage and abundant pale yellow blooms. Tolerant of partial shade. Use in medium-sized ponds.

'Perry's Baby Red' Deep wine red flowers, which are borne quite freely. Use in containers or small ponds.

'Texas Dawn' Spectacular yellow blooms with a hint of pink that sit well above the water, showing well from a distance. Use in medium-sized ponds.

'Colorado' Like 'Texas Dawn' it flowers above the water, but it bears salmon-pink to peach-coloured blooms. Use in medium to large ponds.

'James Brydon' Cup-shaped flowers of deep red, contrasted with bright orange stamens. Blooms well in light shade. Use in containers or small to medium ponds.

'Joanne Pring' A small waterlily that bears a profusion of pale to deep pink blooms, averaging about 2 inches (5 cm) across. Use in containers or small ponds.

'Virginalis' A slow-growing cultivar with large, fragrant blooms of pure white. Use in medium to large ponds.

'Sioux' One of the changeable waterlilies, with flowers that open yellow and turn apricot over a few days. Handsome purple mottled foliage. Use in small to medium ponds.

'Helvola' A miniature waterlily with lightly mottled foliage and diminutive pale yellow blooms 1 to 1½ inches (2.5 to 4 cm) across. Use in containers or small ponds.

DEEP WATER AQUATICS

This is a small group of aquatic plants that thrive with the crown planted at a water depth of 1 foot (30 cm) or more. Hardy waterlilies fall under this category but have been given their own section due to the many varieties available. Deep-water aquatics generally flower and bear foliage on or just above the pond's surface.

Aponogeton distachyos (water hawthorn) A semi-evergreen plant with very fragrant (vanilla-scented) white, waxy flowers that bloom just above the water's surface. Not only does this plant begin to flower in early spring, but it also tolerates partial shade very well. This easy-to-grow deep-water aquatic should really be used more often! Tolerates a crown depth of 1 to 2 feet (30 to 60 cm) below the water.

Nymphoides peltata (water fringe) Tiny waterlily-like foliage floats on the surface, and bright yellow, five-petalled flowers with fringed edges bloom just above. Tolerates a crown depth of 1 to 2 feet (30 to 60 cm) below the water.

Orontium aquaticum (golden club) A member of the Araceae family, it has attractive, finger-like white blooms tipped with yellow, which poke out of the water. The bluish-green foliage will rise above the pond surface if it is placed in less than 1 foot (30 cm) of water. Tolerates a crown depth of 1 to 1½ feet (30 to 45 cm) below the water.

BOG PLANTS

Most of you are already familiar with many bog plants in the guise of common perennials such as *astilbe,* daylilies *(Hemerocallis),* hosta, Siberian iris and creeping jenny — all of which make fine specimens in wet soils. Most of these are herbaceous and will thrive on a moist pond edge, stream side or perhaps a dedicated bog garden created as a temporary overflow area during wet periods. Bog plants in general will tolerate wet soil conditions from autumn through to spring, but they can also endure a drier period in summer.

> *Gunnera manicata* (giant rhubarb) A huge specimen plant with rhubarb-like leaves up to 5 feet (1.5 m) across and bizarre, cone-shaped flowers with a reddish hue. This Brazilian native usually requires a winter mulch of its own leaves (cut and turned upside down) or some straw.
>
> *Iris ensata* or *I. kaempferi* (Japanese iris) Although it is often sold as a marginal plant, Japanese iris is not fond of being in water all the time, so it makes a better bog plant. The large, flattened blooms have cascading petals of purple, lavender, blue or white.
>
> *Onoclea sensibilis* (sensitive fern) The coarsely toothed fronds are not typical of ferns, and spread by means of black rhizomes to form a large clump. The fertile fronds that carry the spores emerge separately and resemble clusters of small beads.

Just Add Fish

MERV ZAKUS, UNIQUE KOI & WATER GARDENS, WHONNOCK, B.C.

Fish add life to any pond and they can actually help to create an ecologically sound water garden when introduced in the proper numbers. Their brightly coloured scales help to focus attention on the water and many become pets over the course of time. On the practical side, goldfish and koi actually like to munch on that pesky string algae, and with the spread of West Nile virus across North America, both could play a very important role eating mosquito larvae, which aid in the transmission of this disease.

Regardless of your budget or the size of your water feature, there is a fish for every circumstance — from a small container water garden with 1 or 2 Sarasa goldfish, to a large filtered pond complete with specimen koi. I prepared this with novice water gardeners in mind; it should provide you with basic information to guide you through your initial fish purchases. Should you decide to take this hobby to the next level, I advise you to seek out the services of a qualified water garden consultant or contact a reputable dealer in fish stock.

COMMON POND FISH

While there are only a few types of pond fish to choose from, there are enough body forms, colour and fin variations among goldfish and koi to allow any pond enthusiast a great selection. Here are a few of the most common pond fish available in the Pacific Northwest.

Rosy Red minnow

This pale gold to light rosy-orange minnow averages 2 to 3 inches (5 to 8 cm) long (the males are longer). They are often mistaken for young Golden Orfes (and sold for a premium as such). Rosy Reds proper are quite

Koi (Photo: Merv Zakus)

inexpensive, breed very well and have an average lifespan of about three years, although I have had some for five years now. This is a great choice for people having trouble with blue herons, as rosy reds are very fast and difficult to catch. They enjoy swimming in schools, which adds to the visual pleasure.

Koi

Koi are long-lived members of the carp family with an average lifespan of 25 to 30 years, although some are capable of living up to 50 years under ideal circumstances. In Japan, koi are often passed onto family or friends in people's wills. Koi (the Japanese word for carp) are also known as *nishikigoi* (brocaded carp) in collector's circles. These ornamental carp grow an average of 1 inch (2.5 cm) a year in our temperate climate, with some reaching a length of 2 to 3 feet (60 to 90 cm) in the right conditions. Koi come in many shapes and colour combinations, including variations or solid tints of red, white, black, yellow, blue, grey and even metallic tinted scales of gold and silver. Some breeds, such as butterfly koi, have long, elegant fins that show very well — which is why these are one of my favourite pond fish.

You will pay according to the colour or quality of your koi and prices can vary from five dollars to several hundred dollars for average specimens of various ages. In Japan, exceptional specimens of collector's koi have come close to fetching a million dollars. Regardless of the cost or breeding, you should purchase koi that appeal to you personally and leave those expensive fish for the breeders or collectors.

Koi reach sexual maturity in an average of seven years. A ratio of two males for every female is recommended, as a single female is capable of laying more eggs than one male can fertilize. Natural pond vegetation, such

Stewartia pseudocamellia
bloom (Japanese stewartia)
see p. 36 (Photo: Kim
Kamstra)

Cornus kousa fruit (Kousa
dogwood) see p. 52

A mixed tulip and forget-me-
not spring bedding display
see p. 45

A mixed bulb display of grape
hyacinth (*Muscari armeniacum*) and *Tulipa* 'Abba'
see p. 46

A late summer display of
Miscanthus 'Morning Light,'
Sedum 'Matrona' and
Phygelius 'Moonraker'
designed by Michael Lascelle
see p. 49

Acer x *truncatum* 'Pacific
Sunset' fall foliage (Pacific
Sunset maple) see p. 51

The heritage villa at Foxglove
Farms covered in the fall
glory of Boston ivy
(Parthenocissus tricuspidata)
see p. 51

Autumn foliage of *Hamamelis* x *intermedia* 'Diane' (hybrid witch hazel) see p. 51

Early winter display of *Camellia sasanqua* (winter camellia) and a few pink tuberous begonias that survived the frost see p. 56

Above An informal random slate path with low groundcover
Right A curved path draws the viewer's eye into the garden
see p. 62–63 (Photos: Frank Schortinghuis)

Left A meandering random stone path with a garden
bench destination
Above A formal path of pavers leading to an elevated gazebo
see p. 62–63 (Photos: Frank Schortinghuis)

Left *Gazania* 'Daybreak Red Stripe' see p. 82
Above *Magnolia stellata* blooms (star magnolia) see p. 79

Above A shade planter of sword fern (*Polystichum munitum*),
Hakonechloa macra 'Aureola' and *Heuchera* 'Can Can' see p. 86
Right A winter planter of *Carex buchananii,* winter pansies,
variegated English ivy and lingonberry (*Vaccinium vitis-idaea*)
see p. 85

Left *Helenium* 'Kanaria', *Nepeta yunnanensis* and *Monarda* 'Feuerschopf'
Above *Papaver orientale* 'Turkenlouis' (oriental poppy)
see p. 100 (Photos: Elke Knechtel)

Left *Astrantia* 'Ruby Wedding'
Above *Monarda* 'Jacob Kline' (bee balm)
see p. 100 (Photos: Elke Knechtel)

Left *Aquilegia* 'Ruby Port' ('Ruby Port' columbine)
Above *Sedum oregonam* and *Sempervivum* 'Rogin' (hens and chicks)
Below *Paeonia* 'Nippon Beauty' ('Nippon Beauty' peony)
see p. 100 (Photos: Elke Knechtel)

Jekyll garden in
Hestercombe,
Somerset, U.K.
see p. 110
(Photo: Clare Philips)

Mixed herbaceous
perennial wall
garden
see p. 109–111
(Photo:
Clare Philips)

Datura sanguineum (red angel
trumpet) see p. 115

Tibouchina urvilleana
(princess flower) see p. 117

Floating plant, *Salvinia natans*
see p. 147

Water lettuce *(Pistia stratiotes)*
see p. 121

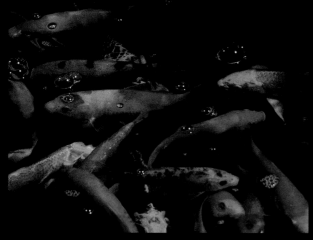

Young koi showing range of colours
see p. 127 (Photo: Merv Zakus)

Nymphaea 'Perry's Baby Red'
(Perry's Baby Red waterlily)
see p. 125

Helleborus corsicus or *arguitifolius*
(Corsican hellebore) see p. 167

Rosa 'Glowing Amber' miniature
rose see p. 173, 176

Rosa 'Wenlock' see p. 177

Rose arbor planted with Rosa 'Eye Paint' see p. 174

Rosa 'Danielle' see p. 172

A selection of New Zealand flax: Phormium 'Sundowner,' 'Yellow Wave,' 'Dusky Chief' and 'Apricot Queen' see p. 117

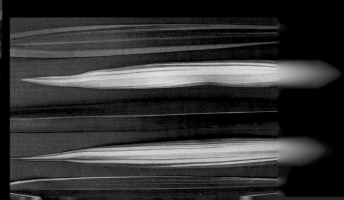

Sedum spathulifolium
see p. 183

A lined pond pond edged with basalt boulders
see p. 161

Mahonia nervosa (low Oregon grape)
see p. 189–190

Newly emerging sword fern *(Polystichum munitum)*
fronds in a carpet of false lily-of-the-valley
(Maianthemum dilatatum) see p. 187

Helleborus niger (Christmas
rose) see p. 57

Snowdrops *(Galanthus nivalis)*
see p. 57

Echinacea purpurea 'Alba'
(white coneflower) see p. 191

Gaillardia (blanket flower)
see p. 192

Pale tiger swallowtail
see p. 193–197
(Photo: Hendrik Meekel)

Painted lady
see p. 193–197
(Photo: Hendrik Meekel)

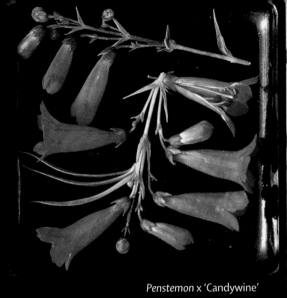

Penstemon x 'Candywine'
see p. 203

Penstemon 'Garnet'
see p. 202
(Photo: Calvor Palmateer)

Winter-flowering
Mahonia x *media* 'Charity'
see p. 201

Red-flowering currant
(*Ribes sanguineum*)
see p. 202

Blueberry and *Montbretia*
see p. 210
(Photo: City Farmer)

Quince fruit *(Cydonia oblonga)*
see p. 205

Aronia melanocarpa 'Autumn
Magic' see p. 217

An assortment of lavenders
see p. 215

as parrot's feather *(Myriophyllum),* or the roots of floaters, such as water hyacinth *(Eichornia)* or water lettuce *(Pistia),* often serve as the breeding ground for the eggs (artificial breeding mats or spawning grass can also be used). Koi require a large pond that is properly filtered with a depth of 4 feet (1.2 m). It should have straight sides (no shelves or ledge) to eliminate the chance of predators catching smaller fish.

Despite their initial expense, koi are very personable pets that can be taught to be hand-fed. I know many gardeners who have actually taken the time to name them.

Goldfish

There are many different forms of goldfish commonly available, all of which readily breed once established.

Common goldfish. The standard, short-finned form which is usually a deep orange colour.

Comet goldfish. Basically, a long-finned form of the common goldfish, hardy and durable.

Feeder fish. These are usually very young comets or common goldfish which are sold to feed carnivorous fish. They are very inexpensive, but many die due to terrible conditions — regular goldfish are shipped 250 per box, feeder fish are shipped 1000 to the same box — and the resulting stress. Remove the ones that don't make it as soon as possible; the rest should go on to live long and healthy lives.

Sarasa Comet. My favorite goldfish, with brightly contrasting red and white colours and long graceful fins and tail. In my opinion, they closely imitate some of the showy koi breeds (such as Kohaku), yet they are not demanding and are less expensive to purchase.

Shubunkin goldfish. A breed of goldfish that quite often exhibits a patchwork of different colours (including orange, red, yellow, black, violet and blue) on a translucent body. There are both short and long-finned forms (Comet Shubunkin). The darker specimens can be very difficult to see against the black pond liner, but this can prove to be an advantage if blue herons are catching your fish.

FEEDING YOUR FISH

Goldfish and rosy reds are usually capable of foraging for themselves, once the pond is established and the sidewall algae is present. You may feed them a floating, pelleted food if you enjoy watching them come up to eat, but only feed them as much as they consume in several minutes and be sure to remove the rest. Excess food will decompose in the water and contribute to water-borne algae and green water conditions. It is very important to be sure that fish food is fresh (not more than 6 months old), otherwise you are feeding your fish empty calories with few vitamins.

Do not feed fish when the water temperature is below 50°F (10°C) (the exception is a few Cheerios — no protein — if your koi happen to be active and are looking for food). Like carp, koi are bottom feeders. In the wild they forage for live vegetation, decaying vegetation and even dead animals and fish, so their diet is truly omnivorous. Cultivated koi are much the same, although processed koi food tends to contain fish meal, wheat germ, krill and shrimp meal (high protein) as the main ingredients. Choose a pellet size that suits the size of your fish, but since it softens and falls apart, smaller fish need not go without. Koi often enjoy eating small floaters, such as Azolla and duckweed, and are often notorious for eating water hyacinth roots to the quick. They will also eat lettuce (just wash the roots and throw it in whole), cabbage leaves (chopped fine), boiled barley, small pieces of cantaloupe or even clean carrot peelings. I often start them off in spring with a treat of small pieces of brown bread with some natural yogurt on it; this helps to kickstart their digestive system.

ADDING NEW FISH TO YOUR POND

There are a few simple rules to observe when transporting and adding new fish to your pond. First of all, get them home as soon as possible! (That means you should finish your other errands first and not leave the fish in your vehicle while you finish the shopping.) When you get them home, immediately float the bag on the surface of your pond to allow them to adjust to the new water temperature. After about five minutes, open the bag and add some of the pond water to it — an amount equal to 10 percent of the bag's volume. Repeat this procedure every 5 minutes and, after about 20 minutes, you should be able to add your new fish to the pond. Be careful not to add the water in the bag, as a precaution against water-borne diseases. Check them frequently during the first hour. This is the time when disoriented newcomers may try to jump out of the pond due to unfamiliar surroundings and other factors, such as pH and water temperature.

OVERWINTERING YOUR POND FISH

All of the fish referred to in this chapter are perfectly hardy in the Pacific Northwest and may be left in any good-sized pond during winter. The 4-foot (1.2-m) water depth that koi prefer helps to moderate water temperatures and control temperature fluctuations that can seriously weaken fish during the winter. In those areas where ice may form for short periods of time, be sure to maintain a hole in the ice to prevent the buildup of toxic gases that can kill your fish. This is best achieved with a small, floating water heater or a shallow, submerged pump that stirs a small surface area to keep it from freezing over. Do not try to break ice that has already formed with a hammer (or similar object), as the sound waves are very hard on fish. Instead, use hot water from a kettle to gently open a small hole in the ice. Fish kept in small, containerized water gardens will probably need to be transferred to an indoor aquarium until spring.

A simple tub garden with a fountain feature and *Salvinia natans* floating on the water surface

Container Water Gardens

JACK & JEANIE WOOTTON, HAWAIIAN BOTANICALS AND WATER GARDENS, RICHMOND, B.C.

A visit to any large garden show will illustrate the fact that water features are now considered almost indispensable to modern landscape designs. A large, well-maintained pond covered with blooming lilies provides an impact that few other landscape features can match, but not everyone has the space or the time for a full-sized pond. Fortunately there is an alternative. Container water gardens, popularly known as tub gardens, provide many people with a simple way to engage in the hobby of water gardening.

A tub garden can be anything from a lined oak half-barrel containing a colourful mix of aquatic plants to the exotic look of an awe-inspiring lotus bursting forth from a glazed ceramic pot. One advantage a tub garden has over ponds is the temperature of the water. It is surprising just how warm the water can become in a tub garden on a sunny day, thus enabling gardeners in temperate climates, such as the Pacific Northwest, to grow aquatic species that would normally languish in a cool pond. This subject will come up again as we examine two different themes that can be used in the design of tub gardens.

A typical mini-pond tub garden set-up

THE MINI-POND TUB GARDEN

The pond style of tub garden is a miniature aquatic ecosystem that, in its most ambitious form, can even include fish. A lined wooden half-barrel can be used for a container if a rustic look is desired, or a glazed ceramic pot can be chosen for a more formal appearance. If you plan on having fish, install a small water pump to ensure that there is sufficient oxygen, particularly on warm summer days. The pump can supply water to a spouting ornament, such as a figurine or bamboo pipe, and you may find the concept of moving water appealing, even if you choose not to have fish.

A wide variety of aquatic and semi-aquatic plants will thrive in such a habitat. It is beyond the scope of this section to discuss all of them, but a well-balanced selection will include leafy submerged oxygenators, such as pondweed or hornwort *(Ceratophyllum demersum)*, and some marginal aquatics, such as arrowheads *(Sagittaria)*, irises and rushes, to name a few. A few of the tropical floating aquatics, such as water hyacinth *(Eichornia crassipes)* and water lettuce *(Pistia stratiotes)*, will help clarify the water and prevent algae blooms. If a sunny location is available, it is even possible to add a dwarf waterlily to your mini-pond. Although there are hundreds of varieties of hardy waterlilies, with flowers in shades of red, pink, yellow, white and orange, only a handful of varieties are diminutive enough for tub gardens. Examples of hardy waterlilies suitable for tubs are the red-flowering 'Perry's Baby Red', the pink-flowering 'Joanne Pring', the yellow-flowering 'Helvola', the white-flowering 'Walter Pagels' and the orange-flowering 'Aurora'.

It is customary when setting up your mini-pond to confine each plant to its own pot, rather than filling the bottom of the tub with aquatic soil and planting directly into the mud. There are several reasons for using the individual pot method. The optimum water depth for aquatic plants varies depending on the species, and by placing bricks (or inverted flower pots) on the bottom of the tub, you can place each plant according to its needs. The nutrient requirements of aquatics varies as well; for example, it is recommended to feed waterlilies with special slow-release fertilizer tablets several times during the growing season in order to promote blooming. Individual pots allow you to feed only those plants that require an extra boost of nutrients. The pots will also confine the more rambunctious aquatics and prevent them from crowding out their neighbours in your tub garden.

You will also find potted plants an advantage when preparing for winter, particularly if you are using a glazed or terra cotta bowl for your tub garden. If you live in an area subject to below-freezing temperatures, the bowl is in danger of breaking if left outside full of water over the winter. Ceramic pottery has no flexibility whatsoever, and even a few inches of ice may exert enough pressure to crack it. It is therefore advisable to remove the plants and empty the bowl, which can then be stored upside down or in a dry location. Unglazed terra cotta requires even more protection; even a hard frost can cause spalling (flaking) of the surface.

Your plants also need to be protected and perhaps the most convenient way to do this if you're living in a temperate zone is to purchase a large plastic tub, commonly known to gardeners as a muck bucket. Simply transfer your hardy aquatic plants into the bucket, fill it with water and you're all set for winter. The plastic is flexible enough to accommodate the ice without cracking. In climates colder than Zone 8, store your plants in a cool location indoors, unless you have access to a pond. Tropical floating plants, such as water hyacinths, are usually considered to be the water gardening equivalent of bedding plants and are composted or similarly disposed of by late fall. Tropical marginal plants, such as taros or umbrella plants, are quite happy to spend winter indoors on a sunny windowsill in a secondary role as houseplants.

THE SPECIMEN TUB GARDEN

The mini-pond tub garden is essentially an outdoor aquarium — the main difference is that an aquarium is observed from the side and the mini-pond tub garden is viewed at an angle from above. The specimen tub garden, on the other hand, is a bold landscape feature, usually with a single plant per tub, and is worthy of a prime position on the deck, patio or lawn, where

A specimen tub garden with giant papyrus

it can be appreciated from a distance. This is not a new concept, for tubs of lotus and tropical waterlilies have traditionally graced the courtyards of Bali and Thailand for many years.

A tub garden situated in a sunny location allows even a gardener in the cool Pacific Northwest to transfer that prized tropical waterlily from the confines of the greenhouse to the outdoors. A small hardy waterlily can also be used, but there are several reasons why a tropical is more rewarding (albeit requiring more effort). Tropical lilies are available in stunning shades of blue and purple, colours that are impossible to obtain in the hardy varieties. Tropicals are also profuse bloomers, a single plant often producing multiple flowers simultaneously. The blooms of certain varieties of tropical lilies are intensely fragrant, an important bonus if the tub is placed on a deck or patio. Unlike the hardies, tropical lilies raise their flowers up to 12 inches (30 cm) above the water, a pleasing effect even from a distance. This characteristic is even more pronounced in the lotus. A mature lotus can produce blossoms on stems 4 to 5 feet (1.2 to 1.5 m) tall, rising above the huge leaves, which, in turn, are elevated 3 feet (90 cm) or more above the water. Unlike the tropical water lilies, lotuses are hardy perennials in many parts of Canada and winter care is similar to that of the hardy water lilies.

If your landscape scheme calls for a more subdued statement, you may want to consider the giant papyrus *(Cyperus papyrus)* for your specimen tub garden. This striking species, although not hardy in Canada, is surprisingly easy to grow and will readily fill a container 3 feet (90 cm) in diameter in a single season. If winter storage of a large tropical aquatic presents a problem, there are hardy species that are showy enough to serve in specimen tubs. Even the lowly cattail, inhabitant of marshy ground across Canada, has a desirable green and white striped form, *Typha latifolia* 'Variegata', which is perfectly suitable as a show plant. If the tropical look appeals to you, consider featuring a clump of hardy thalia *(Thalia dealbata)*, a hardy marginal aquatic plant resembling the famous bird-of-paradise.

At first glance, it might seem that water gardening within the confines of a container is an uncomfortably restrictive proposition. But perhaps it is just the limits of our imagination that truly binds us and keeps us from enjoying water gardening in its smallest form.

Waterfall and Stream Design
ROB BOUCHARD, COASTAL CREATIONS LANDSCAPE, SURREY, B.C.

The most alluring part of a water feature is movement, with its soothing, ever-changing sound. Moving water can be achieved in many ways; the outcome is completely up to the imagination of the person installing it.

Here are a few techniques for installing beautiful, natural-looking waterfalls and streams, and some of the equipment involved in making them work.

A well designed waterfall is always natural looking when completed (Photo: Shibusa Pond Services Ltd.)

WATERFALLS

There are so many different ways to build a waterfall that I could fill an entire book on various techniques and styles. For simplicity, this focuses on the easiest and perhaps the most natural-looking style.

Don't try to build it too tall

Try to stay close to the height of the tallest boulder you have to work with. Don't stack up several small boulders to achieve the height you want, as it will look unnatural. If you really want a waterfall 4 feet (1.2 m) high or more, anticipate hiring a contractor with machinery to help install the boulders, as a large waterfall will require large boulders that are in scale with the overall height.

Don't forget to build a berm

Mounding soil around the base of the waterfall to create the illusion of height is critical when building a natural-looking feature. Typically, you will be able to use all the soil you excavated from the pond as your berm — this way, there is no soil to truck away and you will get a nice-sized, natural-looking berm.

Choose the right rock

Rock selection is important. Avoid sharp, blasted quarry-type rock: it doesn't look natural and the edges can cause damage to the pond liner. Rounded river rocks or mossy basalt boulders will look beautiful and natural in a pond setting.

Assemble the necessary equipment

You will need a prefabricated biological filter or biofalls (as the basis for the waterfall), 45 mm EPDM (rubber) pond liner, black expanding waterfall foam and rocks. The biological filter is placed at the appropriate depth, which is whatever you decide is the final height of your waterfall. The plumbing is hooked up to the biological filter, then the filter is levelled and

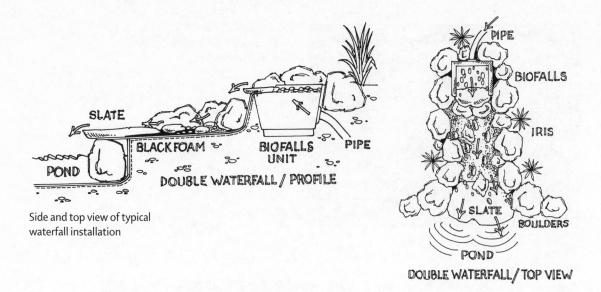

Side and top view of typical waterfall installation

backfilled. Finally, the liner is affixed to the filter using the screws and latex silicone that come with the unit.

Using a biological filter as the base for the waterfall will ensure that you have a leakproof system — and there is no need to have filters elsewhere in your pond. Now you are ready to start building the waterfall.

Start by placing larger rocks on either side of the waterfall unit, making sure they are as tall as or a little bit taller than the highest point on the filter. Next, smaller rocks will go underneath the water spillway to conceal the front of the filter. The filters we use have a rim around the inside of the unit for placing small rocks to hide all of the plastic. Then find a really nice piece of flagstone that comes close to matching the width you'll need to fit the water spillway. This piece of flagstone will need a bit of trimming with a masonry hammer in order to fit between the rocks. Spray the black waterfall foam into all the nooks and crannies behind the rocks to force the water over them, rather than allowing it to pool behind. Lastly, the flagstone is placed on a bed of foam and held level until the foam dries. One small tip is to wait until the foam is almost dry, then press in some pea gravel to conceal the foam…and that is all there is to it!

STREAMS

Creating natural streams is part art, part skill and part hard work. Streams are considerably easier to build than waterfalls — you can use smaller rocks and you don't have to be as precise when figuring out where there might be water leakage. Every stream is going to be different, but here are a few basics.

Don't build in a straight line

In nature, streams never go in a straight line; they twist and turn and find the path of least resistance. When building a stream, try to imagine what the water would do if it were naturally running a course through the grade in your backyard. If you ever made miniature rivers when you were a kid, you'll know what I mean! Try flooding a small slope of slightly loose soil with a garden hose and watching the water as it picks its route, eroding the loose particles of soil to find the easiest way to the bottom.

Variety is key

If you have a 10-foot (3-m) section of stream, use at least three large boulders (12 to 24 inches/30 to 60 cm) and fill the remainder with smaller boulders (12 inches/30 cm or under). This will eliminate the "pearl necklace" look, where dozens of smallish rocks are all lined up in a row. When we install streams, we use river rock in a variety of sizes for the gravel between the edging boulders. It is mixed approximately 1 part 2- to 6-inch (10- to 15-cm) rock to 3 parts 1-inch (2.5-cm) rock. This mix provides the most natural effect.

Assemble the equipment

Use the same equipment and procedures for a stream as for a waterfall — streams are just longer waterfalls! Streams can originate from a waterfall or from a small pool that the waterfall feeds into. For this type of stream, we will assume that the yard has a slight grade, and you should cut across the slope and curve downwards into the pond.

We generally sink the biological filter into the ground quite deep so there isn't much of a drop from the beginning. Again, we use 45 mm EPDM liner for most residential ponds. For streams, we like to use one piece if possible, to avoid any seams that could leak in the future. For most applications, we use a 10-foot-wide (3-m) liner by whatever length your stream will be. With liner this wide, you will have lots of room to curve the stream bed and experiment with different shapes.

On either side of where you have decided to route the water, excavate and flatten an area about 2 to 3 feet (60 to 90 cm) wider than the stream bed. The bed for the stream does not have to be very deep, especially on the uphill side. Dig only enough on the uphill side so that it will lie just slightly higher than the majority of the rocks in the stream. Place the liner

Use plants and small boulders to soften the edges of the stream

BASIC STREAM / CROSS - SECTION

on the excavated area, making sure that it is long enough to overhang the pond by about 1 foot (30 cm). Now picture this flat black liner as your canvas. The water level in your stream will be approximately 3 to 5 inches (8 to 13 cm) deep, depending on how wide you make it. This means that you must allow at least 6 to 10 inches (15 to 25 cm) extra liner on the edges, so it can be folded up to contain the water.

Starting from the top of the stream, start laying boulders in whatever shape you desire — twisting and turning the liner to make sure it looks natural. Once you've finished a couple of feet, step back and have a look at it. Does it look good? Are you sure? Don't be afraid to rebuild it at this stage. We have actually torn apart finished waterfalls that we were not completely happy with, and rebuilt them at our expense.

If you want to add a small drop in your stream, pull the liner up and over the rocks that you have already placed. Dig down into the soil as far as you want the drop to be. Be careful to make sure that you have enough slope for the water to flow towards the pond. Continue with the boulders until you reach the water, prepare a nice drop into the pond, and you're almost there.

Next, fold up all the edges of the pond liner against the back side of the boulders in the stream. With edges held up, soil is placed against the liner, pinning it against the rocks and giving your stream the ability to hold water. The mix of river rocks is then installed gently, throwing it in with a shovel and hiding all of the liner in the stream. Once the river rock is placed, turn on your stream and check for leaks and overflows. Pull up the liner if there are any leaks and trim any excess liner. Cover the top edge of the liner with more river rock. This will help separate the soil from the stream.

Remember that this is just one method used to build a stream, but it is by far the simplest. I think you will find that the results are outstanding.

Ornamental Ponds

GERALD THOM & GORDON EDMONDSON, SHIBUSA POND SERVICES LTD., DUNCAN, B.C.

The recent popularity of water gardening should come as no surprise. The simple pleasures ornamental ponds provide have been enjoyed for centuries, by people of all ages. The fascination with ponds goes back thousands of years to ancient Egypt and Greece, where water gardening was first practiced.

Water gardens are a natural focal point in any location. The tranquil beauty of ponds is created by the contrasting colours of the water, plants and fish, and the reflection of the pond's surroundings. To be able to enjoy a trouble-free pond, take the time to plan well. Inform yourself before you decide on pond siting, design, construction and, eventually, stocking the pond with plants and fish. An understanding of the biology of your pond will increase your interest and reduce the effort required to maintain a healthy and attractive ornamental pond.

TYPES OF WATER FEATURES

Water features vary from simple reflecting pools to complex recirculated and filtered koi ponds.

Reflecting Pond Reflecting ponds are generally still ponds with little or no aquatic life. As the name implies, they are intended to reflect the surroundings and create a relaxing environment. Black liners provide excellent reflective qualities, an illusion of depth, and easy, inexpensive construction. Reflecting ponds are often formal in design and may incorporate surrounding plantings to provide colour and interest. Chemical solutions are usually added to maintain water clarity and eliminate mosquitos.

Water in Motion Running water features include formal fountains and waterfalls. The flowing water masks background noise, creates a sense of privacy and adds interest. Most flowing features are powered by submersible pumps, which are quiet and quite inexpensive. The flow rate can be varied by installing a plastic ball valve in the return line after the pump, to restrict the flow. Changing the flow rate can change the mood and makes the water feature more versatile. A source of electricity is required near the water feature to power the pump (and possibly light the water feature for maximum effect at night). Many running water features are devoid of aquatic life, as organics can clog pumps and fountains and create extra maintenance. Water clarity can be maintained with chemical solutions.

Still Plant Ponds Still plant ponds can function as both reflective pools and low-maintenance aquatic gardens. Many aquatic plants (especially lilies) require still water and 3 to 10 hours of direct sun per day for proper growth and flowering. Almost all aquatic plants are herbaceous, so these ponds can look quite barren in winter. Evergreen plants, such as *Viburnum davidii,* and winter-flowering shrubs, like *Erica carnea,* can be planted around the pond to provide winter colour and interesting reflections. We recommend that all aquatic plants be potted to contain the soil and reduce maintenance. Many varieties of aquatics are invasive and can quickly take over the pond if not contained. Fertilizer will be required occasionally and is available in tablet form, made specifically for aquatic plants. A few small goldfish make excellent inhabitants in these ponds, as they consume pests (mosquitos and aphids) and provide some interest. Many plant ponds in the Pacific Northwest are 18 inches to 2 feet (45 to 60 cm) deep.

Ecologically Balanced Ponds Balanced ponds are a fascinating exercise in ecology. Planted and stocked to mimic a natural pond, they should contain water plants, snails and a few goldfish. The correct balance of plants and animals is required to create a healthy and attractive environment, but once a pond is balanced it requires very little maintenance, other than the removal of bottom debris once or twice a year. Balanced ponds are not crystal clear: they are natural ponds and therefore go through natural cycles. They normally stay quite clear except for a few weeks in early spring when the combination of accumulated nutrients, reduced plant growth and intense sun creates algae blooms. Balanced ponds can incorporate flowing water, but the amount of flow and surface disturbance should be kept to a minimum for proper water plant growth. In the Pacific Northwest these ponds are usually 18 inches to 2½ feet (45 to 75 cm) deep.

Fish Ponds Fish ponds are designed to hold larger numbers and varieties of fish, such as koi. They usually require constant recirculation and filtration to remove wastes and provide oxygen for the fish. Fish in these systems require regular feeding; unlike balanced ponds, there is not enough natural food available. The ponds are an excellent hobby for enthusiasts interested in raising fish. They require more maintenance and are usually more expensive than balanced ponds. The initial cost and ongoing maintenance can be reduced by proper design and construction. If you are contemplating a fish pond, we strongly suggest professional advice on design and construction to create an aesthetically pleasing, yet functional pond. Koi ponds are the most common type of fish pond and should be a minimum of 4 feet (1.2 m) deep in the Pacific Northwest. They may incorporate biological filters and ultraviolet lights to maintain water quality and clarity.

Gamefish Ponds Trout ponds require large open areas and a minimum depth of 8 feet (2.4 m). On rural acreage they are an excellent source of recreation and even the occasional tasty meal. To keep trout you will require a permit and site inspection by the government agency in your area. Trout ponds normally take three to four years to establish and require a good source of water. If the water temperature exceeds 70°F (20°C) the fish may die.

Indoor Ponds Indoor ponds are the latest trend in water gardens. They can be as simple as a still plant pond or as complex as a recirculated and filtered koi pond. Indoor water features can be very attractive and relaxing in the home or office, but special precautions are necessary. For large installations, professional design and construction is highly recommended due to concerns of weight, humidity, water damage and aesthetics. Do not attempt large indoor water features without consulting a professional.

PLANNING AND SITE SELECTION

Once you have decided on the type of water feature you want, the next step is to choose the appropriate site. Listed below are the site selection criteria in approximate order of importance.

Proximity to House and Vantage Point Water gardens provide a natural focal point, so they should be located where they are readily accessible and easily viewed. Take advantage of the relaxing effects of the water and make the most of both sight and sound by allowing for a comfortable seating area adjacent to the pond. Be sure to allow room for background and surrounding planting to soften the landscape and provide winter interest.

Safety and Underground Services Ponds and toddlers do not mix! Ponds are usually located in the backyard for safety and privacy. Check with the city or municipality to find out about the underground services (hydro, telephone, gas lines, septic, perimeter drains, etc.), and water depth and fencing guidelines to protect yourself and others. Provide at least one point of easy access with a stable edge to allow for close viewing and service. For large ponds, the area adjacent to this should be stepped to facilitate entry and exit during service or in case someone falls into the pond.

Light Exposure Water gardens require 3 to 10 hours of direct sun per day (during the summer) for proper plant growth and flowering. In full sun locations, provide midday shade with floating plant material, a structure or deciduous shade trees set back from the south side of the pond. Fish ponds do not require as much direct summer sun — locate them where they get a maximum of 8 hours of sun per day.

Trees Trees can provide an excellent backdrop and some shade. They should not overhang the pond as leaf drop and roots are a nuisance. Use evergreen trees close to the pond to provide winter colour and minimize leaf drop. Keep in mind the maximum height and spread of trees and locate them accordingly. Skimmers are useful to remove leaves and surface debris.

Drainage Do not locate a pond in low, boggy areas, as draining the pond may be impossible and runoff may float the liner or contain toxins. If drainage is a problem in winter or spring, choose a different location or provide drainage. When planning the pond, determine where to locate the overflow and, if possible, consider a bottom drain for ease of maintenance.

Power Supply If you want water movement or night lighting, you will need to install a ground fault interrupter (GFI). It can be in the breaker box or at a weatherproof receptacle near the pond. For ease of access, the weatherproof receptacle should be located in a planting area at the opposite end of the pond from the waterfall. Consider using a control switch inside the house for convenience.

Water Supply Ornamental ponds use less water than most other landscaped areas. Only add water to make up for evaporation. Evaporation loss in still ponds is minimal, so generally adding water with a hose once a week is all that is required. For large, flowing water features, a float valve can be installed to make up automatically for losses due to increased evaporation.

DESIGN

Once you have chosen the type of feature you want and its location, it's time to create a design that suits the area. Consider the site from all vantage points, both inside and outside the house. To visualize the pond, it helps to lay out a garden hose in various sizes and shapes. The rule of thumb on size is that the pond should take up ¼ to ⅓ of the total space to be landscaped. Be sure to leave enough area adjacent to the pond for seating, viewing, access and complementary plantings. Locate decks and patios for easy access and optimal viewing. Try to visualize feature plants

Pond construction, top view
(Illustration: Shibusa Pond
Services Ltd.)

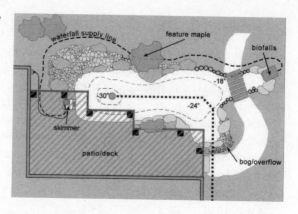

and traffic flow. Leave the hose out for a few days to experiment with the proposed size and shape.

The next step is to consider which pond features or accessories you desire. Are you interested in a waterfall, fountain, island or overhanging decks or bridges? Be careful not to clutter the landscape. Ponds are normally open areas, so only choose a few features as focal points. Orient features for maximum effect, keeping both sight and sound in mind.

You should also consider how the services (pumps, return lines, electrical, float valves, etc.) will be hidden. Overhanging decks and bridges are very effective for hiding the mechanics. Plants (terrestrial and aquatic) can also be useful to cover services.

The pond bottom should be terraced to accommodate the various aquatic plants. Marginal plants are usually located to the sides and rear of the pond on shelves 8 to 12 inches (20 to 30 cm) deep. Most marginal plants provide an excellent backdrop or transition due to their vertical height and the profusion of foliage they provide. Waterlilies and oxygenating plants prefer 18 to 24 inches (45 to 60 cm) of water depth. A variety of depths in this range is beneficial, so that individual plants can be raised or lowered to suit their growing habit and the seasonal growth.

CONSTRUCTION MATERIALS

When shopping for pond construction materials the main concerns are toxicity, life expectancy, aesthetics and price. Do your homework and you will likely save money and end up with a much better finished product. The obvious place to start when considering pond materials is deciding what will hold the water.

Sheet Liners Sheet liners are the best choice for the do-it-yourself person. They are flexible, easy to install and adaptable to any design. Be sure to check toxicity, life expectancy, puncture resistance, thickness, stretch and cost. The most common types of liner used today in North America are PVC (polyvinyl chloride), EPDM rubber and a variety of polyethylene.

In our opinion, fish-safe EPDM is currently the best buy in pond liners. It is inexpensive, long-lived (usually guaranteed for 20 years), strong and has excellent stretch. When shopping, beware of roofing membranes, as

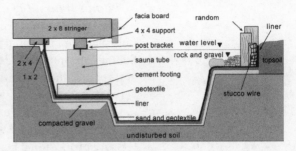

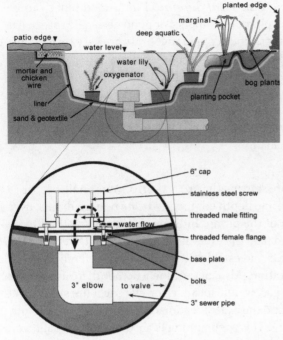

Top left Pond cross section
Top right Edge detail, deck and post
Left Bottom drain
(Illustration: Shibusa Pond Services Ltd.)

most varieties are toxic. Only buy roofing membrane if the supplier will guarantee it is fish safe. Pond suppliers are the best source for EPDM. This is a heavy pond liner and seaming can be done with a solvent cement glue, which is applied like contact cement with seam tape. Seam work should only be done by professionals.

Clay Clay can be used to hold water and is sometimes a viable alternative for large ponds. It is generally only cost effective if it is found on site. Clay ponds tend to remain muddy and vegetation control can be a serious problem.

Concrete Concrete is a traditional material but is no longer considered a good choice. It is labour-intensive, expensive, requires sealing, tends to crack and leaches toxic lime.

On the plus side, concrete ponds are long-lived — 30 to 50 years if properly built with at least 4 inches (10 cm) of concrete, galvanized mesh and rebar.

Fibreglass Fibreglass is a good pond material but it is expensive and should also be professionally installed. It is strong, puncture resistant and quite long-lived (20 to 30 years). Preformed fibreglass ponds come in limited shapes and sizes, and are quite expensive. A variety of preformed ponds are available from most pond suppliers and some garden centres. A disadvantage is that they are difficult to transport and install.

Edge Support Pond edge support can be provided by rocks, bricks, timbers, patio slabs and/or mortar. These materials are generally available at local building or masonry suppliers. Be sure to ask about toxicity to fish when using any materials around or in the pond.

Pumps, Plumbing and Electrical Supplies Pumps and pipes can be purchased from your local plumbing supplier or pond dealer. Be sure to use only plastic pipe and fittings, since copper and brass are very toxic to fish. Submersible pumps are recommended because they are quiet, inexpensive and require little maintenance. (The new magnetically driven pumps are very energy efficient.) Be sure the submersible pump you buy is specifically designed for fish pond use. Electrical supplies can be purchased from most building supply stores; we recommend GFI (ground fault interrupter) outlets and professional installation.

POND CONSTRUCTION

Planning Ahead Before starting the excavation of your pond, prepare a sketch showing the shape and depth contours. Locate bottom drains, overflow points and location of the pump. Indicate the edging method to be used around the pond and plan the excavation accordingly. Determine the desired finished water level and establish a fixed point of reference, which can be used during excavation. Also, determine whether there are any services buried in the area (gas, water, sprinkler or electrical lines). Contact the utility companies to find the exact locations and expose them carefully by hand before excavating. This preplanning is absolutely essential if you are considering excavating with a machine.

Excavation Excavation equipment can save a lot of time and effort and is well worth considering. If you excavate with a machine, dig 12 inches (30 cm) to the inside of the finished pond edge and 12 inches (30 cm) deeper than required. The finishing detail can then be done by hand to maintain bank stability and the remaining material can be used to fill and contour the bottom. The proper machine is very important to minimize the mess and handwork necessary. If you are contracting the machine and operator, be sure to be present during the entire excavation to supervise, so you achieve the best possible results.

If you are digging the pond by hand, dig it according to the plan. Keep the sides as steep as possible and slope the pond bottom gently (5 to 10 percent) as the debris accumulates in one spot for easy removal. Shape the pond as desired, leaving shelves for plants and edge detail as shown on your sketch. The soil removed from the hole can often be used to create berms along the back side of the pond to accommodate a waterfall or complementary plants. Soil may also be required to build up the low side of the pond, to level the top edge. This is very important since water is always level! Constantly check the edge levels by using a carpenter's level and board, string and line level. Laser levels make the job easy and are now reasonably priced.

Once the pond is excavated and graded, cut back all visible roots as short as possible, or pull them out and rake out any large rocks or debris. Use 1¼ to 2 inches (2 to 5 cm) of masonry sand to line the excavation, providing a smooth padded base. For extra protection against stones and roots, geotextile (heavy landscape fabric) or old carpet and underlay can be placed over the sand. Be sure to check the carpet and underlay for staples and nails.

Lining the Pond Lining the pond is the next step. To determine the size of liner required, measure the maximum width and length of the excavation. Add twice the excavation depth to each dimension. These dimensions will be the size of liner required. Double-check your calculations by draping a string or rope in the hole across the widest and longest points. Mark the string, then measure both lengths. We usually recommend adding approximately 12 inches (30 cm) to each dimension, to allow for some leeway during installation.

To install the liner, drape it over the excavation and centre it over the hole. If you are installing a bottom drain, clamp the liner in position now. Weight the outer edges of the liner (5 lbs. per ft./7.5 kg per m) using smooth stones or bricks, so the liner just touches the bottom in the middle of the pond. Then start filling the pond with a garden hose to mould the liner to fit the excavation. During filling we recommend combining small wrinkles on the sides into 3 or 4 folds where required. Continue to fill the pond to the overflow point and let the liner settle for at least 24 hours.

Edge Detail To complete the edge detail, drain the pond down to 4 to 6 inches (10 to 15 cm) below the edge shelves. Do not drain the pond completely, as the water will help to support the sides while you are finishing the top edge. Take your time and complete the edge detail combinations as decided earlier. Remember to allow for the pump return line and power cord, if it is deemed necessary to hide it from view. When completing the edges, an artistic touch is beneficial to blend one edge to another and obtain a natural look. Try to use more than one edge detail to maximize both function and aesthetics.

If mortar is required to stabilize the edge, use the following mixture.

- 6 shovels of clean sand (no aggregate)
- 1 shovel of Portland cement
- 1 shovel of masonry cement

Mix with water to trowel thickness (it should stick to a trowel that is held almost vertical).

Add cement colour to the water if desired.

Once the mortar is set and the edge detail complete, backfill the soil against the liner to obtain the highest water level possible. Then fill the pond and trim off the excess liner. Cut it about ½ inch (1 to 1.5 cm) lower at the planned overflow point. Drain and clean the pond after waiting a few days for everything to settle. A pump and wet/dry shop vacuum will be required if the pond is not equipped with a bottom drain. Then refill the pond.

Install the pump and return lines, and test the waterfalls and creeks. In a balanced pond, the pump should be sized to recirculate the pond volume every 2 to 6 hours. Fish ponds are usually recirculated once every

1 to 2 hours. We recommend using flexible plastic pipe for the return lines for ease of installation and less restricted water flow, as it resists freezing damage and requires fewer fittings (please note that the hose size should be twice as large as the pump outlet to maximize flow). Supply electrical and water source to the pond if required (don't forget the GFI). Plant the pond and surrounding landscape to complement the site and provide seasonal reflections.

STOCKING THE POND

Successful pond-keeping requires an understanding of nature: you must work with it and not against it. This is especially true when stocking a new pond, which will go through a natural process of adjustment. New ponds can be built, filled with water and stocked with plants, fish and snails in less than a month. In nature, the same process takes several years. The inevitable result of combining all these ingredients in a new pond is murky green or brown water. Your pond grows algae, which is a natural and harmless condition. Do not empty and refill your pond, as this will only extend the problem by providing new nutrients and minerals. The pond and its inhabitants need time to adjust before they can work effectively together to create a balanced ecosystem.

Balancing Formula The first concern after filling a new pond is chlorine and/or chloramines. These chemicals are added to municipal water to kill pathogens and bacteria. Unfortunately, they will also kill your fish and beneficial pond bacteria. To remove these chemicals, you can aerate your pond or use a commercial chlorine-chloramine remover. To establish the beneficial bacteria and enzymes, you may want to add a water conditioner like Microbe Lift to speed up the natural process.

Once you have conditioned the water, you can add plants and animals to your pond. The correct numbers and combinations of these organisms are important for a healthy, functional pond. The following "recipe" is a good starting point. Some adjustment may be required, as ponds differ in light intensity, depth, surface area, nutrients, water movement and temperature.

For each square yard (m) of pond surface, use
- 1 medium waterlily
- 3 bunches of oxygenating plants
- 12 pond snails
- 3 goldfish, which should be less than 4 inches (10 cm) when stocked

This combination is not written in stone, but any changes to the proportions of plants and animals should be compensated for. The lilies provide surface coverage to limit the amount of light available for algae (50 percent of the water surface should be covered during summer). This can be achieved with waterlilies, floating plants and marginal plants. Dur-

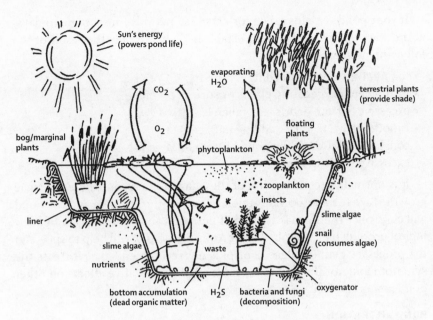

Sun's energy
(powers pond life)

evaporating
H₂O

terrestrial plants
(provide shade)

CO₂

O₂

floating
plants

bog/marginal
plants

phytoplankton

zooplankton

insects

slime algae

liner

snail
(consumes algae)

slime algae

waste

nutrients

bottom accumulation
(dead organic matter)

H₂S

bacteria and fungi
(decomposition)

oxygenator

Simplified pond ecosystem
(Illustration: Shibusa Pond
Services Ltd./Brian Morgan)

ing winter, very little surface coverage is required, as there is less sunlight and the low water temperatures slow all the pond processes.

Oxygenating plants provide oxygen and food for the fish while consuming carbon dioxide and dissolved nutrients. Because of this, they are extremely effective at starving algae of their required nutrients. Snails also control algae by consuming it. The number to stock will vary, depending on species and size. Although fish eat excess plant material, algae and pests, be careful not to overstock. Start with small fish, so the new pond will be able to provide enough food and the fish will grow to suit the pond. Fish should not be added until two weeks after the introduction of plants. This allows the plants to get established and condition the water. After stocking, the length of time required for the pond to balance and clear will vary depending on the weather, water chemistry and other pond conditions. It may take 60 to 90 days, so be patient and allow nature to run its course. Don't be alarmed at the sight of algae. It is part of the balancing process and is the basic food for aquatic life. Ponds containing natural life are not always crystal clear.

Once balanced, most ponds will remain in balance for years. The occasional algae bloom may occur, especially in the spring, when there are long sunny days prior to vigorous plant growth. Don't be overly concerned with the accumulation of bottom debris, as some material is required to provide the plants with nutrients. You should not vacuum the pond bottom more than once a month. For most ponds, vacuuming twice yearly is sufficient to prevent an over-supply of nutrients. However, don't allow large quantities of bottom debris to accumulate for more than one year or algae will flourish and toxic gases may be produced, which can kill pond life.

If your pond remains green for extended periods (more than 90 days) at the start-up or is green once established, it is usually the result of the following problems:

- too many fish or overfeeding
- insufficient oxygenating plants or surface coverage
- excessive bottom debris (e.g. fallen leaves)
- runoff or lawn fertilizer adding nutrients
- constant agitation of the pond bottom by large fish or excessive water motion

It is normally a combination of these factors that contributes to algae growth. Take the appropriate action to correct the problem and the pond will clear once the algae is starved of nutrients and light. The use of a biological product like Microbe Lift or Aqua Bacta Aide will help to speed up the process. Chemical algae control is not recommended as it treats the symptom and not the problem, and it will have negative effects on other pond plants and fish.

POND FILTRATION

Recirculation and filtration is not required for a properly balanced pond. If, however, you want to keep higher densities of fish or species that demand high water quality (such as trout), recirculation and filtration will be required. Serious koi enthusiasts often use filtration; it allows them to keep more fish and maintain water clarity so they can see them. Recirculation and filtration can be expensive and requires regular maintenance, so consider the advantages and disadvantages carefully before making a decision.

All types of pond filtration require water circulation, which is usually provided by pumps. The objectives of a recirculated filtration system are to:

- provide adequate oxygen and remove carbon dioxide
- remove suspended and bottom solids (fish wastes and detritus)
- remove dissolved toxins produced by fish and decomposition (ammonia and nitrite)
- neutralize chlorine and maintain desired pH

There are three types of filtration systems, which can be used separately or in combination. They are chemical, mechanical and biological filtration. The following is a brief explanation of each type, but if you decide to employ filtration you will need to do further research and consult a professional to assist you in designing a low-maintenance, efficient system.

Chemical Filtration Chemical filtration usually employs either carbon or zeolite which function by absorption and ion exchange. Both materials are commonly used in aquarium systems to remove dissolved toxins (e.g. ammonia and nitrite) and to neutralize chlorine. The aquarium or pond water is pumped through these materials constantly to maintain water quality. Activated carbon is usually considered disposable as it has a limited absorption capacity, after which it can only be recharged with extremely high heat. Because of this, activated carbon is usually too expensive to be considered for ornamental ponds. Zeolite removes pond toxins by ion exchange and also has a limited capacity. Fortunately, it can be recharged with a salt solution. For complete pond filtration, you would require 2.2 pounds (1 kg) of zeolite for every gallon (5 litres) of pond water, which also makes it expensive and bulky. Chemical filtration is also maintenance intensive.

Mechanical Filtration Mechanical filtration is commonly used in combination with both chemical and biological filtration. Most systems use particle size or weight to trap and remove the suspended and bottom solids produced by fish. Mechanical filters include cartridge filters, sand filters, centrifugal filters, screens and settling sumps. The objective of mechanical filters is to remove particulates which would quickly clog chemical and biological filtration systems. Depending on the filter design and pond loading, maintenance levels will vary.

Biological Filtration Biological filtration employs naturally occurring bacteria to convert ammonia and nitrite to nitrate, which is harmless to fish unless it is in very high concentrations. The bacteria which perform this function (Nitrobacter and Nitrosomonas) must be present in large quantities and require a constant supply of well-oxygenated water containing ammonia (fish wastes). There are many designs for biological filters, but the essential components are a large surface area (bacteria-growing surface), lots of oxygen and consistent water flow through the media. The efficiency of a biological filter depends on several factors:

- quantity and quality of the media (gravel and lava rock are commonly used)
- fish density in the pond
- contact time between the water and the media
- effectiveness of solid removal, prior to filter
- water flow rate through the filter
- oxygen level in the filter
- water temperature and pH
- the age of the filter (number of bacteria present)

There is a lot to consider in a biological filter design but once properly designed and constructed, it is inexpensive to operate and requires little maintenance. Biological filtration is the same process that occurs naturally in the bottom of streams, where water runs through the gravel that contains trillions of these beneficial bacteria. Ultraviolet (UV) sterilizers are commonly used in fish-rearing systems to kill algae and pathogens in the water. Normally, the water passes in a thin layer around the light (the water should also be free of particles). Ultraviolet clarifiers use a lower dose of UV light to clump algae together for removal by mechanical filtration.

With all filtration systems, supplemental feeding is required, since there is usually not enough aquatic life to support the dietary needs of the fish.

CHAPTER 7
Designing with Plants

There was one shrub in particular, set in a marble vase in the midst of the pool, that bore a profusion of purple blossoms, each of which had the luster and richness of a gem; and the whole together made a show so resplendent that it seemed enough to illuminate the garden, even had there been no sunshine.
Nathaniel Hawthorne, "Rappaccini's Daughter"

There is often controversy among garden designers and landscape architects as to whether it is the plants that highlight the garden or the hard landscaping that provides an elegant framework in which to place a few trees and shrubs. Regardless of your opinion on this aesthetic matter, I think most gardeners are willing to admit that when the right plant is given an ideal location, the results, even if simple in design, can be truly spectacular.

Landscapes centred around specific plant groups need not be boring botanical displays. There is room for a sophisticated palette of texture, colour and seasonal interest. This narrow approach to garden design may seem a bit naive to some, but the truth of the matter is that it takes a very talented designer to pull it off, someone who is intimately familiar with all aspects of the plants being used.

The writers in this section of the book are as passionate and knowledgeable about "their" plants as any gardener is capable of being. Perhaps a spark of their design inspiration will light your own creative fire and some of their ideas will find a place in your garden.

Helleborus corsicus or
argutifolius (Corsican
hellebore)
Colour photo p. 138

Les Jardins Vertes

MICHAEL LASCELLE, AMSTERDAM GARDEN CENTRE, PITT MEADOWS, B.C.

The predominantly green garden is not a design aesthetic that appeals to most novice gardeners. It seems to be an acquired taste that develops after years of experimenting with various colour schemes.

My first experience with such a garden occurred early in my career and, unfortunately, it was my job to dismantle it and discard the plants. The new owner of a large and established property had made the decision that rhododendrons were the only shrubs worth planting. Consequently, vast portions of an established landscape were gutted and rhododendrons planted in a grid pattern throughout.

This particular garden was a peninsula that divided two open portions of the landscape, with a meandering walkway of random slate threading its way from one side to another. The path was flanked at both ends with a pair of bold Corsican hellebores *(H. corsicus* or *H. argutifolius),* the quintessential green plant with its lustrous, serrated foliage and prominent chartreuse blooms. The bed was built around a small stand of mature deciduous trees, which were limbed to a height of about 18 feet (5.5 m). Well-spaced clumps of *Kerria japonica* and *Acer circinatum* (vine maple) formed the understory, thriving in the light that filtered through the canopy above. Each clump was encircled with tall Solomon's seal *(Polygonatum commutatum),* which nicely covered the bare lower stems and gracefully arched outwards.

The balance of the bed was a simple melange of green and variegated hostas, including the two-tone *H. undulata* 'Albo-Marginata', three species of fern — deer fern *(Blechnum spicant),* sword fern *(Polystichum munitum)* and crested lady fern *(Athyrium filix-femina* 'Vernoniae Cristatum')

— and a combination of sweet woodruff *(Galium odoratum)* and periwinkle *(Vinca minor)* sweeping through the open areas and covering the edge of the slate path. I took a long, slow look as I walked down this path for the last time; as you can see, much of this garden has remained with me for over 20 years and that is why I am able to share it with you. While I was unable to save the garden, the work of that original designer still lives on.

FOLIAGE GREEN

In a garden with an absence of (or at least limited) flower colour, foliage textures play a much more important role. Without the distraction of brightly coloured blooms, it becomes easier to appreciate the subtle colour variations of foliage, the shape or form of individual leaves, plants and groupings, and foliage contrast between adjacent shrubs.

Suddenly, those ordinary green plants almost seem to have a life of their own, and are no longer simply a foil for flowers. The essence of a green garden lies in paying close attention to foliage detail and the varying shades of a colour most of us take for granted in our landscapes.

The problem is that few of us go to our local garden centre in search of green plants and even fewer retailers seem to offer many plants for this purpose. So to help you find some potential candidates, here are a few of my favourite lime, chartreuse, emerald, jade and olive foliage textures, most of which can be found at any well-stocked garden centre.

Abies balsamea 'Nana' A very slow growing conifer with dense, deep green needles that emerge a bright lime colour in spring. Full sun. Height 2 feet (60 cm). Zone 3.

Acer shirasawanum 'Aureum' Golden full-moon maple flushes bright gold in spring, stays a clear lime in summer and turns orange to red in fall. Height 12 feet (4 m). Zone 5.

Adiantum pedatum Maidenhair is a herbaceous fern with lime to pale green fronds arranged in a fan shape, accented with pure black stems. Shade. Height 2 feet (60 cm). Zone 2.

Arum italicum This hardy perennial features lustrous arrowhead-shaped winter foliage (in zone 5+) with pearly highlights on the veins. Shade. Height 1 foot (30 cm). Zone 5.

Asarum europeum A semi-evergreen woodland groundcover composed of lustrous, rounded leaves of deep green. Shade. Height 6 inches (15 cm). Zone 3.

Asplenium scolopendrium Hart's-tongue fern has evergreen, undivided fronds that emerge a shiny pale green and deepen in colour with age. Height 18 inches (45 cm). Zone 4.

Bergenia cordifolia An evergreen perennial with large, glossy deep green leaves (tinted burgundy in winter) and for the most part, pink blooms. Part to full sun. Height 1 foot (30 cm). Zone 3.

Carex 'Ice Dance' An evergreen sedge with arching, deep green blades clearly edged in ivory. Shade to part sun. Height 1 foot (30 cm). Zone 6.

Clematis armandii An evergreen vine with simple, elongated foliage of a deep glossy green and fragrant white blooms in early spring. Part to full sun. Height to 20 feet (6 m). Zone 7–8.

Fatshedera lizei A hybrid of Fatsia japonica and Hedera helix which forms a climbing evergreen shrub with glossy palmate foliage. Shade. Height 9 feet (3 m). Zone 8.

Fatsia japonica Japanese aralia is a bold broadleaf evergreen with very tropical foliage of a dark forest green. Shade. Height 9 feet (3 m). Zone 7.

Hosta 'Royal Standard' Deeply veined foliage of dark green accented with pure white, fragrant summer blooms. Shade to part sun. Height 22 inches (55 cm). Zone 2.

Ilex crenata 'Convexa' A dense broadleaf evergreen shrub with lustrous, deep green convex foliage and insignificant black berries. Part to full sun. Height 6 feet (2 m). Zone 6.

Laurus nobilis Although bay laurel is not extremely cold hardy in all regions, it makes a fine foliage standard when grown in a container. Full sun. Height 6 feet+ (1.8 m+). Zone 9.

Lonicera nitida A broadleaf evergreen shrub with fine-textured, boxwood-like foliage of a glossy forest green. Part to full sun. Height 4 feet (1.2 m). Zone 6.

Miscanthus sinensis 'Strictus' A late-season ornamental grass with upright blades of rich green, horizontally banded with gold. Full sun. Height 6 feet (1.8 m). Zone 5.

Pachysandra 'Green Sheen' A new form of this evergreen groundcover with congested, deep green foliage that is very glossy. Shade. Height 8 inches (20 cm). Zone 3.

Salvia officinalis 'Icterina' This evergreen culinary sage features gold to pale lime foliage irregularly marked with deep green in the centre of the leaf. Full sun. Height 1 foot (30 cm). Zone 4.

Salvinia natans A wonderfully textured floating fern for the pond, it is mid-green in colour and is not winter hardy. Part to full sun. Height ½ inch (1 cm). Frost tender.

Sarcococca ruscifolia A broadleaf evergreen shrub with lustrous deep green foliage, an arching form and fragrant white winter flowers. Shade. Height 4 feet (1.2 m). Zone 6.

Sasa palmata A running bamboo with thick, leathery bright green leaves up to 15 inches (30 cm) long. Shade to full sun. Height 5 feet (1.5 m). Zone 7.

Taxus baccata 'Fastigiata' Irish yew has a thin, columnar form with deep emerald green needles. Shade to full sun. Height 10 feet (3 m). Zone 6.

FLOWER GREEN

Some gardeners are under the impression that a green flower doesn't really qualify as a bloom, simply because it happens to be in the same colour group as most leaves or needles. Nothing could be further from the truth! It can actually be easier to appreciate the detail of a green bloom without the distraction of brilliant colours — the elegant stamens, the delicate veining on the petals and sepals, or the subtle contrast of golden pollen grains.

Flowering plants, along with green foliar shrubs and vines, are the building blocks of the green garden and they can be set off by the occasional clump of burgundy or bright yellow. *Milium effusum* 'Aureum' (golden millet) or *Hakonechloa macra* 'Aureola' are good choices for shade gardens. Use *Heuchera* 'Amethyst Myst' or 'Ruby Ruffles' for part sun, or *Ber-*

beris thunbergii 'Aurea' or 'Royal Burgundy' for full sun. It only takes a few burgundy or gold foliage specimens for enough contrast to appreciate the various hues of green.

Here are some of the many green-flowered annuals, perennials, bulbs, vines and shrubs for you to choose from.

Alchemilla mollis Lady's mantle features delicate sprays of yellowish-green flowers and unique, pleated leaves that hold the morning dew. Part to full sun. Height 1 foot (30 cm). Zone 3.

Daphne laureola This broadleaf evergreen shrub is often considered a weed due to self-seeding, but is still quite attractive with its lustrous deep green foliage and pale lime flowers. Shade to part sun. Height 5 feet (1.5 m). Zone 6.

Eucomis bicolor An exotic bulb with green basal leaves topped with an unusual pineapple crown, covering purple-edged chartreuse blooms. Full sun. Height 2 feet (60 cm). Zone 7.

Euphorbia amygdaloides **var.** *robbiae* An evergreen perennial with dark, leathery foliage and attractive lime green flowers. Shade to part sun. Height 2 feet (60 cm). Zone 5.

Helleborus argutifolius A bold evergreen hellebore with glossy, serrated foliage and apple-green bloom clusters. Partial sun. Height 2 feet (60 cm). Zone 6.

Helleborus foetidus A durable, evergreen hellebore with blooms of pale lime tipped in burgundy. Part sun. Height 18 inches (45 cm). Zone 5.

Hydrangea paniculata 'Limelight' This hardy hydrangea bears midsummer, cone-shaped blooms of lime to mid-green. Part to full sun. Height 6 feet (2 m). Zone 3.

Leucojum vernum A bulb that resembles a large snowdrop, with jade green foliage and nodding, pure white blooms, each petal also tipped with green. Part sun. Height 1 foot (30 cm). Zone 5.

Molucella laevis Bells of Ireland is an annual (often grown as a cut flower) with tall spikes of tiny white blooms, each surrounded by a lime green calyx. Full sun. Height 2 feet (60 cm).

Nicotiana alata 'Lime Green' A fragrant annual form of flowering tobacco best suited to warm sites. Part to full sun. Height 1 foot (30 cm). Frost Tender.

Rhododendron 'Shamrock' An early-blooming, dwarf rhododendron with pale greenish-yellow flower trusses. Part to full sun. Height 2 feet (60 cm). Zone 6.

Rosa 'Green Ice' A miniature rose with clusters of fully double, pale green blooms on a short plant. Full sun. Height 1 foot (30 cm). Zone 6.

Rudbeckia 'Green Wizard' This hardy perennial starts blooming in June, with small green petals clustered around an enormous black cone. Full sun. Height 30 to 40 inches (75 to 100 cm). Zone 4.

Tulipa 'Spring Green' A late blooming viridiflora tulip with attractive ivory white flower petals, each barred with apple green. Full sun. Height 20 inches (50 cm). Zone 3.

Zantedeschia 'Green Goddess' Your typical white calla lily, except that the spathes are bright green with a white throat. Part to full sun. Height 18 inches to 2 feet (45 to 60 cm). Zone 8.

Zinnia 'Envy' An annual with large, dahlia-like blooms of pure green. Best grown in areas where there are warm summers. Full sun. Height 2 feet (60 cm). Frost tender.

Designing a Rose Garden
TED BROWN (PART 1) & BILL MEAGHER (PART 2), FRASER PACIFIC ROSE
SOCIETY, COQUITLAM, B.C.

Part 1

START WITH ROOTSTOCKS

Before you begin to design your rose garden, or prior to the purchase of that first rose, you need to consider the various rootstocks available and their impact on long-term growth habits. Most garden roses available today are grafted plants. The rose you see when in leaf or flower is usually grafted onto the root of a more vigorous rose that provides it with a stronger growth habit, not always provided by the grafted plant itself. This rootstock has a great bearing on how the rose will perform in your growing area. To help you choose the right rose for your region, here are descriptions of some of the rootstocks used for grafting.

'Dr. Huey' Unfortunately, many of the roses sold in the Pacific Northwest are grafted onto this rootstock. 'Dr. Huey' is a vigorous, large-flowered climber that produces a dull red bloom and foliage that is prone to mildew. This rootstock tolerates alkaline soil and is popular in the American Southwest where it is able to withstand the irrigated desert soils. Most soils in the coastal region of the Pacific Northwest are basically acidic in nature and with our colder winters, 'Dr. Huey' is really not a good choice.

Multiflora In my opinion, this is the best rootstock for the Pacific Northwest, as it prefers damp, cool soils that are acidic in nature. Knowledgeable gardeners in our region have for many years chosen this rootstock for the many benefits it offers and its capacity to produce vigorous bushes. It is winter hardy, resistant to black spot and easy to root.

Laxa This rootstock is the dominant choice in the United Kingdom, which has similar climatic conditions as the Pacific Northwest, and it is as acceptable as multiflora. While some roses purchased from the U.K. with this rootstock are initially smaller, they tend to produce large plants in succeeding years.

Canina Canina rootstock is used predominantly in parts of Europe, particularly in Germany. It is also an acceptable rootstock for the Pacific Northwest. Canina does have the annoying habit of producing abundant suckers. The rootstock grows independently of the rose and may eventually cause it to fail by taking over.

Own Root Some rose varieties grow quite well on their own roots (not grafted onto a rootstock). Those that root and grow most successfully on their own roots are usually vigorous roses such as climbers, shrubs and some floribundas, as well as some old garden roses.

Rosa 'Danielle' *Colour photo p. 139*

Most miniature roses are also propagated and sold on their own roots. However, beware of overblown claims that are made about "own root" roses. These roses are not necessarily more scented, disease resistant or hardy than grafted roses.

Some last words of caution when purchasing roses. Many well-known roses do not grow well in the Pacific Northwest. Quite often, novice gardeners purchase them, and local retailers stock them, simply because the variety or cultivar is well recognized. For example, the sought-after rose 'Climbing Peace' does not develop many blooms here. It will produce strong growth up to 10 or 15 feet (3.2 to 5 m), but very few flowers will adorn the plant. Another consideration is the petal count of the rose bloom. Roses with more than 50 petals per bloom may have difficulty opening in our damp climate and will tend to "ball."

THE VERTICAL ELEMENT — CLIMBING ROSES

Some people assume that a climbing rose is just a plant that will grow to great heights and fill a desired location, but this is far from true. There are short climbers (or pillar roses) which grow to about 6 or 7 feet (2 to 2.3 m), and very large climbers (or ramblers) that can reach 40 or 50 feet (13 to 17 m). Choose a rose that will fill the area you have available, rather than purchasing the rose and then wondering where to plant it.

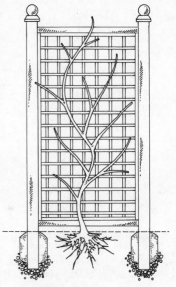

For urban areas there is a relatively new form of climber introduced for smaller-scale gardens. The miniature climber grows only to 6 to 8 feet (2 to 2.6 m) and bears small flowers in abundance. The word miniature pertains to the bloom size and not necessarily the ultimate height of the plant. Some miniature climbers can reach a height of 10 feet (3 m); however, this is the exception.

These climbers can be used in a myriad of landscape situations. One simple and effective way to display them is to place a 4- × 8-foot (1.2- × 2.4-m) trellis between two upright 4 × 4 posts, with 2 × 4 supports on the top and bottom. This will provide a firm structure on which to train the rose, and both sides can be used if you wish to plant a second miniature rose. A second method is to simply sink a 4 × 4 post into the ground and train the rose around the post by tying it with soft yarn at intervals (eye hooks can also be used to fix the yarn). Some very good miniature climbers include 'Nice Day' (orange-pink), 'Laura Ford' (yellow), 'Good as Gold' (yellow), 'Warm Welcome' (orange), 'Jeanne LaJoie' (pink) and 'Love Knot' (red).

A simple support trellis for miniature climbers

The larger climbers vary widely in height and width. All should be grown horizontally as soon as the canes are long enough to be tied in such a position. If left to grow vertically, the flowers will only come from the very tip of each long cane. When tied horizontally, each eye (the bump where the previous year's leaves were) will grow what is called a lateral branch. The lateral growth is where the bloom is produced, so it is important to promote as much lateral growth as possible along the length of each cane.

Rose arbor with *Rosa* 'Eye
Paint' in the foreground of
the garden of Bill and Reiko
Meagher of Maple Ridge, B.C.
Colour photo p. 139

Many climbing roses have a very stiff growth habit and are somewhat
difficult to bend sideways all at one time. A more horizontal position can
be obtained by moving the cane in several stages a little at a time, over a few
months. The thinner canes on some climbers are easier to train laterally
— many of these are ramblers that bloom only once in the season. There
are also quite a number of modern climbing roses with supple canes that
bloom repeatedly. It is very important when building a structure (or purchasing one) that it be of very sturdy construction that will last, since roses
are long-lived and are quite heavy when fully leafed out.

Very tall climbers can be used in many interesting ways — such as
adorning an old dead tree or growing through an existing tall conifer.

When roses are trained this way, you will not have to prune, spray or dead-head; just plant them and let them grow out on their own. The only maintenance occurs early in their training — you may have to guide the canes up into the tree until it gets established. The reward (which will occur in about 3 years) will be a cascade of bloom throughout the crown of the tree, adding colour and height to your garden. Some varieties that work well under these circumstances are 'Bobby James' (white), 'Treasure Trove' (apricot), 'Chevy Chase' (red), 'Seagull' (white), 'Francis E. Lester' (white/pink) and 'Kiftsgate' (white). These are only a few of the "tree scramblers" available to the gardener who is looking for something a little different.

Part 2

A ROSE FOR ANY CLIMATE?

Rose hardiness will vary with the type of rootstock used, but beyond that, not every rose will thrive in every climate zone — even if it is cold hardy enough to survive there. Some cultivars prefer warmer, interior summers (for proper flower production) while others need mild winters just to survive until spring. Here is a brief listing of strong rose cultivars which have proven to be adaptable in a range of climate zones, but still perform well in the cool summers of the Pacific Northwest.

Hybrid Teas 'Savoy Hotel' (light pink), 'Liebeszauber' (red), 'Sunset Celebration', also known as 'Warm Wishes' (apricot)

Floribundas 'Iceberg' (white), 'Amber Queen' (Apricot), 'Glad Tidings' (red), 'Many Happy Returns' (light pink)

Shrub Roses 'Armada' (pink), 'Sally Holmes' (white), 'Fred Loads' (orange), *Rosa glauca*, also known as *R. rubrifolia* (small pink flowers, reddish-purple foliage)

Ground Covers 'Nozomi' (light pink), 'Flower Carpet Pink' (deep pink), 'Snow Carpet' (white)

Hedge (Any type of rose can be used for hedging, depending on the purpose and height in mind.)
TALL (6 feet+/2 m+) 'Queen Elizabeth' (light pink), 'Maigold' (fragrant apricot, very thorny)
MEDIUM (3 to 4 feet/1 to 1.3 m) 'Top Rose' (yellow), 'Ballerina' (pink)
SHORT (2 to 2.5 feet/60 to 75 cm) 'Regensberg' (pink), 'Trumpeter' (orange-red)

Many hardy varieties have been developed by Agriculture Canada, such as the 'Explorer' series. Kordes of Germany has bred roses for northern climes, as has Poulsen of Denmark and Buck of the United States. Species roses (which grow true from seed) native to Canada and other northern areas of the world do very well in Canadian gardens. These are good choices for a cabin or recreational property in interior climates, where low maintenance is necessary. Following are some examples of hardy roses (zones 3 to 4) for colder climates.

'Alexander MacKenzie' (Explorer) Light red.
'George Vancouver' (Explorer) Light red.
'Morden Blush' (Parkland) White to pink blooms.
'Blanc Double de Coubert' (rugosa) White blooms.
  (Also good in coastal climates.)
'Harrison's Yellow' (shrub) Sulfur yellow flowers.
'Hansa' (rugosa) Crimson-purple blooms. (Also good in
  coastal climates.)

ROSES IN THE LANDSCAPE

Roses come in many guises — climbers, specimen shrubs, groundcovers, as well as tall border plants that blend well with herbaceous perennials. One of their most appealing qualities is the quick repeat bloom cycle of many varieties, so that you can have colour throughout the summer into late fall and even the occasional bloom in early winter.

Roses can be planted in groups (usually in odd numbers), either in one colour or mixed, as part of the overall plan. They can also be trained into an excellent hedge used to separate different aspects of the garden, or to keep that pesky mail carrier from making his or her own path through your side yard!

Besides the climbing roses, which have already been discussed, many roses are well adapted to a specific landscape purpose. Here are a few of the most common.

Groundcover roses grow broader than they grow tall. They are very attractive when planted on an incline, where they will actually cascade down the slope. Some climbers with lax stems can be pegged down and thus become effective groundcovers.

Shrub roses (any variety that is not a hybrid tea, floribunda, climber or miniature) may be underplanted with groundcover perennials such as hardy geraniums or saxifraga; depending on their size, they will fit almost anywhere in the garden.

Standard, or tree roses provide height and can be used as focal points in the landscape. They are very effective when used to line the edge of a pathway, with a display of summer bedding below.

Miniature roses generally have small flowers and leaves, and do not grow more than 2 feet (60 cm) tall (unless they are miniature climbers). They are a good choice for edging the front of a mixed border or for growing in containers on a balcony or patio.

Patio roses, as they are known in Europe (the popular name in the United States seems to be Mini-flora roses) have been bred in the last 20 years as an intermediate size between hybrid teas and floribundas, and true miniature roses. They can be used in the garden where shorter plants are required, or in containers on the patio or balcony.

English roses are the life work of English rose breeder David Austin, of Wolverhampton. They have been bred to have the form of old garden roses but with repeat bloom, which many of the older varieties lack. Most are also fragrant. They come in all sizes and growth habits, and many new varieties are added every year.

Hybrid tea roses bear solitary shapely blooms on long, elegant stems. Most have an upright growth habit which lends itself to an open mixed border or a formal row — where you can access both sides to cut flowers for the house.

Floribunda roses usually bear large clusters of smaller blooms (others, like 'Sheila's Perfume', strongly resemble hybrid teas in form) that show well from a distance. Many have a compact growth habit, which works well for an informal hedge or small mass planting.

Designing with Ornamental Grasses
EWAN MACKENZIE, CAMPBELL VALLEY GRASS CO., LANGLEY, B.C.

There has never been a better time to use ornamental grasses as a part of your gardening plans. With so many varieties to choose from, there is a grass cultivar for every location — large or small, hot or cold, wet or dry.

The form, texture, structure, movement and seasonal changes of ornamental grasses provide interest for most of the year. Many of them come to life when backlit with early morning or evening sun. Especially striking is *Imperata cylindrica* 'Red Baron' (Japanese blood grass). Its red foliage bursts into life as the rising or setting sun strikes it from a low angle. Many ornamental grasses also have very fine, airy flower spikes that catch the sun.

Golden Hakone grass
(*Hakonechloa macra* 'Aureola')
(Photo: Ewan MacKenzie)

You can speak to your grasses and they might actually reply with a rustle or rattle, depending on the mood of the wind. Wind also plays with the grasses, organizing the foliage so it acts much like a weather vane or causing them to dance and flail with more turbulent air movement.

Later in the season, the fine hairy flowers of many ornamental grasses, like *Pennisetum alopecuroides* 'Moudry', catch the early morning dew, which glistens like hundreds of small diamonds in the rising sun. These same flowers also become spectacular with frost, if only for an hour or so before the sun melts it away.

A lot of grasses are perennial and although they may go dormant in the fall, that is not the end of their ever-changing display. For example, most of the *Miscanthus* species will grow from buds under the ground in spring and give lush green foliage as a backdrop for spring bulbs or perennials. As the season progresses, they grow taller, adding form and texture to the border. The flowers, which can be brilliantly colourful for up to a month, appear any time from July to September. As the flower colour fades, the blooms twist and curl, creating a very interesting texture. Many *Miscanthus* have striking autumn foliage tones. When you are ready to tidy the garden for winter, leave these dormant grasses, as they continue to add colour and interest when there is little else in the garden.

COOL AND WARM SEASON GRASSES

Now that your gardening appetite is awakened, you will need some cultural information to make the most of these treasures. Probably the most significant aspect to understand about grasses is the difference between "cool season" and "warm season," as this will help you to choose the right grasses for your needs.

As the name implies, cool season grasses actively grow in cooler conditions (0–24°C/30–78°F). In some areas they grow all winter long and slow down in the heat of summer, still remaining attractive even when dormant. The cool season grasses tend to be smaller in size, up to 2 to 3 feet (60 to 90 cm) tall, and they add colour to the garden in the winter months.

Warm season grasses are much like herbaceous perennials. They grow from dormant buds under the ground in spring, as the soil warms up. They are in their glory when temperatures get above 70°F (20°C), usually mid to late summer. Most have striking fall colour as well as good winter structure. Old foliage can be left until the first sign of new growth appears above the ground, at which time they can be cut back to 2 to 4 inches (5 to 10 cm) high.

USING GRASSES IN THE LANDSCAPE

When planning with grasses, remember to consider all four seasons. This may make it slightly more complicated, but the effort will be worthwhile in the long run.

Ornamental grasses can be used in many ways in the landscape. You might want a specimen grass that will be a feature on its own, such as *Saccharum ravennae*. This works well as a focal point in the garden with plantings around it, such as perennials, shrubs or other ornamental grasses. A very useful specimen grass is *Molinia caerulea* 'Skyracer'. It can be placed near the front of a border, as the foliage stays low, but the flower spikes can reach up to 6 to 8 feet (2 to 2.5 m); the spikes stand very stiff and erect, fanning slightly and allowing a view of the plants behind. 'Skyracer' has a smaller cousin, *Molinia caerulea* 'Moorhexe', which is suitable for smaller spaces or borders, with flower spikes reaching to 3 feet (90 cm).

Some grasses lend themselves to mass plantings. Use upwards of three to five plants in a group, depending on the size of the border and the desired effect. A good choice here would be *Helictotrichon sempervirens* (blue oat grass), with its steely blue spiky foliage. This cool season grass is very hardy (zone 4) and is evergreen, so it has good colour 12 months of the year.

Ornamental grasses are an effective way to highlight perennials with darker foliage (such as burgundy heucheras). They can be used as a contrast for plants with gold foliage, or as a foil for other grasses, such as the fine bronze blades of *Carex buchananii*. They can also be used as a backdrop, or picture frame, for a perennial border. A common problem in the mixed border is highlighting plants with darker foliage, such as *Penstemon* 'Husker Red', *Cimicifuga* 'Brunette' or *Heuchera* 'Bressingham Bronze'. A background of *Miscanthus sinensis* 'Variegatus' makes a striking contrast that is easily seen from a distance.

Spring bulbs look great when planted among drifts of cool season grasses such as *Deschampsia* 'Goldtau'. As the spring flowers fade, the golden flower spikes of this grass hide the dying bulb foliage.

SUN, SHADE, DROUGHT AND BOG

Most grasses are very drought tolerant, but there are some grasses and rushes that thrive in damp soils or even in shallow water. A couple of good choices are *Juncus effusus* 'Carmen's Japan', with its very spiky, blue-green foliage. A similarly coloured rush with curled foliage is *J. inflexus* 'Afro'. Other grass-like plants for wet areas are *Typha* (cattails) and *Acorus* species *A. gramineus* 'Ogon', a vibrant cultivar with gold foliage and fine green vertical stripes that is especially good for damp shaded areas.

For shaded gardens with tall trees, *Luzula* species do very well. *L. nivea* (snowy woodrush) has broad grey-green foliage and snowy white flowers in spring. To brighten up a dull shady corner, try *Milium effusum* 'Aureum'. The chartreuse foliage is very soft to the touch and grows up to 12 inches (30 cm) tall. The flowers are also yellow, but take note that this is a rampant self-seeder and if you don't want it to grow everywhere, cut the flowers off before they set seed. Also good for shade, especially damp shade, are most of the *Carex* species. Some will even tolerate saturated soils or having their roots in water. A particularly striking variety is *Carex elata* 'Bowles Golden'. As the name suggests, the foliage is golden, with lime green edges. For blue foliage, *C. nigra* or *C. glauca* work well.

Molinia, *Panicum* and *Pennisetum* species do well in dry areas with full sun. One of my favourite grasses is *Molinia caerulea* 'Variegata', with its gold and green variegated foliage, golden flower spikes and dark brown flowers. *Panicum* species are used primarily for their foliage colour. *P. virgatum* 'Prairie Sky' has lovely blue arching foliage. Others, like 'Shenandoah', have fantastic red foliage later in the season and striking autumn colour.

CONTAINERS TO MEADOWS

Ornamental grasses do very well in containers. Some are best used as a single specimen, such as *Miscanthus sinensis* 'Strictus'. With its green foliage and horizontal yellow banding it really stands out. Mixing grasses with contrasting foliage in a container gives a very simple, but sophisticated look. Place taller or more upright grasses in the middle or back of the container and grasses that will trail over the edge of a pot in front. *Carex* 'Frosty Curls' and one of my favourites, *Hakonechloa macra* 'Aureola', with its gold and green striped foliage and cascading habit, are both good choices. Mixing grasses with perennials in containers can also give excellent results. Choose contrasting or complementary color schemes; the structure or form of the grass adds interest to the feature.

One grass that is a must for every garden is *Pennisetum setaceum* 'Rubrum' (purple fountain grass). This is a zone 9–10 grass and in most climates it won't survive the winter, so many gardeners treat it as an annual. The striking, burgundy-red foliage cascades over the container and contrasts well with lighter-coloured plants. The flowers resemble bottle-brushes and have a silvery-red sheen as they emerge. These plumes arch up and then cascade 1 to 2 feet (30 to 60 cm) above the foliage, moving with the slightest breeze. This grass looks great in a grass border, especially when combined with annuals and perennials. I wish it were hardier, but it can be dug up, put in a container and overwintered in a greenhouse or sunny window. It will not tolerate any frost, but this grass is well worth growing as an annual and replanting each year — you won't be disappointed!

Some people are ripping out their old, high-maintenance lawns and replacing them with a more environmentally friendly grass meadow. You can create a meadow from just one variety or use a combination of grasses to achieve subtle contrasts. You won't have to get out the mower every week or treat it with chemicals and fertilizers, and your only maintenance will be a light trim once or twice a year.

Many of the *Carex* species are well suited to this kind of planting, such as *C. remota* and *C. tumulicola*. Another good species for mass planting is *Sesleria*. Look for *S. autumnalis*, with its gold to yellow foliage and autumn blooms, and *S. caerulea*, a short blue species. Meadows can look great on their own or they can be punctuated with specimen plants, such as conifers, shrubs, perennials, annuals or even other prominent grasses. Most of these meadow-type grasses will take a bit of foot traffic with very little damage. So when you are planting your meadow, don't be skimpy with the plant material — go wild and enjoy ornamental grasses in their finest natural form!

There are very few plants on the market today that present us with such textural variety, seasonal interest, extended bloom periods and kinetic grace as ornamental grasses do. Just take the time to look a little closer the next time you hear someone comment, "oh, that's just a grass."

CHAPTER 8
Helping Mother Nature

*Strange that so few ever come to the woods to see how the pine lives
and grows and spires, lifting its evergreen arms to the light...most
are content to behold it in the shape of many broad boards brought
to market, and deem that its true success!*
Henry David Thoreau, *The Maine Woods*

One of the things that became clear while I was editing this
book was the realization that most gardeners are deeply concerned about how their horticultural practices impact the environment. Suddenly, all those trends towards organic fertilizers, indigenous plants and beneficial insects seem like genuine
grassroots movements, rather than just sales gimmicks or the
whims of a fanatical few. Don't get me wrong, these have always
been important principles to me, but I was never quite sure
of their general acceptance among my peers. Now, I have no
doubts whatsoever.

Those principles of preserving natural areas, using organic
gardening practices and inviting nature into our landscapes are
well embodied in the pieces in this chapter. That doesn't mean
nature is always convenient in the urban landscape: blue herons
will eat your goldfish, raccoons will wreak havoc in the compost
pile, starlings will decimate blueberry bushes at every opportunity and few crocus bulbs are safe when there are grey squirrels
within half a block. But these incursions are minuscule when
compared to the environmental damage that homo sapiens
have exported from continent to continent.

I'm not one to dwell on past mistakes and the opinions presented here provide me with a great deal of optimism. Perhaps
in the next hundred years, our increasing awareness will allow
us to heal some of the damage we have wrought over the past
century.

Sedum spathulifolium
Colour photo p. 140

Creating Wildlife Habitat —
Right in Your Own Backyard!

ANGELA DEERING, NATURESCAPE BRITISH COLUMBIA, VICTORIA, B.C.

Naturescaping can be described as landscaping to create ecologically sound and aesthetically pleasing urban gardens through the use of plant species native to the region. Naturescaping promotes the creation of landscapes that restore, preserve and enhance wildlife habitat in urban and rural areas.

Naturescaping has a significant role to play in the creation of sustainable landscapes in British Columbia. Conventional landscaping involves the extensive use of lawns and exotic horticultural specimens. Such landscapes are prevalent throughout North America and give very little thought to specific local conditions, regional climates, soils and other possible constraints. Conventional landscapes can also require ongoing intensive horticultural management, including the application of pesticides and chemical fertilizers.

Naturescaping addresses many of the ecological issues surrounding traditional landscaping practices.

- *It reduces water consumption.* Native plants are more water-thrifty because they are adapted to regional weather cycles.
- *It improves water quality.* Reducing or eliminating the use of chemical pesticides and fertilizers from landscape maintenance eliminates this source of pollution and helps keep waterways free of pesticides and fertilizers.
- *It creates habitat and improves biodiversity in urban areas.* Loss of biodiversity and habitat is a serious issue in urban areas. Natural-

ized landscapes can act in conjunction with existing parks and green spaces to connect habitat through urban landscapes.

- *It cuts down on the spread of invasive species.* Many invasive plant species, such as Scotch broom, gorse *(Ulex europaeus)* and purple knapweed, are exotic horticultural escapees. These plants have spread out of gardens and into the natural world, often out-competing many native species of plants.
- *It creates landscapes that have a regional context.* Contemporary landscapes are very similar wherever you go. A natural landscape creates a sense of place and reflects the particular environment in which it is found.
- *It reduces landscape maintenance costs.* Conventional landscapes are very expensive and time-consuming to maintain. Naturalized landscapes are not maintenance free, but the bulk of costs are restricted to the first three years, while the landscape is being established.

DESIGNING A NATURESCAPE

These recommendations for creating a Naturescape have been divided into 3 steps — planning, planting and maintaining.

Step 1 Planning

As with all garden designs, a naturalized landscape should be carefully planned. Before you begin, decide how large you want your habitat to be and break the project into manageable chunks; don't be afraid to have a three- to five-year plan. Trying to do too much can be discouraging. Approach your project on a bed-by-bed, project-by-project basis. Here are some guidelines for planning, planting and maintaining a natural garden.

Shelter Shelter takes many forms. When designing your wildlife habitat, think in layers. Thickets of trees, as well as dense shrubs and hedges, provide cover for birds to hide and nest in. Dead trees, both standing and on the ground, provide excellent habitat. In fact, many birds, such as woodpeckers and chickadees, rely on tree cavities to raise their young. Woodpiles, brush piles and dry stone walls offer habitat for small animals. It is also important to provide areas of meadow and leaf litter, which is important for foraging. Finally, shelter can also be provided in the form of nest boxes.

Food Planting indigenous plants helps ensure the survival of native species and conserves water. Indigenous plants and some very specific non-native plants are food sources in the form of nectar, seeds, berries and associated insects. The list on the next page features a few native plants that have excellent wildlife habitat value.

Vaccinium parvifolium
(red huckleberry)
Colour photo p. 140

SHRUBS

Sambucus caerulea (blue elderberry)
Attracts bees, butterflies and hummingbirds. Berries eaten by birds.

Cornus stolonifera (red-osier dogwood)
Attracts bees, butterflies and hummingbirds. Provides food and cover for wildlife.

Salix scouleriana (Scouler's willow) Attracts
bees, butterflies and hummingbirds. Provides food and cover for wildlife.

PERENNIALS

Fragaria virginiana (wild strawberry)
Attracts bees and butterflies.

Vaccinium (blueberry family) Provides food
and browse for wildlife.

Epilobium angustifolium (fireweed)
Attracts bees, butterflies and hummingbirds.

Sedum (stonecrop family) Attracts bees
and butterflies.

Choosing a diversity of food-producing plants will ensure that a habitat can provide food throughout the year. Diverse vegetation also attracts
many insects that play an important role in any habitat garden. Food may
also be provided in feeders for birds. It is also important to note that in a
wildlife habitat garden you must use biological controls and organic fertilizers, such as compost, to maintain the balance of prey and predator relationships.

Water Clean, fresh water is often difficult to find in developed areas. Streams and creeks have been diverted into culverts and marshy areas have been drained. Yet all animals need water year-round for drinking and bathing, and it is essential for many insects and amphibians to complete their life cycles.

By including a water source in your wildlife habitat you can transform an average habitat into an extraordinary one. Water can be offered in many ways — bird baths, ponds, streams or even a shallow dish.

Step 2 Planting

Once you have designed a plan, it's time to think about planting. Make sure the site you have selected is appropriate for your plants. Woodland plants need shade. Meadow plants need full sun or partial sun. Bog plants require a great deal of water. Plants found on rocky outcroppings require very little. Buy plants from a reputable nursery and never collect plants from the wild.

If you are reducing your lawn size it can be very tiring digging up the sod. An easier method is to lay down a layer of newspaper (about 12 sheets thick). Apply mulch and compost thickly and leave it over the winter. Plants can be planted directly into the mulch the following spring.

Step 3 Maintaining

Much of the maintenance of your landscape will be annual or semi-annual. Be sure to prune plants back in early spring (unless they are spring bloom-ing), prior to leaf growth. This delay in pruning allows seed-eating birds the opportunity to feast on plant seeds during the winter. Ensure that you have plants blooming or providing seed throughout the year. Finally, be sure to make time to enjoy your Naturescape and observe the changing activities of each season.

For more information about Naturescape British Columbia, visit the Web site at http://www.hctf.ca/nature.htm

Lower Maintenance with Native Plants
MICHAEL LASCELLE, AMSTERDAM GARDEN CENTRE, PITT MEADOWS, B.C.

Many gardeners are on a constant quest to find those perfect, low-main-tenance plants — ones that require no pruning, no watering (once estab-lished) and no fertilizer, but still flourish as though you did prune, water and fertilize. Quite a few potential candidates have come to the forefront over the years, including spreading junipers (affected by twig blight), ivy (too invasive), *Viburnum davidii* (eaten by weevils) and 'Otto Lukyen' lau-rels (subject to shot hole fungus). As you can see, many have fallen out of favour due to cultural problems (in part due to overplanting) or because they were not low maintenance over the long run.

Native plants fill this void because they are already adapted to the condi-tions that exist here, so gardeners in the Pacific Northwest can enjoy their beauty with minimum effort. Many of our indigenous plants also flourish outside their natural habitat and quite a few are already used extensively in temperate gardens around the world.

DEFINING A HABITAT

Before you go out to purchase those native plants, it is important to find out which species will thrive in your specific growing conditions. One of the best examples I can provide is the difference between indigenous plants in two communities on Vancouver's north shore, which are only about 10 minutes apart by car. Rockridge, in West Vancouver, receives plenty of sun and has many open areas with gravelly, well-drained soil. Arbutus, Douglas fir and seaside shore pine are the predominant trees here. Oceanspray *(Holodiscus discolor)* and introduced shrubs such as butterfly bush *(Buddleia)*, gorse and Scotch broom have naturalized extensively. On the other hand, North Vancouver's Lynn Valley always seems to have a raincloud hovering overhead and its dense forests are almost like a temperate rainforest. Western red cedar and bigleaf maple thrive here, with thick understories of sword and lady fern, salal and red huckleberry *(Vaccinium parvifolium)*. Despite being only minutes apart, these two communities are like night and day are far as the ecologies are concerned, and very few native plants would be adaptable enough to thrive in both sites. So some discretion must be used, to ensure that even our indigenous plantings are site specific.

WEST COAST PLANT ASSOCIATIONS

Once you've found at least one native plant that seems to thrive in your garden, it may prove easier to select some companion plants, simply by association. In nature, certain plants grow together in small ecosystems that provide ideal soil, light and moisture conditions.

Dry Forest (partial shade to filtered light/dry soil conditions in summer)

Mahonia nervosa (low Oregon grape), *Gaultheria shallon* (salal), *Polystichum munitum* (sword fern), *Philadelphus lewisii* (mock orange), *Goodyera oblongifolia* (rattlesnake plantain).

Streamside (moist shade/tolerant of temporary flooding)

Maianthemum dilatatum (false lily-of-the-valley), *Rubus spectabilis* (salmonberry), *Viola sempervirens* (evergreen violet), *Oplopanax horridus* (devil's club), *Salix hookeriana* (Hooker's willow).

Open Meadow (full sun/generally well-drained soils)

Holodiscus discolor (oceanspray), *Ribes sanguineum* (red-flowering currant), *Rosa nutkana* (nootka rose), *Solidago canadensis* (goldenrod), *Arbutus menziesii* (arbutus).

Damp Forest (shade/even moisture with fertile soils)

Achlys triphylla (vanilla-leaf), *Dicentra formosa* (western bleeding heart), *Acer circinatum* (vine maple), *Tiarella trifoliata* (foamflower), *Smilacina racemosa* (false Solomon's seal).

Forest's Edge (at least partial sun/reasonably fertile soils)

Osmaronia cerasiformis (Indian plum), *Arctostaphylos uva-ursi* (bearberry), *Vaccinium parvifolium* (red huckleberry), *Acer glabrum* (Douglas maple), *Physocarpus capitatus* (pacific ninebark).

Wetland (constant moisture or standing water/bogs or lake edge)

Aruncus sylvester (goat's beard), *Spiraea douglasii* (hardhack), *Myrica gale* (sweet gale), *Athyrium felix-femina* (lady fern), *Kalmia polifolia* (bog laurel).

COASTAL BRITISH COLUMBIA'S TEN BEST

The coastal forests and meadows of British Columbia are home to many fine ornamental shrubs, trees, vines and perennials. As is often the case, we tend to ignore (as far as landscape potential is concerned) the beauty that surrounds us. Even worse, many of us just take it for granted!

Yet in other countries, our native plants are highly esteemed. Red-flowering currant and Oregon grape have adorned English landscapes for many decades now. Several years back, I had a visit from two enthusiastic plantsmen from South Africa who were searching for a seed source for vine and bigleaf maple to take home with them. My gift of a few handfuls of vine maple seed was, to my amazement, received like it was a rare orchid or choice perennial.

So whether you've made a commitment to creating a space for indigenous plants in your garden, or you are just looking for a few reliable shrubs, trees and perennials to add to the yard, at least one of the 10 selections below will undoubtedly capture your interest and fulfill a landscape need.

Acer circinatum (vine maple) Vine maple is probably one of the best urban landscape trees available on the market today. It is usually grown as a multistem specimen and exhibits a very erect form when grown in full sun (the opposite is true in deep shade). In sun, leaves generally turn a brilliant scarlet in the fall. Averages 20 feet (6.5 m). Zone 5.

Achlys triphylla (vanilla-leaf) A much underused woodlander with distinct trilobed leaves and small white bottlebrush blooms that push up just above the foliage. This is a great companion plant for western bleeding heart *(Dicentra formosa),* as they are often found growing together. Averages 1 foot (30 cm) tall. Zone 5–6.

Aquilegia formosa (western columbine) A highly ornamental herbaceous perennial with bicolour blooms of red and yellow on long, drooping stems. This plant is highly attractive to both hummingbirds and butterflies, and it naturalizes well by self-seeding. For this reason, you may want to keep it isolated from other *Aquilegia* cultivars, to prevent cross-pollination. Averages 3 feet (90 cm) tall. Zone 3.

Mahonia nervosa
(low Oregon grape)
Colour photo p. 141

Blechnum spicant (deer fern) A durable landscape fern with flattened
evergreen fronds of deep green (bright green in spring) and fertile
fronds that stand very erect in the middle of the plant. This is a very
consistent plant from season to season and it tolerates a wide range
of growing conditions, including morning or late afternoon sun.
Averages 18 inches (45 cm) tall. Zone 3.

Cornus canadensis (bunchberry) An absolutely stunning (but sometimes difficult to grow) evergreen groundcover with tiny, pure
white dogwood blooms, followed by bright red berry clusters.
I have seen this species growing in gritty subalpine soils, as well as
rotten logs in lower elevations. In either case the soil was coarse
and well drained. Success lies in starting out with larger plants
(1 gallon size is best), so forget those little specimens, as they rarely
succeed. Averages 6 inches (15 cm) high. Zone 3.

Cornus stolonifera or *C. sericea* (red-twig dogwood) A deciduous
shrub with green leaves, airy white flower clusters and bright red
stems that play a prominent role in the winter garden. Red-twig
dogwood thrives in moist to wet soils, making it a useful stream-
side planting. A cultivar with bright yellow stems ('Flaviramea') is
also available and makes a wonderful contrast when planted with
the species. Averages 6 to 12 feet (2 to 4 m) tall. Zone 3.

Lonicera ciliosa (western honeysuckle) Our native honeysuckle is
both vastly neglected by many coastal gardeners and taken for
granted by those who live in its natural environs. The bright yel-
lowish-orange trumpet blooms are borne in whorls and are well
frequented by hummingbirds. Flowers mature to translucent red

berry clusters. This species is easy to grow and provides an unusual flower colour in a forest setting. Averages 18 feet (6 m) tall. Zone 6.

Mahonia nervosa (low Oregon grape) A tall evergreen groundcover that tolerates dry forest sites, such as those found under western red cedar *(Thuja plicata)*. Bright yellow terminal blooms are followed by edible (but tart) blue berries and the foliage will often turn to a beautiful bronze-purple during the winter. Averages 2 feet (60 cm) tall. Zone 5-6.

Maianthemum dilatatum (false lily-of-the-valley) An aggressive groundcover for wet, shaded areas that might otherwise go bare. The heart-shaped foliage is quite dense and provides a good foil for the dainty white blooms and berries (green spotted with brown) that follow. It is often low enough for taller perennials such as *Smilacina* (false Solomon's seal) and *Disporum* to coexist with. Averages 4 to 8 inches (10 to 20 cm) tall. Zone 5.

Ribes sanguineum (red-flowering currant) A spectacular spring-blooming shrub that is popular among coastal gardeners and hummingbirds. Pale pink to rose-coloured flowers are borne in abundance in early spring. It is best grown in part to full sun, with good drainage. Averages 3 to 10 feet (1 to 3 m) tall. Zone 5.

Designing a Pesticide-Free Garden

CONWAY LUM & RENATA TRIVERI-COLIN, MANDEVILLE GARDEN CENTRE, BURNABY, B.C.

Designing a landscape with the purpose of reducing pesticide use presents different challenges, depending on the circumstances of your particular garden. The residential landscape can be as diverse as a sprawling rural estate with high maintenance needs, a small urban garden where flowers are being raised exclusively for show competitions, or even a solitary planter sitting on a high-rise balcony.

One of the first steps in reducing pesticide use, no matter what the nature or size of our gardens, is a change in attitude. As gardeners, we can show a lot more tolerance towards minor plant damage simply by lowering our overall expectations. Even nature has room for decay, disease and death as a normal part of the cycle of life.

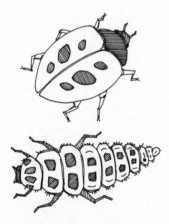

Adult ladybug and ladybug larva

The next thing to consider is increasing your plant diversity — or adding flowers that will bloom over a long period of time — in order to attract beneficial insect populations. Spiders, parasitic wasps, lacewings and ground beetles help to control insect pests by preying on or eating eggs, grubs, pupae or adults. Ornamental plants such as fennel *(Foeniculum vulgare)* provide nectar for parasitoids (predatory insects that parasitize insect pests), and the pollen of yarrow *(Achillea millefolium)* is a source of food for other beneficial insects that prey on insect pests. While more research is being done in this field, you should consider plants from the

Echinacea purpurea 'Alba'
(white coneflower)
Colour photo p. 142

daisy *(Asteraceae)*, carrot *(Apiaceae)*, cabbage *(Brassicaceae)* or mint *(Lamiaceae)* families.

Leaving areas of your garden undisturbed will provide a place for beneficial insects to establish and multiply. This could be simply achieved in the form of a perennial border left unweeded and untended. If your space is limited, try using the following method. Cut up pieces of corrugated cardboard and stack them like a deck of cards. Place them in a partially protected spot, like an open plastic bottle or jug with the bottom cut off. This will provide an alternative hiding place for beneficial insects during the winter months.

Growing a variety of plants can also greatly reduce potential insect problems or diseases, particularly on susceptible plants. For instance, members of the cabbage family are highly susceptible to a fungal disease called clubroot, which can remain in the soil for many years. The best way to avoid the disease is to use long crop rotations with vegetables from another plant family, such as peas and beans. This method ensures that the soil being planted with members of the cabbage family is free of the disease and the alternate crops being planted are not affected by the clubroot fungus.

If you are not willing to give up plants that are known to be susceptible to disease, place them in a prominent location where you can keep a close eye on their progress. When a problem or pest does appear, you can deal with it quickly. Nasturtiums are one such plant. They enjoy widespread favour among gardeners, but black aphids also seem to find them attractive. This pest can be easily controlled at an early stage by simply spraying the foliage with water to wash them off. By keeping careful year-to-year records and checking certain plants at least once — maybe twice — a week, a pest outbreak can be noted and controlled before it becomes unmanageable.

It's important to be able to distinguish friend from foe. Too few gardeners recognize the larvae of ladybird beetles — which are voracious aphid predators — since they hardly resemble the adults. Ants present a similar problem; many people don't consider ants detrimental to plant health, but there is a strong symbiotic relationship between ants and aphids. Ants cultivate aphids for their "honeydew" (the undigested plant sugars that aphids leave behind), which ants use as food. The honeydew can also attract a black fungal growth called sooty mould.

DEALING WITH WEEDS

One of the most time-consuming tasks in the garden can be the lawn. This is also an area where gardeners are most likely to use herbicides and pesticides. Lawns take a great amount of care when compared to a mixed shrub or flower border, so one of the first things to consider is reducing the amount of space in your garden dedicated to turf. If this is not an option, you can reduce herbicide use by overseeding with perennial ryegrass two to four times a year. This keeps the turf thick and chokes out weeds. For a lower-maintenance lawn, seed with sheep fescue, a grass species that is drought tolerant and requires much less mowing.

Random weeds in flower beds can also be easily handled with the use of a hoe. This works well to control chickweed, for instance, by disturbing the soil surface and preventing any dormant seeds buried underneath from sprouting. For larger areas, there are propane burner tools that can be used to eradicate weeds and edge lawns, with much less impact on the environment than chemical weed sprays.

FLOWERS THAT ATTRACT BENEFICIAL INSECTS

Here are some specific members of the mustard family *(Brassicaceae)*, mint family *(Lamiaceae)* and aster family *(Asteraceae)* to consider for your landscape. Many of these plants bloom throughout the season or have overlapping flowering periods, ensuring a continual food source for the most beneficial insects.

Aster Family
Achillea millefolium (yarrow) Zone 2
Coreopsis verticillata (tickseed) Zone 3
Echinacea purpurea (purple coneflower) Zone 3
Gaillardia x *grandiflora* (blanket flower) Zone 2
Leucanthemum x *superbum* (shasta daisy) Zone 4

Mint Family
Lavandula angustifolia (English lavender) Zone 4
Melissa officinalis (lemon balm) Zone 4
Salvia nemerosa (perennial salvia) Zone 3
Thymus vulgaris (common thyme) Zone 5

Mustard Family
Aurinia saxatalis (basket-of-gold) Zone 3
Iberis sempervirens (candytuft) Zone 3
Lobularia maritima (sweet alyssum) Annual

SLUG AND SNAIL-RESISTANT PLANTS

In the Pacific Northwest, slugs and snails are often the scourge of ornamental borders. Yet many gardeners are hesitant to resort to standard slug baits because the active ingredient, metaldehyde, is equally poisonous to birds, wildlife and domestic pets. A wildlife-friendly organic bait (with ferric phosphate) is also available, but another option, planting perennials and bulbs that sustain only minor damage, seems to work quite well for a growing number of gardeners. Here is a list of ten fairly common plants that are not attractive to slugs and snails.

Bergenia cordifolia (pig-squeak) Zone 2
Corydalis lutea (golden corydalis) Zone 4
Dicentra eximia (low bleeding heart) Zone 3
Epimedium x *rubrum* (barrenwort) Zone 4
Euphorbia amygdaloides (wood spurge) Zone 5
Galanthus nivalis (snowdrop) Zone 3
Helleborus niger (Christmas rose) Zone 4
Hosta 'Canadian Shield', *H.* 'Blue Wedgewood' Zone 2
Pulmonaria hybrids (lungwort) Zone 3
Stachys byzantina (lamb's ear) Zone 3

Butterflies in Your Garden
HENDRIK MEEKEL, APRIL MEADOWS LANDSCAPE, WHONNOCK, B.C.

What makes butterflies so important to us? Perhaps it is simply that life on earth, as we know it, would not be the same without them. We can all appreciate the delicate movements of a butterfly flying by or sipping nectar from a flower, but a closer look reveals the incredibly detailed patterns on either side of their wings. These designs are so intricate that even within one species, there are no two exactly the same!

Male and female butterflies are quite often different in design. This is called sexual dimorphism and it helps them recognize each other in flight, so they can find a potential mate. Other species have evolved to resemble a different, poisonous butterfly, in order to avoid being eaten by birds or other predators. The best example of this in North America is the viceroy's

Swallowtail
(Photo: Hendrik Meekel)

mimicry of the poisonous monarch butterfly (which derives its toxins while eating from the milkweed plant in its larval stage).

There are 20,000 species of butterflies in the world and most of them are tropical. All butterflies are first caterpillars, and every species has one or just a few host plants on which the larvae can feed, which makes it all the more important to know a little bit about their life cycles and habitats. The information here focuses mainly on North American gardens and is specific to the Pacific Northwest region.

LEARN AND RESPECT

Butterflies go through a complete metamorphosis; there are four stages in their life cycle — egg, caterpillar, chrysalis and butterfly. The female butterfly lays her eggs on the host plant and in an average of 8 to 14 days, those eggs hatch into tiny caterpillars. These caterpillars usually eat new-growth leaves and moult their skin about four or five times. As the caterpillars get larger, they change their appearance or colour pattern to whatever is best suited for their survival. Swallowtail butterflies are the best example of survival mimicries, often looking like a speck of dirt, then bird droppings, and finally changing to resemble a snake or lizard head in larval stages. When irritated, a Y-shaped organ protrudes from the body to mimic a snake's tongue; it even secretes a foul odour to help repel the threatening predator.

Some species are brightly coloured to indicate their toxins, which they concentrate and store while feeding as caterpillars on their host plants. In a sense, all caterpillars are parasitic, choosing to feed on just one or a few species of plants. When feeding, most only partially defoliate a branch

or leaf so as not to lose their camouflage protection. Others are so viv-
idly coloured they can easily be spotted by a bird, but the bird will soon
learn about the caterpillar's disagreeable flavour and remember not to eat
it again. Some caterpillars live in large groups and can quickly defoliate a
branch or even an entire plant, but these host plants are resilient and can
quickly regenerate after the caterpillars have left to pupate into a chrysalis.
Two good examples of this are mourning cloak caterpillars, which often
strip willow branches, and tortoiseshell caterpillars, which defoliate sting-
ing nettle.

The caterpillar stage takes about a month, so in our region there is usually only one generation a year. In warmer climates there could be two or
even continuous overlapping broods. The winter season in our temperate climate causes every species to find a special niche for survival. That is
why all stages of hibernation can be found in our area, depending on the
species. There is no set length of time for how long a stage of metamorphosis can last, although in the Fraser Valley it generally takes most species 1 to 2 weeks for eggs, 1 month for caterpillars, and 1 to 2 months or
8 to 10 months for the chrysalis, ending with 2 to 3 weeks or 6 months for
butterflies, depending on the species. Many people think butterflies only
live a day or two but this is not the case. Most of them have a lifespan of
about 2 to 3 weeks. This short stage in their life is what most people focus
on, because butterflies have come to symbolize beauty and freedom in the
natural world we live in.

The survival rate of butterflies in nature is usually less than 5 percent.
This means that for every 100 eggs laid, only five or less will make it to
adulthood. So it is always a good idea to provide some room in your garden for the few survivors.

DESIGNING A BUTTERFLY GARDEN

Butterflies are cold-blooded; this means they need sunshine and warmer
temperatures in order to be content in our gardens. If your landscape is
situated on a north slope, it may be difficult to attract butterflies or design
a suitable garden, but as long as the sun can get through, all will be well!

There are some challenges to be met when you attempt to design a butterfly garden. Look to native plant species to find out which ones are beneficial for attracting butterflies and their caterpillars. The local library is a
good place to start, as most are stocked with books on native plants in your
area and how to identify them. Garden centres may also be able to help you
acquire these plants and some of the materials needed in the construction
of your new landscape.

Most gardens are smaller than we realize, so keep this in mind before
you allot a portion for a butterfly garden. Larger trees and shrubs should
be planted on the north side of your property, as this will allow for optimum sunlight. It is also important to provide host species in abundance,

especially if the plants are smaller. Select species rather than cultivars when choosing plants. Even a subtle difference such as variegation on a host plant may cause butterflies to reject it, because the virus that causes the variegation also reduces the plant's vigour.

One thing you will soon learn is that the appearance of your garden will change. What you may have considered a weed will have to be re-evaluated and examined when designing a butterfly garden. It is not necessarily a weed from nature's perspective. In fact, much of what we admire as ornamental plants in our landscapes might be considered as weeds from another perspective.

The chrysalis stage of butterflies relies heavily on camouflage. So it might be helpful to know that your garden should not always be groomed and cut down in the fall. The reason for this is that it is highly likely that you may accidentally discard some chrysalises and inadvertently separate future caterpillars from their food source. So learn to incorporate some rough spots into your landscape.

The single major reason for the decline of butterflies is urban or industrial sprawl and the resulting loss of natural habitat. Most butterflies can be slow to adapt to new host plant species, even if they are in the same plant family.

The prospect of global warming is of incidental benefit to butterflies. Since they are cold-blooded, the higher temperatures allow them to be more active and fly greater distances. So the likelihood of them coming through your garden may be much greater in the future — which is all the more reason to provide some habitat for them in your landscape.

FEEDING HABITS

Water attracts butterflies, so having a water source in your garden is a necessity. Some butterflies like to puddle (sip water) in groups in the morning or late afternoon, when moisture wells up from the ground or where water has collected over the evening. They do this to not only collect water, but also to get minerals. This is why a butterfly may occasionally land on your arm to collect mineral salts from your skin. Also, some butterflies (especially admirals) like to sip on rotten fruit — so the fallen apples from your trees can benefit butterflies as well as birds.

Double flowers are not the best choice in a butterfly garden because there is less nectar available in these and it is much harder for the butterflies to find. Butterflies in general are not known for eating pollen — the exception being a few tropical species and monarchs, which tend to have a longer adult life span. When choosing the right host plants for your garden, indigenous species should always be your first choice. But regardless of your plant selections, nature always seems to find a way to adapt and surprise us yet again.

HOST PLANTS FOR BUTTERFLY CATERPILLARS

HOST PLANT	ZONE	BUTTERFLY SPECIES
Asclepias species (milkweed)	3 to 4	monarch butterflies
Aster novi-belgii (Michaelmas daisy)	3	mylitta crescent spot
Cirsium vulgare (thistle)	2	painted lady
Dicentra formosa (western bleeding heart)	5	Parnassius clodius
Gaultheria shallon, Arctostaphylos (salal, bearberry)	3 to 5	brown elfin
Heracleum lanatum (cow's parsnip)	3	anise swallowtail
Holcus lanatus, Bromus, Festuca (grasses)	3 to 5	woodland skipper
Lupinus, Trifolium (clovers) and other **legumes** (pea family)	3 to 4	western tail blue, sulphurs, gray hairstreak
Malva **species** (mallow)	3 to 6	westcoast lady
Pinus monticola, P. contorta var. *latifolia* (white, lodgepole pine)	5	western pine elfin
Plantago **species** (plantain)	3	North American buckeye
Poa **species,** *Deschampsia* **species,** *Phleum* **species** (grasses)	3 to 5	plain ringlet
Prunus emarginata (bitter cherry)	3	pale tiger swallowtail
Prunus virginiana (chokecherry)	3	two-tailed swallowtail
Pseudotsuga menziesii, *Pinus* (Douglas fir, pine)	2 to 7	pine white
Rumex occidentalis (western dock)	5	purplish copper
Salix **species and cultivars** (willow), **cottonwood, aspen**	2 to 6	western tiger swallowtail, mourning cloak, white admiral
Sedum **species** (stonecrop)	2 to 3	Parnassius phoebes
Spiraea, Holodiscus, Cornus (spirea, oceanspray, dogwood)	3 to 5	spring azure
Thuja plicata (western red cedar)	6	Rosner's hairstreak
Urtica **species** (stinging nettle)	4	anglewing, tortoiseshell, admiral butterflies
Viola **species** (violets)	3 to 5	fritillaries

PLANTS FOR ATTRACTING BUTTERFLIES

Although many butterflies may visit the dandelions and clover in your lawn, this is not the safest habitat, as cats love to pounce on them to play. However, there are many ornamental shrubs and perennials (pink, purple and blue flowers seem best) that will attract butterflies to your garden equally as well. Here are a few of the best to choose from.

Annuals and Perennials

Allium **species** (flowering onion) Zone 3 to 6
Alyssum, marigolds, dahlias (annual flowers)
Hesperis matronalis (sweet rocket) Zone 2
Penstemon **species** (penstemon) Zone 3 to 7
Phlox paniculata (garden phlox) Zone 3
Verbena bonariensis (tall verbena) Zone 7

Shrubs

Daphne **species** (daphne) Zone 3 to 7
Ligustrum **species and cultivars** (privet) Zone 3 to 7
Ribes sanguineum (red-flowering currant) Zone 6
Syringa vulgaris (French lilac) Zone 3
Viburnum **species** (viburnum) Zone 3 to 7

CHOOSING THE RIGHT BUTTERFLY PLANTS

Flowers are designed to be pollinated by insects and understanding this symbiotic relationship will help you appreciate the delicate balance that exists in nature. Sometimes this balance is disturbed by the introduction of a non-native species, as evidenced in the Hawaiian Islands, where aggressive plant species are supplanting indigenous ones. It can be a privilege to create gardens with beautiful plants from around the world, but this can come with consequences. In our area, butterfly bush *(Buddleia davidii)* is quickly self-seeding and becoming a weed that butterflies absolutely adore. So choose your butterfly plants carefully.

Gardening for Birds

CALVOR PALMATEER, FOR WILD BIRDS AND GARDENERS, VICTORIA, B.C.

Many people now realize that gardens only come fully alive when they are home to a number of resident or transient birds. If you want to attract these cheery visitors to your landscape, you must provide them with the basics of food and shelter. The standard bird menu includes seeds, insects, berries, and nectar or sap.

SEED

Most gardeners trying to attract birds start out by placing seed feeders, which are a practical and efficient way to provide seed-eating birds with food. The alternative is to grow plants that produce seed, but as most gardeners quickly discover, seed germinates and creates weeding problems. Although feeders come in various shapes and sizes, that typically doesn't affect the type of bird that uses them (larger species may have some diffi- culty using some feeders but they soon learn to adapt). When choosing a feeder for a garden, remember that the feeder must be easy to clean, thus encouraging regular maintenance. It is important to choose a design that keeps the seed dry, as mouldy seed is a health hazard to birds. And make sure that the feeder is designed to prevent birds from defecating onto the seed, as this is also a source of disease for birds.

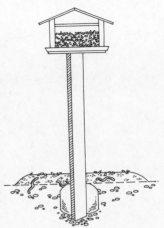

Mulching below bird feeders

Placement of feeders can be critical for bird safety. Those located near the house must be placed within 5 feet (1.5 m) of windows. This ensures that birds that are startled and fly off in a panic will not have enough momentum to break their necks should they hit a window. Proximity to a window also enhances your viewing enjoyment: there's nothing like being close enough to the birds that you don't need binoculars to see them! Inter- estingly, the birds soon become habituated to your movements behind the windows and learn not to fly away. It is also critical to avoid placing feeders near glass deck railings. Birds never learn that there is glass under the rail- ing and you will have regular collisions and possible fatalities. The only way to solve this particular problem is to hang netting in front of the glass.

The type of seed used in feeders is also very important. Even though most people believe that mixed seed is the best choice, this is not true. If you take the time to watch, you will notice that birds seek out the sunflower seeds and scatter the rest. The end result of using mixed seed is unsightly mounds of uneaten seed that ends up on the ground, where it will eventu- ally sprout or rot. From 30 years of experience I have learned that the best seed choice is hulled sunflower. All the birds eat it and very little is thrown to the ground. The odd bird out is the house sparrow, which prefers millet. If more than one seed is offered, it should be provided in separate feed- ers. To further cut down on maintenance, the area under the feeders can be paved for easy cleanup. One excellent method is to put a layer of fine bark mulch under the feeders which extends out for about 4 feet (1.2 m). Add some red compost worms, which will keep the surface clean by pull- ing down the bird droppings and seed chaff. The added bonus is that you provide an area for American robins to search for worms.

INSECTS

Generally, birds will search for insects on their own in the garden. Many seed-eaters change their diet to insects when raising young, which is a bonus for the gardener whose aphids and other pests are thus controlled. To make your landscape even more attractive to insectivores such as chick- adees, nuthatches, bushtits, woodpeckers and wrens, all you have to do is provide them with suet. Remember, however, that cats, dogs, raccoons and rats also consider suet a fine snack. Hang it up high where only birds can reach it, then put a bowl or plate over it to keep it cool and dry. When buying suet, avoid any brand that uses millet or ground corn as a major ingredient. Although these cheap fillers reduce the price, the result is that you are forcing insectivorous birds to eat cereal grains that are not a part of their normal diet. Try to purchase suet only with oily seeds and nuts such as sunflowers, peanuts and almonds. Remember to hang suet close to the window to enhance your viewing pleasure and prevent window kills.

BERRIES

Some species of birds, such as thrushes, switch to berries in the winter. Others, like waxwings, eat berries year-round. When planting a garden, check around for native plants that produce berries. How fast these plants are stripped of their fruit will show you which plants are most popular with your birds. Berries I have had great success with include blueberries, raspberries, elderberries, cotoneaster, viburnums, pyracantha and saskatoonberries. Add these to your garden and you will attract many additional bird species to admire. Although not popular with birds in temperate climates, snowberry *(Symphoricarpos albus)* may be eaten as a hardship food in colder areas.

Please remember that berries make ingenious use of the digestive system of birds as a method of seed transferal — a rather messy process. When eating berries, birds tend to fly to a perch and digest their meal. If cars, paths and patios are below that perch, then deposits will be made.

NECTAR

Hummingbirds are the most common type of bird that thrives on nectar, but other species, such as orioles, tanagers, warblers and house finches, also drink this sweet elixir. If you choose to buy a nectar-feeder, select one that is easy to clean and does not drip. Not only is a clean feeder necessary for bird health, but dripping feeders will attract wasps and ants that can discourage the hummingbirds from feeding. A drippy feeder also creates a sticky mess that will vex most gardeners. It's easy to make your own nectar: just use a solution of ¼ to ⅓ cup (50 to 75 mL) white sugar to one cup (250 mL) boiling water. Do not use red dye, honey or artificial sweeteners.

When designing a garden to attract hummingbirds, remember that the plants should be clustered. Hummingbirds need a large number of nectar-producing blossoms to promote territorial behavior. If the patches of blossoms are too small, the hummingbirds will "trapline," meaning they will fly from patch to patch, feeding as they go. For summer blooms on the west coast I use *phygelius, salvias, penstemons* and *fuchsia* as the backbone of my hummingbird-friendly plantings. In the springtime, *Ribes sanguineum* (red-flowering currant) is the major focus of male Rufous Hummingbirds. Those living in colder interior regions of British Columbia can bring lots of

Mahonia 'Charity'
Colour photo p. 143

hummingbirds into their gardens with *Ribes odoratum* and *Lonicera* 'Drop-more Scarlet' (red honeysuckle). Pacific Northwest gardeners living where the climate is mild will find that winter-flowering plants, such as *Mahonia* 'Charity' and *Grevillea* 'Victoria,' are used by Anna's Hummingbirds.

COVER PLANTINGS

When landscaping a property for birds, plan some areas for cover. An ideal situation is a densely planted area where birds can seek protection from bad weather and elude predators. Evergreen shrubs and conifers are the best choices for cover plants. My garden has dense plantings of *Ceanothus, Pyracantha, Escallonia* and conifers. Birds often use these same plants to nest in during the breeding season.

BIRD HOUSING

Several species happily take advantage of the offer of a nest box when they are provided with one. Swallows, chickadees, nuthatches and wrens are frequent tenants in my nest boxes, although species will vary depending on where you live. Nest boxes also make up for the lack of natural holes in suburban areas that have long-since supplanted traditional bird habitat. In addition, nest boxes can provide shelter for some species at night and during periods of bad weather.

Birds are lively, entertaining and musical — and one of the few reminders of nature's charm that we increasingly urbanized folk can have regular access to. And any landscape, however modest, can become a bird sanctuary. Exploring this low-cost design option will definitely enhance the pleasure that your garden already gives you. When buying a bird feeder, selecting birdseed or choosing bird-attracting plants, it is always a good idea to visit a specialty store or consult with someone with extensive local knowledge to ensure your long-term success.

TOP PLANTS TO ATTRACT BIRDS TO YOUR GARDEN

Berry plants that attract thrushes, waxwings, woodpeckers and jays.

Amelanchier (saskatoonberry) Zone 2

Aronia (chokecherry) Zone 3

Cotoneaster (cultivars and species) Zone 3–8 depending on species

Crataegus (hawthorn) Zone 3–8 depending on species

Malus (crabapple) Zone 3–8 depending on species

Pyracantha (firethorn) Zone 6

Ribes (currant) Zone 3–8 depending on species

Rubus (raspberries and blackberries) Zone 3–8 depending on species

Sambucus nigra (black elderberry) Zone 3

Vaccinium (blueberries) Zone 3–8 depending on species

Nectar plants that attract hummingbirds.

Delphinium (old-fashioned singles) Zone 3

Fuchsia (hardy forms) Zone 6–8 depending on variety

Kniphofia (red-hot poker) Zone 6–8 depending on species

Lobelia (perennial forms) Zone 3–8 depending on species

Lonicera (honeysuckle) Zone 2–8 depending on species

Monarda (beebalm) Zone 3–8 depending on cultivar

Penstemon (including cultivars) Zone 3–8 depending on species

Phygelius (Cape fuchsia) Zone 7

Ribes (flowering currant) Zone 3–8 depending on species

Salvia (sages) Zone 3–8 depending on species

Penstemon 'Candywine'
Colour photo p.143

CHAPTER 9
The Edible Landscape

The garden was planted with a generous supply of useful roots and herbs; but, as manure was not allowed to profane the virgin soil, few of these vegetable treasures ever came up. Purslane reigned supreme, and the disappointed planters ate it philosophically, deciding that Nature knew what was best for them….
    Louisa May Alcott, *Transcendental Wild Oats*

Many gardeners seem to have a serious deficiency of common sense when it comes to dealing with fruits and vegetables. We often have a naive notion that all pests and diseases will stay at arm's length so we can enjoy the fruits of our labour. We don't mind struggling with fussy ornamentals, such as roses or blue Himalayan poppies, but we seem to have less patience when problems arise with our apples, tomatoes, peppers and herbs.

There is also a false perception that in our grandparents' day, fruits and vegetables grew like weeds and they will gladly do so again, if we only take the time to plant them. The truth is that even back then the apples got canker, the vegetable garden sprouted dandelions and the birds got the cherries just as they ripened.

I think you will find the pieces in this chapter both pragmatic and humorous — necessary qualities if you plan to grow fruits and vegetables for any length of time.

Quince fruit (*Cydonia oblonga*)
Colour photo p. 144

Creating an Urban Orchard
MICHAEL LASCELLE, AMSTERDAM GARDEN CENTRE, PITT MEADOWS, B.C.

CHOOSING THE RIGHT TREES

As a nursery manager, I often see more people coming in to buy replacement fruit trees than I do first-time buyers. The reasons are almost always the same — either the trees they purchased have quickly declined into poor health (scab and canker are the most common problems in our wet coastal climate) or they are not producing any fruit, even after maturity. Quite often this is a problem of gardeners buying their favorite eating apple without finding out if it tolerates local conditions or if they need to grow another tree for cross-pollination.

The issue of cross-pollination can be quite complex. I can recall one instance when a gentleman bought two Gravenstein apple trees, thinking they could pollinate each other. Gravenstein is a triploid and produces very little viable pollen, so it needs the pollen from another apple cultivar that blooms at the same time in order to produce fruit of its own. Making it even more complicated is the fact that if the pollinator tree is not self-fertile, it will also require a pollination partner, as the Gravenstein is unable to reciprocate!

Another critical factor in producing fruit successfully is matching your climate zone and weather conditions to the appropriate fruit trees. A good local example is McIntosh apples. Many people want to plant a McIntosh apple tree because it is their favourite eating apple, but the majority of this crop is commercially grown in the Okanagan valley in the British Columbia interior, where the winters are cold and the summers long and hot. This cultivar responds very poorly and declines quickly in the wet springs and often cool summers of the coast.

There are also minimum temperature barriers that affect those gardening in zones 2 to 4. Hardy apples ('Goodland'), pears ('Early Golden') and plums ('Pembina') are available (as are other fruits) for northern or interior B.C. areas, but the selection is not the same as for those living in warmer areas.

Lastly, if you only have room for a few trees in your garden, try to avoid varieties that crop every other year (biennially). 'Green Gage' plum and 'Bramley's Seedling' apple are two examples. Choose cultivars that produce consistent, large yields from year to year. A few coastal varieties have proven to be quite reliable. 'Italian Prune' plum, 'Bosc' pear and 'Lapins' cherry are reliable producers in the Lower Mainland. Refer to local magazines and garden guides and ask questions before you buy.

LESS IS MORE

An urban orchard is just that — urban — and cramming in as many trees as you can fit on a small lot will not result in bumper crops of fruit. But a few mature, well-spaced trees that are properly maintained are quite capable of producing more fruit than the average homeowner is able to consume fresh or possibly even preserve. In the case of an urban orchard, less is definitely more!

One solution for those hoping to raise more than one variety of a particular fruit is to plant trees with multiple grafts. These specialty items have anywhere from 3 to 8 (in the case of some espaliers) different cultivars grafted onto a single stock. The advantage here is that each variety cross-pollinates the others to maximize production.

All fruit trees require good air circulation, ample sun exposure, adequate soil and frost drainage and possibly additional irrigation during

---

COASTAL FRUIT TREE SELECTIONS

Here are a few fruit tree cultivars that are well adapted to our coastal conditions.

Apples 'Jonafree', 'Prima', 'Florina', 'Redfree', 'Liberty', 'Spartan', 'Red Gravenstein', 'Yellow Transparent', 'Elstar', 'Akane', 'Cox's Orange Pippin', 'Lodi', 'Golden & Scarlet Sentinel'.

Pears 'Clapp's Favorite', 'Bartlett', 'Aurora', 'Conference', 'Sierra', 'Bosc', 'Highland'.

Cherries 'Lapins', 'Rainier', 'Compact Stella', 'Aaron', 'Compact Bing', 'Sweetheart', 'Sam', 'SchattenMorello' (sour), 'Montmorency' (sour).

Asian Pears 'Chojuro', '20th Century', 'Hosui', 'Shinseiki', 'Seuri'.

Plums 'Italian Prune', 'Peach Plum', 'Mirabell', Redheart', 'Shiro', 'Santa Rosa',

Peaches and Nectarines 'Frost', 'Renton', Pacific Gold', 'Red Haven', Red Gold'.

Figs 'Brown Turkey', 'Italian Honey Fig', 'Desert King'.

An espalier apple trained into a Belgian fence form at the UBC Botanical Garden, Vancouver, B.C.

dry spells, while the fruit is still developing. Fruit trees that are crowded together will shade each other, compete for moisture and nutrients and slow down air flow. This can lead to the rapid spread of fungal problems and other diseases.

So before you make that trip to your local garden centre or nursery in search of fruit trees, consider their cultural needs and the space required to grow them. Purchase accordingly and, in the end, you'll save both time and money.

ROOTSTOCKS

If you want to attempt an urban orchard, you will have to inform yourself about rootstocks. Not only do they affect ultimate size, they can also determine the age of maturity, the possible need for long-term staking and the types of soil the tree will tolerate. A small selection of fruit trees, known as genetic dwarfs (such as 'Golden Glory' peach) or, in the case of apples, columnar ('Scarlet Sentinel' apple), have a naturally compact branch structure and growth habit — their growth rate is only slightly affected by rootstocks. Rootstocks also have varying degrees of hardiness.

The root stock often affects the ultimate fruit tree size. In apples, these range from dwarf (EM9) to semi-dwarf (M26) with the largest tree crown representing a standard apple

ROOTSTOCKS COMMONLY USED

Apples

M26 is semi-dwarfing, producing trees 40 percent of standard size. It prefers fertile soils.

EM9 is very dwarfing, producing trees 30 percent of standard size. It requires permanent support.

Bud 9 is very dwarfing, producing trees 50 percent of standard size. It is resistant to collar rot and extremely hardy.

Cherries

Gisela is very dwarfing, producing trees 50 percent of standard size. It allows for early fruit production and is very hardy.

Colt is slightly dwarfing, producing trees which average 15 to 18 feet (5 to 6 m) tall. It is not suited for extreme cold or drought.

Mazzard is lightly dwarfing, producing trees 80 percent of standard size. It also produces large crops.

Pears

Quince A produces a medium-sized tree. It is not compatible with all pears and is moderately hardy.

OH x F produces trees up to 13 feet (4.5 m) tall. it is resistant to fireblight and hardy in zones 5 to 9.

Plums

St. Julien A is semi-dwarfing, producing trees up to 13 feet (4.5 m) tall (depending on the cultivar).

Myrobalan produces trees about 18 feet (6 m) tall. It tolerates heavy soils and is hardy.

POLLINATION

There was a time when fruit trees grew in every backyard and empty lots or undeveloped lane allowances fostered healthy populations of beneficial insects. Unfortunately, those days of abundant pollen and pollinators are over. Today's urban gardeners should seriously consider self-fertile trees, particularly if space is an issue.

All peaches, sour cherries *(Prunus cerasus),* mulberries, quince *(Cydonia oblonga)* and most apricots are reliably self-fertile, so you only need one tree to produce fruit. You will have to be quite selective when it comes to choosing sweet cherries ('Sweetheart'), apples ('Golden Delicious'), plums ('Stanley', 'Italian Prune') and pears ('Bosc') but if you choose these, they will be reliably self-fertile in zones 5–9. (In colder regions, the varieties will differ.)

Just having self-fertile trees does not always solve pollination problems. Beneficial insects are still needed to transfer the pollen and fertilize the flowers. You can attract natural pollinators such as bumblebees, wild honey bees, mason bees *(Osmia lignaria)* or leaf-cutting bees to your garden by planting flowers to lure them (see the following checklist) and by providing artificial nesting sites, such as bee boxes.

If you want to encourage wild pollinators (including mason bees) in your garden, here is a short list of ornamental shrubs, trees and perennials known to attract them.

Cercis canadensis (eastern redbud) Zone 4
Doronicum caucasicum (leopard's bane) Zone 3
Erica carnea (winter heather) Zone 6
Erysimum/Cheiranthus (wallflower) Zone 3 to 6
Mahonia aquifolium (Oregon grape) Zone 6
Myosotis alpestris (forget-me-not) Zone 3
Pieris japonica (lily-of-the-valley shrub) Zone 6
Viola odorata (sweet violet) Zone 6

BUILDING A BEE BOX

Keeping those wild pollinators close to your garden is as easy as providing them with a nesting box. You can create your own with a 4 × 4-inch (10 × 10-cm) block of wood that is 6 inches (15 cm) long. Using a ⅜ inch drill bit, drill a succession of holes on the 4-inch (10-cm) face that are ¾ inch (2 cm) apart and 4 inches (10 cm) deep. The wood should be untreated, and pine, fir or hemlock are the best choices (do not use cedar). A similar habitat can be achieved by purchasing cardboard straws of the same diameter and length (4 inches/10 cm), and bundling them in a weatherproof shell, such as a 2-litre plastic pop bottle with the top cut off.

The nesting box should be mounted on its side, under the eave of a building, preferably on a south exposure where it gets some morning sun and protection from the rain. These artificial nesting boxes are suitable replacements for the stems of dead shrubs or weeds that used to exist in many undeveloped areas. From April to late June, try to provide a source of mud nearby, as the female mason bee lays an egg on a bed of pollen in the tube (or hole), then seals it up with a layer of mud. She repeats this process until the tube is full and then she applies an extra thick layer of mud to close the opening.

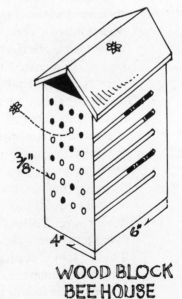

WOOD BLOCK
BEE HOUSE

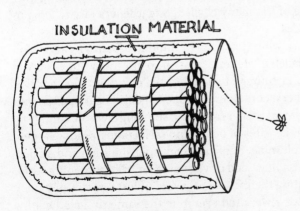

INSULATION MATERIAL

CARDBOARD STRAW BEE BOX

The compost demonstration garden in Vancouver, B.C. (Photo: City Farmer)

Watch Your Step — Food Gardening in Small Spaces

SPRING GILLARD, CITY FARMER, VANCOUVER, B.C.

"I've fallen and I can't get up," said a voice from inside a large yellow chrysanthemum. I was walking along a stretch of community gardens in Kitsilano when I heard a woman cry out. One of the gardeners had fallen and was suspended inside the bush; she couldn't reach the ground to push herself back up. Compost Hotline Operator to the rescue! Apparently, falling into large bushes is just one of the many challenges gardeners face when gardening in cramped spaces.

I work for City Farmer, which has been promoting urban agriculture for 25 years now (rescuing fallen gardeners is just one of my many duties). Over the years, we have met, encouraged and educated countless food gardeners. Community gardeners, container gardeners, guerilla gardeners, budding green thumbs, master gardeners and even smoking environmentalists have all passed through the gates of our Compost Demonstration Garden in Vancouver, British Columbia. Some are seeking inspiration and advice, others just want to share a new seed or vegetable, or tell a gardening story. Whether they're cultivating their whole backyard or just one tiny patch on their front boulevard, we always tell everyone the same thing: a healthy garden begins with healthy soil.

"Okay, so the first thing to do is build up your soil with good topsoil and compost to hold the moisture in the soil," said Sharon Slack, our intrepid head gardener. She was teaching her annual four-week "Introduction to Organic Food Gardening" course to a group of eager new students and I was eavesdropping. Most of the students have small plots or only a balcony to garden in.

"When you have lots of organic matter in the soil, earthworms are drawn to the site and they will keep your soil well aerated," said Sharon. "You'll want to mound the soil up to 12 inches, as we have done here in our beds." She gestured towards the dozen or so neat beds that make up our food garden. Herbs and vegetables need about six inches (15 cm) of soil to thrive and root crops need 10 to 12 (25 to 30 cm). "If you like, you can frame the bed with untreated wood or rocks."

Raised beds are recommended for vegetable gardening, even in small spaces. Planting above the ground ensures good drainage. It also helps protect crops from heavy rain runoff or frost and is ideal for shallow or clay-based soils. And because the soil warms up more rapidly in the spring, you'll be harvesting your vegetables earlier. Then you can phone your friends back east and rub it in.

In small spaces, good soil is even more critical to keeping pests and diseases at bay, so you may want to begin with a soil test. You can pick up a kit from any garden centre. If your soil is acidic, as most local soils are, you'll want to add lime (except for potatoes).

Once you've added some compost and maybe some lime to your soil, you can amend it from there for the specific needs of each vegetable. For example, carrots usually need lighter, sandier soils. Zucchini and Swiss chard are heavy feeders and may require extra compost or manure. Leafy veggies need extra nitrogen so their leaves will grow faster and be more tender. Fruiting vegetables need phosphorus (we use rock phosphate) and nitrogen. Root crops need more potassium (try untreated wood ash when preparing the soil in the spring and fall).

Size is another consideration when planning a vegetable garden. Typically, a community garden plot is about 3 feet wide by 10 feet in length (0.9 × 3 m). Ideally, you want the bed to be an arm's length across, so you can get to the plants easily from either side. But your little plot does not have to be rectangular or square, it can be any size or shape. And if you're really in a tight corner, consider growing upwards. Beans, cucumbers and squash can be trained up stakes or trellises. A bean teepee doubles as a fun place to hide from the kids in the summer or it can block the view of a neighbour's unkempt compost bin.

One of Sharon's students wanted to know how much light she would need.

"You'll want six to eight hours of sun per day," Sharon answered. "Especially if you want to grow tomatoes, eggplants, peppers or cantaloupes. They need very hot conditions."

There are tricks to heating soil up, mind you. We often lay black plastic over the entire bed and then cut holes into it and plant the peppers into the holes. The plastic really helps intensify the heat. And it's a heck of a lot easier to control the temperature than neighbouring gardeners.

"The environmentalist in the plot next to mine is growing nothing but tobacco this year," said a new community gardener.

Sharon nodded sympathetically. She had picked her share of butts out of our broccoli bed.

"Doesn't tobacco get really large and leafy?" she asked. "I'm worried that it will shade my vegetables too much."

"Yes, it does," said Sharon, "but you can still plant root veggies such as carrots, radishes and salad greens in shadier areas."

We tend to plant quite intensively in our garden to show just how much food it is possible to grow in a relatively small area and to help hold the soil in place. You might start with some lettuces, carrots, radishes, pole beans and maybe some tomatoes, broccoli or kale.

"But don't plant too many seeds. Plant only what your family will eat and in quantities that you can consume fresh, or are able to preserve for winter."

Sharon began handing out copies of the West Coast Seeds catalogue. "This catalogue is your bible," she said.

And she's right. It tells you all about planting times and gives lots of other good information. Don't forget to read the seed package, too. If you're not planting from seed but are using nursery plants, check with the nursery on when the plants should go in the ground. Each has its ideal planting time and conditions. In other words, plant the right plant in the right place at the right time.

CITY FARMER'S COMPOST TEA

Fill a burlap sack with finished compost to the quarter mark. Set it into a five-gallon (20-L) bucket and fill with water. Brew for about a week or so and then water your heavy feeders with it.

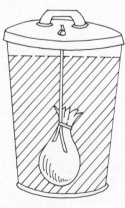

We like to grow a great diversity of crops at City Farmer. We grow high-protein crops like beans and amaranth *(Amaranthus caudatus),* and exotics like artichokes, ground cherries, mizuna, red celery and edame (soybeans). And we have our favourites, like the mesclun salad mix from West Coast Seeds — a cut-and-come-again blend that kept staff, volunteers and a local hospice in greens all summer long.

We tend to plant some crops that are not only edible but serve as ornamentals as well. For example, amaranth, cardoon *(Cynara cardunculus)* and quinoa all look as pretty as they taste. And by companion planting — interplanting flowers like marigolds, nasturtiums or even a chrysanthemum with the veggies — you not only fool the pests, you can fool the public. A visiting television reporter once asked Sharon where the vegetables were because with all of our crops in bloom, it looked more like a flower garden.

Diversity is also an important biological pest control strategy. If you grow vegetables that belong to the same plant family in the same spot two years in a row, they will be more prone to specific pests and diseases.

Underplanted bush beans
(Photo: City Farmer)

And in addition to confusing pests, flowers can also help attract beneficial insects and birds.

When you harvest your lettuces or radishes, plant more to keep yourself in salad fixings all summer long. In fall, Sharon plants garlic at the same time the tulip bulbs are going in. Garlic doesn't take up much room while it's growing, then when you take the garlic out in early- to mid-July, you can plant fast-growing bush beans, lettuces or radishes.

"Okay, so soil, drainage, light and right plant, right place, right time are all important considerations," Sharon summarized. "But there's something we haven't talked about yet."

"Water?" a student called out.

"Right," said Sharon.

She began to give her group the water conservation tour. We use a variety of systems to water our crops. We have several rain barrels placed strategically around the garden for quick filling of a watering can. Our food and ornamental beds are wired with either soaker hoses or drip irrigation. We find these systems are best for getting water directly to the plant root. They also minimize evaporation, help prevent disease caused by watering the leaves of plants, and conserve water.

"We're lucky on the west coast because we can grow vegetables almost year round," said Sharon. Cool-weather crops grow well here in winter, including Asian greens, cabbages and chois as well as the European winter veggies like kale, celery, mustard greens, chard and broccoli.

"And we can extend the growing season by growing a crop in the cold frame," said Sharon. "We get nice salad greens into late fall and then again early in the spring."

"What about extra fertilizing," a keen student wanted to know.

According to Sharon, if you've amended your soil well in the spring and fall, the plants should just need sunlight and water. We usually spread a ½-inch (1-cm) layer of compost on the beds in fall and then dig more in come spring. But you could give the heavy feeders an occasional boost during the growing season with an organic dry fertilizer blend, compost tea or a seaweed foliar spray. You can buy seaweed fertilizers at most garden centres and there is one available from the West Coast Seeds catalogue.

It's also a good idea to mulch your small plot in the fall with leaves or straw. Mulching helps hold the soil in place and keeps it from leaching nutrients during the rainy season. The mulch can then be dug into the soil in the spring.

Another technique to boost nutrient levels is called green manuring. In the early fall, empty beds can be seeded with annual rye grass or red clover. These overwintering crops help to fix nitrogen in the soil and hold the soil in place over the winter. They, too, are dug into the soil come spring.

To find out more about organic food gardening, visit the Vancouver Compost Demonstration Garden at 2150 Maple Street or phone the Compost Hotline (604-736-2250) to find a demonstration garden in your area. In addition to food gardening, most compost demonstration gardens also offer information on worm composting, natural lawn care, soil care and biological pest control. You can also visit our web site for more information at www.cityfarmer.org.

In the meantime, if you find yourself gardening in a small space, watch your step!

BREAKFAST, LUNCH AND DINNER — STARTING YOUR SEEDS

Wes Barrett, our former head gardener, used to swear by this formula for indoor seed starting. He gives California gardening guru John Jeavons credit for it. The idea is that you grow your seedlings and transplants in increasingly rich mediums. The seeds are started in pots and set in a bright, sunny window or even on top of a fridge — unless of course, you have a greenhouse.

Sow your seeds in a soilless "breakfast" mix (2 parts peat moss to 1 part vermiculite to 1 part perlite), and transplant into a small pot of "lunch" mix fortified with soil and compost (3 parts soil to 2 parts peat moss to 1 part perlite to 1 part compost). This mix will help minimize root shock and foster growth. Finally, set the plants into a well-prepared, compost-enriched soil for a gourmet "dinner." If you are gardening in containers, use one part compost to one part perlite to one part potting soil.

According to Wes, since seeds contain a sufficient food supply to grow to the two-true-leaf stage, a rich sowing mixture is not required. In fact, the seeds may rot in such a medium as pure compost. If the starting medium contains soil, there is a risk of weed, fungus or pest contamination as well.

An assortment of lavender
species and cultivars
Colour photo p. 144

The Edible Ornamental

SHEENA ADAMS, URBAN GREENERY & TREES, PORT ALBERNI, B.C.

Over the past few years, there has been a steady increase in the popularity
of edible gardening. As well as vegetables, gardeners are filling their residential landscapes with herbs, edible flowers, fruit and nut trees and small
berry bushes. Look up and you will even find grapes and kiwis decorating
arbours and softening the appearance of brick walls. And why not — these
are all easy plants to grow and they can be very ornamental in a landscape,
as well as providing us with the satisfaction of growing and harvesting our
own food.

Ornamental edibles can be planted in containers or nestled into mixed
shrub borders. They can even provide the underlying structure of the landscape itself. They can be annuals, perennials, deciduous shrubs or small
trees. The important elements in planning are knowing what is available,
deciding what you would like to harvest and determining what growing
conditions you have. Even on a small balcony you can have a hanging basket with tomatoes (such as 'Tumbler') and a few containers with lettuce

Aronia melanocarpa 'Autumn Magic' **Colour photo p.144**

and mixed greens. Whatever the situation, there is definitely a way you can enjoy ornamental edibles.

A great place to start with any design is planning for trees. Trees lend height, add structure and will eventually create the canopy of the garden. Most fruit trees are available on a variety of rootstocks, which means there are trees suitable for everything from growing in containers to shading the chicken coop. Seek out the appropriate rootstock for the space you have. Most fruit trees are highly ornamental in bloom, as well as producing attractive edible fruit. Pears have lovely white blossoms, peaches are a radiant pink and apples offer a soft pink flower. The fruit and foliage can be just as lovely, from the glossy colour of crabapples to the tropical foliage of the nectarine. The next time you need a tree, think edible and ornamental, and be prepared to enjoy both worlds.

The next step in the design process is planning of shrubbery. Shrubs are the backbone of any design; they provide structure throughout the year, offering height, texture and form from season to season. There are many ornamental and edible shrubs (most are deciduous) that will brighten up any garden and work well with the conifers and other broadleaf evergreens commonly grown for winter interest. Like fruit-bearing trees, deciduous fruiting shrubs offer both blossoms and fruit, and many also provide fall colour. Remember to keep in mind the growing space available — and be aware of those suggested sizes at maturity. For spring bloom you may want to try pink-flowering currant *(Ribes sanguineum),* which produces flowers for you and small berries for the birds, or *Aronia melanocarpa* 'Autumn Magic'. For late summer colour look for summer-fruiting shrubs such as blueberries, gooseberries, tayberries or jostaberries (a thornless cross between black currants and gooseberries). You can expect a great display in autumn when the foliage of blueberries (especially 'Hardyblue') takes on brilliant hues of deep orange to burning red.

The next stage is the planting of perennial edibles. These plants come up year after year, but generally die down to the ground in winter. While not offering much to look at in the cold season, they are certainly a nice way to add life to the garden in summer. Asparagus is a fabulous perennial for the orchard or the understory of ornamental trees; it also makes an attractive border for the front of any bed. Second on my list is rhubarb. A favorite spring treat, this plant will add a tropical look to any garden border or container. The third plant that strikes me is cardoon, which is a popular delicacy in Italy. This large perennial boasts style, texture, summer bloom and, above all, bold architectural form. The peeled stalks of this cousin to the artichoke are often enjoyed steamed with butter. A fourth favourite edible perennial is *Wasabia japonica* (Japanese horseradish). This tasty plant is a great edible perennial for a shady location. While the whole plant can be eaten, it is usually the roots that are enjoyed and the leafy foliage adds softness to any landscape. There are many other great perennial edibles that you can add to your landscape to give you and your kitchen year after year of culinary pleasure.

Another great way to add colour to your border is to use the flavorful foliage and colourful fruits of annual vegetables. You can hang them in baskets, tuck them into containers or allow them to climb up small trellises. From climbing spinach to tumbling tomatoes to compact peppers, the opportunity for colour, both in the garden and in the kitchen, is endless. When planning your next hanging basket, try thinking salad, stir-fry or veggie dip. You can actually grow these in containers around the patio and guests can help themselves to really fresh veggies. All you need to provide is a little salad dressing.

Groundcovers are the bottom pieces of the puzzle in garden design. They are grown to mulch the soil, thereby reducing weed growth, conserving water and reducing erosion and compaction. There are a few edibles that work very well as groundcovers. Ever-bearing strawberries are a perfect example; they are fast growing, spread easily with runners, offer attractive blooms and fruit all summer long. Another good option is the American cranberry *(Vaccinium macrocarpon)*. This 6-inch-high (15-cm) beauty will readily spread through a moist location. If blueberries are more your style, seek out a lowbush variety. They generally get about 12 to 18 inches (30 to 45 cm) high and there are several cultivars available. If you are looking for flowers and foliage, try an evergreen thyme. With all the new varieties available, there is sure to be one that will keep your soil cool and your soup tasty. My favourite is silver thyme because it has wonderful pink flowers and silvery foliage that I enjoy all year round.

Herbs are another group of edibles that are not only attractive and tasty, but are also grown for their fragrance. They can be evergreen, deciduous or perennial and they are wonderful to both cook and decorate with. Small evergreen shrubs include bay laurel *(Laurus nobilis)* and rosemary. For a small border consider any of the lovely lavenders (great for baking) and to fill your containers, try sage, cilantro and thyme. Other favorites that not only look great but help to attract beneficial insects are parsley, fennel *(Foeniculum vulgare)* and garlic. When planning to add herbs to your garden, remember to plant a few extra of your favourite plants and be sure to use them often. A little rosemary can turn those roasted potatoes into a heavenly dish, lavender adds fragrance to any kitchen and parsley will brighten up those summer salads.

There is no end to the plant material that can be incorporated into our landscapes and still be enjoyed in the kitchen. So the next time you need a plant for that special spot in the garden, think about planting an edible ornamental and be prepared to enjoy its beauty, taste and diversity.

ORGANIC MULCHES FOR YOUR EDIBLES

Apply these yearly in early spring to safely feed your edibles all season long.

Veggie Mulch
   1 wheelbarrow full of composted
   chicken manure
   ½ cup (125 mL) bone meal
   1 cup (250 mL) kelp meal
   1 cup (250 mL) alfalfa meal
   ¼ cup (50 mL) crushed oyster shell
   ¼ cup (50 mL) rock phosphate
Mix all together; apply a small handful around vegetables at planting time.

Fruit Tree and Berry Mulch
   5 shovels leaf mould
   5 shovels garden compost
   5 shovels peat moss
   1 cup (250 mL) bone meal
   ¼ cup (50 mL) rock phosphate
   ¼ cup (50 mL) alfalfa meal
   ¼ cup (50 mL) green sand
Mix and apply a 2 inch (5 cm) layer around the tree drip line in early spring.

Herb Mulch
   1 cubic foot peat moss
   2 cubic feet bark mulch (not cedar)
   5 lb. (2.2 kg) fish compost
   2 cups (500 mL) bone meal
   1 cup (250 mL) lime
Mix thoroughly; place a 2-inch (5-cm) layer around plants and water well.

INDEX